Detlev Blanke

International Planned Languages
Essays on Interlinguistics and Esperantology

Edited by Sabine Fiedler and Humphrey Tonkin

For Katrin, Michael and Henry

Detlev Blanke

International Planned Languages

*

*Essays on Interlinguistics
and Esperantology*

Edited by
Sabine Fiedler and Humphrey Tonkin

New York
Mondial
2018

Mondial
New York

Detlev Blanke

International Planned Languages
Essays on Interlinguistics and Esperantology

Edited by Sabine Fiedler and Humphrey Tonkin

Copyright © 2018 Detlev Blanke
All rights reserved.

ISBN 9781595693778

Library of Congress Control Number: 2018948508

www.mondialbooks.com
www.librejo.com

Contents

Foreword. *Sabine Fiedler* i

I. Planned languages – a survey of some of the main problems 1

II. The term 'planned language' 29

III. (*with Wera Blanke*) Is scholarly communication possible in a so-called 'artificial' language? 45

IV. Terminology science and planned languages 73

V. Causes of the relative success of Esperanto 99

VI. Paths to the scholarly literature on interlinguistics and Esperanto studies 115

Afterword. *Humphrey Tonkin* 167

References 171

Foreword

The author of this book, the German interlinguist and Esperanto researcher Detlev Blanke (1941-2016), has influenced the study of planned languages like no one else. It is to a large extent due to his lifelong scholarly devotion to this area of research that Interlinguistics and Esperanto Studies (Esperantology) have become serious subjects of study in the academic world. In his seminal monograph on international planned languages published in 1985 and numerous other publications, Blanke gives an overview of the history of language creation. He describes the most important planned language systems, their conceptual frameworks, features and the motives of their creators, presents various systems of classification and completes these with a typology of his own. A special focus is put on Esperanto initiated by L.L. Zamenhof in 1887.

Detlev Blanke was strongly influenced by Eugen Wüster, the father of terminology science. He once went so far as to say that no matter what topic in interlinguistics he delved into, he ended up back at Wüster. It is therefore no surprise that Eugen Wüster takes centre stage in one of the articles in this collection. It was he who introduced the term *Plansprache* (planned language), using it as a translation of Jespersen's *constructed language* in his 1931 dissertation on terminology standardisation. Following Wüster, Blanke defines a planned language as 'a language consciously created by an individual or group of people, in accordance with defined criteria, with the goal of facilitating international linguistic communication'. This definition serves as a starting point for the serious study of the phenomenon and has become even more important of late with the advent of another burgeoning group of artificial languages, those created for fantasy and science-fiction literature or films (e.g. Klingon). These languages are constructed to render pseudo-authenticity to fictitious characters or ethnic groups, but they are not planned languages according to Wüster's definition, as they do not aim to facilitate international communication.

Detlev Blanke's body of work in interlinguistics includes works on a wide variety of topics, such as word-formation in various planned language systems, the peculiarities of translations from and into planned languages, the use of Esperanto as a language for special purposes, the relationship between language planning and planned languages, and the potential role of Esperanto in solving problems in international communication, to name but a few. To me, his most significant contribution however, was the classification of planned language projects according to the real role of communication that they played or play. This accords with the view that languages are social phenomena and cannot be reduced to structural elements. Indeed, the majority of deliberately created languages have not grown beyond publication; only a small group of systems have found real-life applications and can be considered semi-languages. This is true for Volapük, Occidental-Interlingue, Novial, Interlingua, Ido, Latino sine flexione, Basic English and some others. However, after having begun to take shape as languages, the majority of them ceased to develop and eventually fell out of use altogether; the only planned language that has remained in use up to the present is Esperanto. In an indirect way, by means of this classification, Blanke also answers the question of whether it is possible to invent a language: a language cannot truly be created. A language project can be initiated, but it needs a speech community to turn it into a language.

In this volume, the most important ideas from Detlev Blanke's research are collected in English translation, thus making them available to a larger readership. In a number of studies, Blanke bemoaned the fact that the specialised literature on interlinguistics had not attracted sufficient scholarly attention. He attributed this to a certain extent to the language of publication, i.e. to the fact that interlinguistic literature is mainly written in planned languages, above all in Esperanto. Today, in interlinguistics as in other fields, authors must publish their research in English for it to reach an international readership. Detlev Blanke did not content himself with criticising the insufficient access to interlinguistic research, but took efforts to contribute to a change. This book is a result of just that endeavour. The seven collected contributions address terminology, the development and classification of planned languages, and the use of Esperanto – the planned language that has been most successful thus far – in various domains, with a focus on its use as a language for special purposes.

Chapters One and Two should familiarise the reader with the most crucial concepts in interlinguistics. Blanke presents his definition of planned languages, discusses the authors' motives for publishing their language projects and describes the most important planned language systems. He presents the common typology of planned language systems based on linguo-structural features, i.e. the distinction between a-priori and a-posteriori projects, and he describes Esperanto's transition from a language project to a fully-fledged language, introducing a framework consisting of a series of developmental steps, such as the use of the language for the creation of literature, in oral communication, in radio programs and as a family language.

Chapters Three and Four are devoted to Esperanto as a scholarly language (or language for special purposes, LSP), a research interest that Detlev Blanke shared with his wife, Wera Blanke. They discuss the use of Esperanto in specialised organisations and journals, the development of specialised dictionaries and principles of terminology planning. In Chapter Four, Blanke sheds light on Eugen Wüster's intensive preoccupation with Esperanto and other planned language systems and argues that this was a decisive influence on Wüster's future work in terminology standardisation. This is only one of many examples where Esperanto, over the course of its 130 years of existence, has had an impact on the work of eminent scholars, philosophers and writers. Blanke calls this 'the heuristic aspect of the value of planned languages' (p. 15).

Chapters Five and Six focus on future research in interlinguistics. Blanke gives a comprehensive overview of available literature on planned languages. These include specialised libraries and archives, bibliographies, university studies and dissertations, periodicals, handbooks, monographs and anthologies, conference proceedings and Internet materials. As Chapter Five is an updated version of Blanke's previous work on the topic, it represents the state of the art in interlinguistics and I recommend it as a starting point for other scientists in the field.

At the end of the book, in Chapter Six, Blanke examines the reasons for Esperanto's relative success. Against the backdrop of our globalised world where English is the dominant means of communication, it does not seem appropriate to mention Esperanto and 'success' in the same breath. The planned language has not become a means of international communication widely used by people alongside their respective mother tongues as Zamenhof had hoped. Nevertheless, it has proven that a language project can become a fully-fledged language; it has won out over linguistic rivals and outlived the more than one thousand other deliberately created languages, so that today the phenomenon of planned languages is generally synonymous with Esperanto. Therefore, Blanke speaks of a 'relative success', supplying both intra- and extralinguistic arguments for his case.

As such, Esperanto offers an alternative in an increasingly monolingual and monocultural world, and is a serious and intriguing research topic. The reader will find that in some of his articles Blanke developed his ideas further, and that this collection therefore also reflects the advancement of the discipline over time. I am delighted that it has become possible to realise Detlev Blanke's plan to publish this book and hope that it fulfils the author's intention to extend the audience of interlinguistic studies beyond the Esperanto community. As it focuses on the most fundamental knowledge on planned languages and provides insights into key sources of interlinguistic research I can also imagine Detlev Blanke's book being used in university lectures and seminars – a matter close to his heart.

Sabine Fiedler

I

Planned languages – a survey of some of the main problems[1]

1. The term 'planned language'

The term *planned language* was created by Eugen Wüster (1898-1977), founder of the science of terminology, and appeared first in its German original as *Plansprache* in Wüster's fundamental text on the creation of norms for technical language (Wüster 1931/1970).

Following Wüster's definition, we understand a planned language as a language consciously created by an individual or group of people, in accordance with defined criteria, with the goal of facilitating international communication. The phenomenon of conscious intervention in language processes, *language planning*, *Sprachplanung*, might suggest that also languages which have been strongly influenced in their development, such as Bahasa Indonesia in Indonesia or Ivrit in Israel, should be called planned languages. Nevertheless, the term is traditionally linked mainly to the problems of interlinguistics, the problems of international language communication.

In the linguistic literature, the term *planned language* is still not widely used, although it is gaining ground in the interlinguistics literature, particularly in German.[2] It also appears in publications in other languages, often as an adjective-noun combination, but also as a compound. Thus one finds *langue planifiée* (French), *planovyj jazyk* (Russian), *lingua pianificata* (Italian), *plansprog* (Danish), *plantaal* (Dutch), and *planový jazyk* (Slovak), among others. The language systems described by these terms are better known under various other names. It is possible to

---
[1] First published in Schubert 1989a: 63-87. See Blanke 1989. Translated by Dan Maxwell. This version edited by Humphrey Tonkin.
[2] See the literature cited in Blanke 1985: 53.

distinguish two groups of terms which overlap to some extent and can cause many misunderstandings:

(a) *artificial language, constructed language*, sometimes *synthetic language*,

and

(b) *universal language, world language, auxiliary language, common language, international language, interlanguage.*

The terms in group (a) indicate the way the language first came into existence and those in group (b) indicate its function. The modifiers in group (a) generally have pejorative connotations when linked with the word *language*, while the terms *universal, world, common, auxiliary,* and *international* can give rise to misunderstandings about the goals and actual functions of the languages. Wüster's term is preferable, since it indicates only the fact that a plan preceded the language.

2. Research barriers

In addition to the variety of terminology referred to (and which we can only briefly touch upon here – but see Blanke 1987), other factors also negatively influence the readiness of many linguists to concern themselves with the phenomenon of consciously created languages, although such readiness has increased in the last few years, as the growing number of publications shows (Blanke 1985: 302-381).

Among these factors are influences from linguistic Darwinism, evident in such dichotomies as 'living' vs. 'dead' languages, and 'natural' vs. 'artificial' languages. Furthermore, certain phenomena apparent among adepts of planned-language systems such as *Volapük, Esperanto, Ido,* and others have served as barriers to research, particularly an amateurish approach to language problems and an exaggeratedly enthusiastic belief in the value of an international language for social change, and – according to some followers – promotion of the brotherhood of humankind. Such attitudes hardly awaken interest in the objective observation of a phenomenon which in the case of *Esperanto* nevertheless reveals an actually functioning language representing one of the longest, most diversified and successful linguistic experiments in the history of language science.

We must also mention an additional barrier to information: more than 60 percent of the specialised literature on planned languages is published in these languages. Of this amount, 95 percent is written in *Esperanto* and the rest is mainly in *Latino sine flexione, Ido, Occidental-Interlingue, Novial*, and *Interlingua*. Accordingly, only 40 percent of the literature is in ethnic languages, mainly English, German, Russian, and French – as the author's own collection of about 10,000 bibliographic items shows. None of this has done much to stimulate linguists to concern themselves with languages whose origin and development are also not linked to the earliest period of humankind. André Martinet (1946: 37) accurately characterised the common opinion of his colleagues concerning planned languages more than 40 years ago: '*Le domaine de la création interlinguistique reste pour beaucoup celui où la fantaisie débridée d'amateurs irresponsables se donne necessairement libre cours*' (The area of interlinguistic creation remains for many a place where the unbridled fantasy of irresponsible amateurs is of necessity given free rein).

3. Planned-language systems

Before discussing some of the aspects of planned languages of general interest for modern linguistics and other scientific disciplines, we will attempt an overview of the planned languages themselves. Several existing studies provide a detailed consideration of many planned language systems,[3] so we will glance only briefly at the main issues here.

3.1 Number of systems

The number of planned-language systems (including pasigraphic systems – international writing or sign systems) has probably already reached upwards of a thousand. In a then still unpublished manuscript, the Soviet interlinguist Aleksandr Duličenko (1976: 117) had by 1973 collected bibliographic and other references to 912 systems. About 600 systems have appeared since the publication in 1887 of L. L. Zamenhof's 40-page outline of the project on the basis of which Esperanto eventually developed.

3.2 The authors' motives

The motives of the authors who start projects are very diverse. Often several such motives exist simultaneously. Let us mention the most important ones:

(a) The humanistic motive of **pacifism** and **harmonious international relations**. The authors hope, by means of a (universal or international) language to reduce or even eliminate conflicts among peoples, races, or political units of different languages. Pompiati (1918: 1), the author of *Nov Latin Logui*, expressed this opinion most concisely as follows: '*Wenn die Menschen alle einander verstehen können, wird es keinen Krieg mehr geben*' (When people all understand each other, there will be no more war).

---

3   See Bausani 1970, Blanke 1985, Couturat & Leau 1979, Drezen 1931/1991, Guérard 1922, Haupenthal 1976, Jacob 1947, Large 1985, Libert 2000 & 2003, Monnerot-Dumaine 1960, Pei 1958/1968, Rónai 1969, Szerdahelyi 1977, and in addition the extensive bibliography in Blanke 1985: 302-317. [See also the bibliography in Blanke 2006 – SF]

(b) Motives related to *language philosophy* have played a role for the creators of a-priori pasigraphies or planned languages. Particularly philosophers of the seventeenth century, among them Leibniz and Descartes, laid out ideas for an ideal rational language which, since logically constructed, would promote logical thinking and accordingly the development of new ideas. Also, Albert Liptay (1892), in his *Langue catholique*, sought to follow the evolutionary tendency that he found in European languages. In this regard his views resembled the theories of Otto Jespersen (1894) on the progression of language evolution or the thesis of Nikolaj Ja. Marr (1928) positing the development of a single language of humanity resulting from assimilation of present-day languages. Jespersen (1928a, b) himself created *Novial* and tried to model his linguistic ideas in his project. *Interlingua*, too, has a background related to the philosophy of language. In his project, which was partly based on previous work of the International Auxiliary Language Association (IALA), Alexander Gode (Gode et al. 1951) attempted to model the ideas of Benjamin Lee Whorf on linguistic relativism, particularly the Whorfian notion of a *Standard Average European* (*SAE*) language.

(c) ***Purely nationalistic and chauvinistic ideas*** motivated other authors. Oswald Salzmann (1915), for example, created *das vereinfachte Deutsch* on the basis of standard German, and Adalbert Baumann (1915) *Wede* (*Weltdialekt*, later named *Weltdeutsch*) with the hope that simplified German could become the international language of humanity after the First World War.

(d) Besides these, the psychologically explainable motive of ***language games***, the simple joy of creating or manipulating language elements, is not uncommon.

3.3 Classifications

There are several ways of classifying planned-language systems, of which we will mention only the most significant ones.

The traditional classification of Couturat and Leau is based on the *relationship of planned language systems to ethnic languages*, especially concerning lexical material. On this basis, the authors distinguish three characteristic groups:

(a) a-priori systems,
(b) a-posteriori systems,
(c) mixed systems having elements of both (a) and (b).

A-priori systems form their phonological and lexical system independently of the models in ethnic languages, often on the basis of philosophically motivated classifications of human knowledge, as in the projects of George Dalgarno (1661) and John Wilkins (1668), for example, or other systems such as the notes of the musical scale (*Solresol* by Sudre 1866). The grammar of a-priori systems is rigorously regular.

A-posteriori systems follow ethnic language models by borrowing lexical material from specific ethnic languages or groups of ethnic languages (according to various criteria) and adapting this material to the structural features of the planned language. The grammar is regular, but, since it often follows the models of ethnic languages, not as rigorously as a-priori systems. In this group, we find the many systems with a Romance-based lexicon, such as *Esperanto* by Zamenhof (1887), *Ido* by Beaufront and Couturat (1907), *Latino sine flexione* by Giuseppe Peano (1903), *Occidental-Interlingue* by Edgar de Wahl (1922), *Novial* by Otto Jespersen (1928a, b) and *Interlingua* by Alexander Gode (Gode et al. 1951).

Germanic systems, such as the already mentioned *Wede* by Baumann or *Tutonish* by Elias Molee (1902), and Slavic systems such as *Neuslavische Sprache* by Ignaz Hošek (1907), also belong to this group.

Mixed systems combine a-priori and a-posteriori traits. An example is provided by the heavily modified – hardly recognisable – ethnolinguistic materials and the very detailed and regular grammar in *Volapük* by Johann Martin Schleyer (published in 1879: see Schleyer 1982). In fact, all systems have both a-priori and a-posteriori elements. The a-priori systems, too, in some way reflect ethnolinguistic systems, at least in their foundations, since even they use vocalic and consonantal phonemes and often employ grammatical rules derived from ethnolinguistic models. On the other hand, the strong regularity of the grammar or the systematisation of an ethnolinguistic lexicon is done on an a-priori basis. Using as a measurement the relative influence of a-priori and a-posteriori systems, it would be possible to put every planned language system on a scale between the end points of 'a-priority' and 'a-posteriority'. A strong component of a-priori elements can be found in the schematic subgroup of the a-posteriori systems, including Esperanto and Ido, because of, among other things, their regularity in morphology and word-derivation. The naturalistic subgroup is characterised by a greater degree of imitation of (Romance) ethnic languages and for this reason regularises the word derivation and morphology less strongly. *Occidental-Interlingue* and *Interlingua* are examples.

Marcel Monnerot-Dumaine (1960) and Sergei N. Kuznecov (1976) go beyond Couturat and Leau (1979) to attempt a more detailed classification on the basis of linguistic criteria. Nevertheless, they, like their predecessors, limit themselves to a structuralist classification, making no clear distinction between planned language *projects* on the one hand – worked out with a great variety of quality and detail – and, on the other hand, actual planned *languages* supporting a community of users and functioning as vehicles for human communication.

For this reason we must add a classification assessing the **actual communicative role** played by given planned language systems. Many overviews of planned language systems in encyclopaedias and linguistic handbooks, compiled by individuals who are not specialists in interlinguistics, lack such a classification. The result is that insignificant projects and a functioning language such as Esperanto are treated as equal linguistic (or pseudolinguistic, in some cases) phenomena. We must emphasise that a language should not be reduced to mere structural elements, but is fully realised only within society – as an instrument of communication, thought, and information exchange. Planned-language *projects* lack these three important language functions.

Ignorance of the social aspect of language is one of the additional causes for the creation of new projects or the reform of existing systems (for example, Volapük and Esperanto, among others, led to many proposals for reforms). In such cases, linguistic details are overemphasised as decisive for the social acceptance of a language.

This erroneous viewpoint was clearly shared by the followers of Occidental (among others), who erroneously suggested that *'Li problema del lingue international es un problema linguistic-technic, ne politic. Occidental va triumfar proque it es linguisticmen superior al altri systemas*[4] (The problem of an international language is a technical problem of linguistics, not a political problem. Occidental will triumph because it is linguistically superior to other systems).

A certain structural linguistic coherence is of course generally a precondition if a planned language is to function socially. But, as the history of planned languages shows, non-linguistic factors are more important than linguistic factors in determining the relative success of a given planned-language system.

To explain the process of making planned language systems part of society, that is, the **transition from a language project to a language** – we

4   *Cosmoglotta* (Helsingfors) 21 (1932): 29.

I: Planned languages – a survey of some of the main problems

can distinguish a series of parallel and sequential steps, which the various systems have followed to different degrees. Such steps were necessary to establish structural precision and stability and to achieve the level of semantic functionality necessary for any kind of language communication.

The life of more than 900 projects ended immediately after the first stage, namely

(1) **publication of its structure.** In other cases, there often followed

(2) **production of texts**, sometimes in the form of a small newsletter, accompanied by discussion of linguistic details and information to be used as propaganda. *Ro* by Edward Powell Foster (1908) reached this stage, for example. Often the authors of the projects managed to find a few interested persons from different countries who learned the system and used it, mainly for

(3) **international correspondence.** Texts were created. The socialisation process had begun. Further steps were characterised by

(4) a certain **organisation of the users** and somewhat systematic publicity. This stage was reached, for example, by *Idiom Neutral* by Woldemar Rosenberger (published in 1898: Rosenberger 1902) or *Neo* by Arturo Alfandari (1961). Further steps worth mentioning as steps toward becoming a full-blown language are

(5) the creation of **literary texts**,

(6) the appearance of certain (small) **journals**,[5] and

(7) a certain application to **specialised texts**. Except for step (6), these steps were achieved by Peano's already mentioned *Latino sine flexione* later named *Interlingua* – not to be confused with Gode's project of the same name (Barandovská-Frank 2002). Ido, Occidental-Interlingue and Interlingua-Gode were also

---

5   Particularly valuable is *Novialiste* [1933-1938] for Otto Jespersen's *Novial*. Stojan 1973: 188-190 mentions 28 small journals of this sort up to 1929.

(8) *taught* to a certain extent and were

(9) applied internationally in *speech*. This holds to a limited extent for *Ido* and *Interlingua* up to the present, but hardly for *Occidental-Interlingue* or, at the end of the nineteenth century, for *Volapük*. Only *Esperanto* went further:

(10) further specialised practical usage (***specialised journals and organisations***),

(11) a developed ***network of national and international organisations***,

(12) a ***wide range of literature***,

(13) relatively ***wide formal instruction*** (sometimes state-supported),

(14) large ***periodically occurring international events***,

(15) ***regular radio programs***,

(16) ***clear social and political distinctions*** in the already established language community and its linguistic reflection,

(17) an independent ***youth movement***,

(18) a certain evolution of ***independent cultural elements*** linked to the language community,

(19) ***bilingualism*** (involving an ethnic and a planned language) of children in (most often international) families.

This collection of evolutionary steps is of course incomplete – and some details might be questioned – but it shows quite clearly that it is easier to construct a planned language system than it is to introduce it in practice. In line with these steps, one might locate all projects on an axis from (1) to (19), and distinguish three main groups:

I. Planned language *projects* (steps 1-4),

II. Planned *semi-languages*, i.e. systems which have gone part way toward realisation and in principle might have become, or still could become, full-blown languages, given the right political conditions. They have passed through steps 1-9.

III. Up to now, the only planned language to gain full functionality by reaching the nineteenth step of the socialisation process is Esperanto, initiated by L. L. Zamenhof in 1887.

All three groups merit the interest of linguists. A consequence of this classification, if rigorously followed, is that we cannot speak of planned *languages* in the plural. If we do, we must understand that plural as an ellipsis, denoting planned language *systems*, employed to contrast such systems with ethnic languages.

4 Main representatives of planned language systems

We will mention only those systems that allow us to demonstrate the main approaches to the construction and evolution of planned language systems, and the partial errors and successes accompanying them. On details of language structure, the literature cited in note 3, above, provides abundant information.

4.1 Pasigraphic systems

Pasigraphies are international notion-to-symbol systems or writing systems. They are planned language systems with only graphics, not phonetics or phonology: 'une langue universelle exclusivement écrite' – a universal language exclusively written (Couturat & Leau 1903+1907/2001: 1). If the signs or pasigrams are replaced by pronounceable letters or letter combinations, pasigrams become parts of pronounceable systems. The number of such systems is estimated at between 120 and 150. Most were created in the 17th and 18th centuries. Pasigraphies may be either a-priori or a-posteriori. They are based on systems of knowledge classification and signal the elements of classification found by symbols, signs, or letters. The a-priori pasigraphic classificatory system of Joseph de Maimieux (1797a, b), who created the term, is particularly worth mentioning.

More recently, the a-posteriori system *Safo* by Andre Eckardt (1952) has appeared. This combines complex notions, and relationships between notions, relatable to 180 basic signs, essentially according to the model of the Chinese writing system.

Examples of the basic signs are: ⊣ 'man', ⊢ 'woman', ⊗ 'wheel', ♀ 'child', ⵧ 'birth'. From these it is possible to form: ⊣ⵧ 'father', ⊣♀ 'boy', ⊣⊗⊗ 'bicyclist', ⊣ⵧ⊢ 'parents'.

No pasigraphic system is really extensively used: active international pasigraphic communities have not evolved. Today, such pasigraphic systems may be of interest in the elaboration and refinement of internationally used symbol sets, for example in sports, traffic, and tourism, and for signs used as aids in consecutive translation, since these are also notion-based, and accordingly closely related to pasigraphic systems.[6]

4.2 A-priori systems

A-priori planned languages are often based on the classification of ideas and accordingly present a sort of encyclopaedic world view. Wilkins (1668), for example, divided the knowledge of his time – according to his understanding – into 40 main classes, which with subgroups form approximately 3,000 words, for example: *Da* 'world', *De* 'element', *Di* 'stone', *Do* 'metal'. *De* can be further extended into *Deb* 'fire', *Debi* 'lightning', and so on. These systems are closed. Their further development

---

[6] See, for example, Herbert 1952, who gives a list of symbols which could be pasigrams if internationally used.

depends on their world view, which would necessitate changes in classification over time. Study of these systems nevertheless acquaints us with a type of historical semiotic thinking. Philosophical languages have a bearing on the problem of language universals, and they have also stirred some interest among creators of decimal and other classification systems – those used in libraries, for example. In addition, they provide potential models for large thesauri and dictionaries oriented towards onomastics, such as Roget and Browning (1966) and Hallig and Wartburg (1952). Studies of pasigraphs and a-priori planned languages also could be interesting for the definition of general semantic units of words (semantic markers, sememes), or notions ('noemes') and the creation of formalised ideal languages of science (a universal scientific code).

A direct link to modern concepts of the philosophy of language is provided by James C. Brown (1960), whose non-classificational a-priori project *Loglan* (Logical Language) tests the hypothesis of language relativism developed by Sapir and Whorf since it is based on the supposition that according to certain criteria a constructed language can influence the thought of the user.

A-priori systems have largely failed to achieve social functionality, since they have been unable to create international communicative collectives.

4.3 A-posteriori systems

4.3.1 Modified ethnic languages

The group of planned languages consisting of modified ethnic languages is based on classical or modern languages. Especially interesting is *Latino sine flexione,* already mentioned. Its author Giuseppe Peano did a great deal of research on the Romance component of the modern European languages (Peano 1915). He in fact used traditional Latin without its complicated inflectional system, in this way making it an isolating language. Here is a sample text:

> *Post publicatione de manuscriptos de Leibniz in 1903 me adopta in plure scripto Latino sine flexione; id es lingua composito ex vocabulos latino, sine flexiones grammaticale.*[7]

Latino sine flexione can be classed as a planned semi-language, since for a certain period of time it was in practical use for scientific and general language texts.

Modified modern ethnic languages are often based on English. Charles K. Ogden's well-known *Basic English* (1931) attempts to cover general vocabulary by means of circumlocutions, using 850 basic words ('things, qualities, operators'). Although it has been often proposed simply as a methodical introduction to Standard English, many of its followers have conceived of Basic English as an international auxiliary language. In fact it is less an introduction to English than a variant of the language that must be learned separately: *To descend* becomes *to come down/to go down* and *to wander* becomes *to go from place to place without aim.*

Basic English was influential in the planned-language movement in the 1930s and still influences efforts to provide basic introductions to national languages, using vocabularies based on word-frequency statistics. Examples are *Basic Slovak* (Mistrík 1985) with 800 of the most frequent Slovak words, *Français Fondamental*, and *Grunddeutsch*.[8]

Since Basic English has also played a role as an international means of communication, it can be considered a planned semi-language, according to our classification.

---

7 'After publication of manuscripts by Leibniz in 1903, I am applying Latino sine flexione in several writings. It is a language based on Latin words without grammatical inflections' (Peano 1915: 9).

8 On these two projects, information can be found in Ronai (1969: 153-159).

4.3.2 Reformed ethnic languages

Another group of planned language systems, the reformed languages, were strongly shaped by ethnic languages. In *Wede*, for example, Adalbert Baumann (1915) greatly simplified the orthography and inflectional system of German, hoping in this way to advance the hegemonic goals of the German imperialistic regime in this way. Here is an example of Wede:

> *T spraklie mangelhafikeit fon Wolapik hawen gefiret su ferhengnis-fole streitikeita.*[9]

4.3.3 Zone languages

Related to the reformed languages are zone languages: those languages with material taken from a single language group – e.g. Elias Molee's *Tutonish* (1902):

> *Dis sprak must bi so rein tutonish as mogli.*[10]

Again there is an evident component of language chauvinism.

4.3.4 Selective systems

A large group of planned-language projects, the *selective* systems, choose their material from diverse language families or from two languages (*compromise languages*: see below). Systems designed to create the appearance of 'natural-looking' languages by imitating ethnic languages (almost always Romance languages) produce *naturalistic systems*. If the Romance elements are mixed with other material and are more thoroughly elaborated so that the system has an autonomously functioning system of morphology and word derivation, the result is an *autonomous (schematic)* system. Attempts to select material and principles of construction from diverse planned language systems, thereby constructing new ones, result in *integrated* planned languages.

---

9 The original German is: *Die sprachliche Mangelhaftigkeit von Volapük hat zu verhängnisvollen Streitkeiten geführt* ('The linguistic flaws in Volapük have led to fatal quarrels').

10 'This language must be as pure Teutonic as possible.'

Let us look at each of these four types – compromise languages, naturalistic languages, autonomous languages, and integrated languages – in a little more detail.

Compromise languages. The group of compromise language projects includes, for example, *Anglo-Franca* by Henderson (under the pseudonym Hoinix 1889), a project which mixes properties of English and French:

> *Me pren the liberte to ecriv to you in Anglo-Franca.*[11]

Naturalistic languages. One of the most important groups of planned-language systems is without doubt the one based on naturalism. To a certain extent it repeats principles of the group of modified classical languages (for example, *Latino sine flexione*), but qualitatively on a higher level. The authors of naturalistic projects take as a starting point a view influenced by Eurocentrism, viz., that the international planned language must be a more or less 'natural' compilation of the actually functioning Romance lexicon. Accordingly, such a system is relatively easily read and understood by an educated European, or a scholar educated in a western culture. This group of projects takes its philosophical basis, as we have noted, from the *linguistic relativism* of Sapir and Whorf (Whorf 1956), according to which languages influence the thought of their speakers. For Europe (mainly the Romance and Germanic regions), Whorf defined an average European language – what he called *Standard Average European (SAE)* – which, in the view of language relativists, determined 'European thought.'

The best-known planned-language systems in this group, *Occidental-Interlingue* by Edgar de Wahl[12] and *Interlingua*, which is partly based on the research of IALA,[13] but was finished by Alexander Gode,[14] fit into

---

11 'I take the liberty of writing to you in Anglo-Franca.'
12 On Occidental-Interlingue, see the good overview in Pigal 1930.
13 On the valuable work of the International Auxiliary Language Association (1919-1953), see IALA 1945.
14 See Gode et al. 1951, and Gode & Blair 1951.

this category. They have become the most important alternatives to the autonomous systems of Esperanto and Ido because of their language structure and language philosophy.

Occidental-Interlingue and Interlingua are based exclusively on Latin lexical material. The first system is arranged more schematically than the second. Interlingua is accordingly still more 'natural' and, concerning word derivation, must to a still greater extent imitate the models of the Romance European languages than Occidental-Interlingue does, since this latter language has a certain limited amount of autonomy.

A typical text[15] rendered in both languages reveals their striking similarity:

> *Altestimat seniores!*
> *In li yeral jurnal de vor cité yo ha leet, que vu sercha un contorist.*
> (Occidental-Interlingue)

> *Estimatissime seniores!*
> *In le jornal de heri de vostre urbe io ha legite, que vos cerca un commisso.*
> (Interlingua)

Both systems have been put to some practical use and therefore can no longer be considered simply projects. In this case we are dealing with planned semi-languages – on the way to becoming languages. At the time of writing, this developmental process seems to be coming to an end for Occidental-Interlingue, but will take a while longer for Interlingua. In both systems, journals and some literature, mainly of a specialised sort, have appeared in the past, though for Occidental-Interlingue this development has apparently ended. International meetings with roughly 20-40 people from eight or ten countries have taken place

---
15 'Esteemed sirs! In yesterday's edition of your local newspaper, I read that you are looking for an office worker' (Waringhien 1959: 102).

sporadically, very rarely for Occidental-Interlingue, more often for Interlingua. There are in fact about a hundred supporters of each of the two systems, too few to guarantee sufficient application and linguistic evolution.

Autonomous languages. The other important group of planned-language systems is that of autonomous systems. They are also based mainly, but not as exclusively as the naturalistic systems, on Romance lexical material. But they are more strongly regularised on the graphemic, lexical, morphological, and grammatical levels. If the naturalistic systems derive their orientation mainly from etymology, the autonomous systems derive theirs mainly from their function.

The most important representative of this group is *Esperanto*, the main features of which are summarised below.

Besides Esperanto (1887), the *Ido* system originated in 1907 by Beaufront and Couturat, merits attention. To a certain extent it is a more Latinised and, especially with respect to word order, a more regularised version of Esperanto. Ido nevertheless never developed as dynamically or achieved the stability of its parent system. It played a certain role before and after the First World War. Two or three small journals are still being published. There are occasional small international conferences, with 30-40 people from approximately ten countries. All things considered, Ido has stimulated Esperantology – the science of the sources, structure, evolution, and communicative application of Esperanto – in important ways. Ido is without doubt the most evolved, with – after Esperanto – the largest corpus of text and the most fully developed dictionaries. We can use the example cited above to demonstrate the marked similarity of Esperanto and Ido:

> *Altestimataj sinjoroj!*
> *En la jurnalo de via urbo mi legis, ke vi serĉas kontoriston.*
> (Esperanto)

Altestimata siori!
En la jurnalo di via urbo me lektis, ke vi serchas kontoristo.
(Ido)

Integrated languages. Also worthy of mention are representatives of integrated planned-language systems, that is, attempts to combine the characteristics of various systems. *Novial*, created by Otto Jespersen (1928a, b), belongs to this group. It is in essence a combination of Esperanto and Ido and a step in the direction of naturalism. Although Novial never played an important role in the history of interlinguistics, it is nevertheless interesting because of the fact that Jespersen, the Danish linguist who had profound knowledge of many planned languages apart from Ido, presents detailed arguments for the individual characteristics of his system. A journal in Novial appeared for ten years with, among other things, interesting linguistic texts by Jespersen himself.

4.4 A-priori / a-posteriori mixed types

The first planned language system that functioned in practice was Volapük, created by Johann Martin Schleyer.[16] Because the lexical material of Volapük came from ethnic languages, especially English and Latin, and secondarily from German and French, it has an a-posteriori component. The roots have nevertheless been changed to the point of unrecognisability (e.g., *vol* 'world', *pük* 'speak', *vola'pük* 'world language'), and the morphology and grammar are very regular and highly elaborated. Thus, Volapük has strong a-priori characteristics. We see this quality in Volapük's version of the text already cited:

Söls palestimöl!
Eliladob in gased zifa olsik, das nedols konodeli sevöl.
(Volapük)

---

[16] Esperantologists have recently studied Volapük in the context of interlinguistics. Haupenthal especially has reprinted several valuable articles (Schleyer 1982, Schmidt 1981).

The fate of Volapük offers several interesting lessons, among them the fact that it is not the details of language structure that are so decisive, although indeed important, for the success of a language. Volapük, although in its language structure much inferior to various projects published before Schleyer's system, nevertheless had a certain success for more than a decade. Journals, books, and dictionaries were published. Congresses took place in 1884, 1887 and 1889. The last of these (in Paris) was conducted in Volapük itself and clearly showed the linguistic defects of the system.

4.5 Conclusion of the survey

In reviewing the history of publication of planned-language projects, we see that their various designs tend to reflect the spirit of their period in regard to philosophy and the philosophy of language. In the middle ages, when Latin functioned as a lingua franca among educated people, there was no awareness of a language problem. In the seventeenth century, when great geographic discoveries were made and international commerce developed, the need for an international language grew stronger. The development of scientific objectivity under the influence of rationalists and encyclopaedists provided additional impetus, and a-priori systems and pasigraphies appeared. Latin lost influence as the role of nation states expanded and standard national languages emerged. As a result, more projects based on ethnic languages, classical and modern, were proposed. This development grew stronger, especially in the nineteenth century. During the twentieth century projects of every type appeared, but especially reforms of a few partially successful systems such as Volapük, Esperanto, Ido, and naturalistic planned languages. Although on average two or three new projects appear each year, they no longer offer anything really new that hasn't already been tested earlier in some system.

For this reason, it is hardly imaginable that a new project could repeat the more than one-hundred-year development, the practical experience, and the theoretical insights which Esperanto, Zamenhof's century-old language, has gained. In contrast to projects and planned semi-languages, it is the only system in which a project has become a fully developed language, has become part of society, and is constantly making further inroads in this direction. For this reason, only Esperanto makes possible the study of the phenomenon of planned languages in its full complexity and in the intimate linkage between language and society.

5 Esperanto

It is impossible to present the structure of Esperanto in any detail here: textbooks, dictionaries, and grammars of Esperanto are available in the major languages of the world, and there is abundant information about structure and specific characteristics in the interlinguistics literature. So we will confine ourselves here to a broad examination of the main properties of this language.

(a) Esperanto is the only existing planned language for which the exact date of birth is known: on July 26, 1887, the first booklet (40 pages long) with a sketch of the project appeared in print in Russian as *D-r Esperanto: Meždunarodnyj jazyk. Predislovie i polnyj učebnik. Varšava: Kel'ter, 1887* (Dr Esperanto: International language. Preface and complete grammar. Warsaw: Kelter, 1887)

This booklet contained only sixteen main rules, three prose texts, three poems, and a list of 900 roots and affixes with a Russian translation. In the same year, Polish, French, and German versions appeared. On the basis of this outline, the language gradually expanded and continued to be developed by its community of users.

(b) The phonological orthography, the mainly agglutinative morphology (with isolating properties), the modern Romance quality of its basic lexical material (about 70%), the autonomous and very elastic system of derivational word formation (and at the same time the possibility of assimilating international words), and the regular grammar have in practice proved sufficient for relatively easy acquisition and application compared to other foreign languages.

(c) The main structural property of the language is the immutability of its phonemes and morphological elements and their relatively easy combinability in syllables, words, and syntactic units.

(d) Practical application over more than a hundred years in an ever greater number of fields and countries has led to a language capable of increasingly nuanced communication. This process has taken place in a field of tension among diversifying forces (for example, ethnic influences and different communicative needs of the users) and unifying forces (increasingly international applications). An adequately codified norm has developed and become stable.

(e) Esperanto is characterised by all properties which are observable in practice in human language: the development of polysemy, homonyms, synonyms, specialised vocabularies, styles, and levels of language. Nevertheless, the fact that the main communicative goal of the language and its practical application is to serve internationally as a means of communication among people with different parent languages has led to a particular awareness of norms that is more closely controlled, controllable, and subject to conscious influence than in ethnic languages. This specific property of a planned language – though not of an ethnic language – keeps the development of polysemy, homonymy, synonymy, and ethnic influences within certain limits.

I: Planned languages – a survey of some of the main problems

The main tendencies within the actual practical application[17] of Esperanto are characterisable in the following way:

(1) The number of users of the language is sufficient to guarantee an increasing amount of usage in more and more areas of application by members of an ever increasing number of different language groups.

(2) The users show an increasing variety in social background (class, stratum, and generation). This is also reflected in the language itself.

(3) To the well-developed everyday language and the literary language, more and more different specialised sublanguages are constantly being added.

(4) The use of Esperanto in recent decades has spread further around the world, that is, outside Europe. Relatively strong Esperanto movements have developed, for example, in Asia (China, Japan, and Vietnam) and in Latin America (Brazil and Cuba).

(5) The spoken application of the language has grown considerably stronger, among other ways in a framework of more than 400 international events per year of various sizes and quality and because of its use in radio.[18]

(6) In general, the production of texts in journals, books, and other materials is accelerating.

(7) Because of these tendencies, and others, the practical application of Esperanto is increasingly recognised as an international cultural and

---

17 The practical application of Esperanto up to about 1974 is well summarised in the encyclopaedic work of Lapenna, Lins and Carlevaro 1974 and the series *Esperanto Documents*, published by the Universal Esperanto Association (Rotterdam). [Much of this material is now available on line at www.uea.org and elsewhere – HT]

18 [Massive amounts of spoken and visual material are now available electronically – HT]

political factor. This development was expressed in the resolution of the 23rd General Conference of UNESCO in 1985 (Sofia, Bulgaria) on the occasion of the centenary of Esperanto:

Resolution of UNESCO 23 C/Res. 11.11. Celebration of centenary of Esperanto

The General Conference,

Considering that the General Conference in its Session of 1954 in Montevideo by its resolution IV. 1.4.422-4224, takes note of the achievements through the international language Esperanto in the field of international intellectual exchange and mutual understanding of the peoples of the world, and recognises that these results agree with the aims and ideals of UNESCO,

Recalling that Esperanto has made in the meantime considerable progress as a means for the advancement of mutual understanding of peoples and cultures of different countries, penetrating in most regions of the world and most human activities,

Recognising the great potential of Esperanto for the international understanding and the communication among peoples of different nationalities,

Taking note of the considerable contribution of the Esperanto movement and especially the Universal Esperanto Association for the spreading of information about the activities of UNESCO, as well as its participation in its activities,

Aware of the fact that in 1987 Esperanto celebrates its centenary of existence,

1. *Congratulates* the Esperanto movement on its centenary,

2. *Requests* the Director-General to continue following with attention the development of Esperanto as a means for better understanding among different nations and cultures,

3. *Invites* the Member States to mark the centenary of Esperanto by suitable arrangements, declarations, issuing of special postal stamps etc., and to promote the introduction of a study programme on the language problem and Esperanto in their schools and higher educational institutions,

4. *Recommends* to the international non-governmental organisations to join the celebration of the centenary of Esperanto, and to consider the possibility of the use of Esperanto as a means for the spreading of all kinds of information among their members, including information on the work of UNESCO.

6 The scientific value of planned languages

As we have shown, the existence of planned-language projects and the functioning of some of them is a phenomenon requiring scholarly consideration – and not only by specialists in linguistics, but scholars in other fields as well. Let us try to summarise a few aspects of this scientific value, all of which have been considered in greater detail elsewhere.[19]

(a) Planned languages – as the most thoroughly developed products of language planning – are linguistic facts and for this reason an object of language science. The fully functioning Esperanto and also the well-developed projects and planned semi-languages are proofs of successful language creation by humans. Esperanto by its existence and functioning raises a series of fundamental questions for language science. These

---
19 See the overview in Blanke 1986b.

can be examined under laboratory conditions, because the language is very young and it is possible to get an overview of its texts fairly easily. In the last decade, the number of linguistic studies of planned languages, especially of Esperanto, has been growing. This is the **linguistic aspect** of the value of planned languages.

(b) The Esperanto language community can be regarded as a micro model of optimal language communication which can be examined from the point of view of various disciplines: politics, economics, sociology, linguistics, psychology, historiography, cybernetics, cultural studies, and others.

The functioning model of Esperanto should be able to point ways to future effective, non-discriminatory, international communication across languages. As for applying the micro model in wider international practice, non-linguistic factors, especially political and economic ones, will nevertheless play the decisive role. This is the **interlinguistic aspect** of the value of planned languages.

(c) In addition, the study of planned languages in general, especially Esperanto, can offer valuable data concerning the solution of problems not specifically linked to planned languages and their goals as such, for example the value of instruction in Esperanto as an intensive general introduction to the learning of foreign languages, the role of a planned language as a bridge language in computerised automatic or semi-automatic translation, or the significance of planned language studies as a stimulus for the formation of a science of terminology.[20]

It would be interesting to consider the educational effects of Esperanto for the personal development of students or adults who have studied the language and applied it.

These and other approaches open to scientific investigation belong to the **heuristic aspect** of the value of planned languages.

---

20 See the study by Wera Blanke in this volume.

I: Planned languages – a survey of some of the main problems

Postscript to this chapter by Sabine Fiedler

In section 3.1.2 of this article, Detlev Blanke presents his typology of planned language projects, semi-languages and Esperanto as a functioning planned language on the basis of individual developmental steps (or levels of application) that a project attains on its way to becoming a living language. This ground-breaking approach is not only of theoretical value as it takes the social character of language into consideration, but also of great practical relevance. Projects that have never been applied in communication cannot be compared to Esperanto with its rich communicative history. This is implied when authors use formulations such as 'artificial languages such as Volapük and Esperanto' or 'planned languages such as Esperanto or Basic English', as often done today.

In the article, first published in 1989, Blanke describes Esperanto's development from concept to reality using a 19-level system, from 'manuscript' (step 1) to 'family language' (step 19). In later works, Blanke (2001a: 52-57; 2006: 65-71) revises his typology of developmental steps, expanding it to a system of 28 levels, rearranging some types of application and adding further levels, among which are the role of the language in electronic media, the emergence of elements of an original culture and the factor of language change. I was delighted at the latter additions, as they accord with the view that development does not end with 'use as a family language'. Native Esperanto is not the culmination of the journey from a project to a living language, because the status of Esperanto native speakers cannot be equated with the status of native speakers of an ethnic language (Fiedler 2012). The development of an original phraseology reflecting cultural features of the speech community and the evidence of language change are certainly more important levels of language application that speak to the status of the language. Detlev Blanke's revision of his typology is therefore significant for a realistic evaluation of Esperanto.

II

The Term 'Planned Language'[21]

1 Terminological confusion

In the field of linguistics and its subfield interlinguistics there is much inconsistency in the expressions used to describe a language such as Esperanto, with terms like 'world language', 'universal language', 'auxiliary language', 'artificial language', and 'international language', used almost interchangeably by specialists and non-specialists alike. Some of these expressions indicate the origin or genesis of a language, while some indicate its communicative function. A few are mixed. Of the terms describing origin or genesis, 'artificial' often carries pejorative connotations. It also has half a dozen or more meanings. The term 'constructed language' was coined by Jespersen, but also seems somewhat colourless. Wüster created the German term Plansprache (planned language). Among the terms describing communicative function, 'universal' has a long history but normally describes the only language for a future humankind. Hence it is not suitable as a description of most modern language projects. 'World language' is often used as a term for ethnic language of wider diffusion. 'Auxiliary' implies an incompleteness, as though such a language is merely a facilitating device. Other terms include 'common language', 'lingua franca,' 'vehicular language,' and 'interlanguage.' The present author prefers the term 'planned language,' defined (see Chapter 1, above) as 'a language consciously created by an individual or group of people, in accordance with defined criteria, with the goal of facilitating international communication.' Esperanto is a **planned language in its genesis** and an **international language in its function**. In this essay the author provides abundant examples of use of the terms he describes by scholars writing in several languages.

---

[21] The original text was first published in Tonkin 1997: 1-20. See Blanke 1997b. Translated by Humphrey Tonkin.

A term is a notionally defined technical word whose meaning contains those elements that – in conformity with the theory of the discipline concerned – represent the essential characteristics of a technical or scientific object or phenomenon (Schippan 1984: 245). Terms form a finite and defined part of the technical lexicon and are characterised, among other things, by lack of ambiguity, preciseness, and a fixed position in a terminological system. This system derives from the systematic quality of the science or discipline in question. The concrete semantic nuances of a term may help or hinder our understanding of the object or phenomenon described. Hence terminology should be consciously, not haphazardly, created.

In interlinguistics, and particularly in the non-specialised literature dealing with means of linguistic communication consciously created for international use, a kind of terminological chaos has gradually been created, and this has had a highly negative influence on our understanding of these phenomena. 'World language,' 'universal language,' 'auxiliary language,' 'artificial language,' 'international language,' 'worldwide language' – these are just a few of the wide choice of terms, half terms, and expressions often used for the same object. Because many of these expressions are polysemantic, they hinder our rational understanding of the phenomenon in question, for example, Esperanto, and aid the development and adoption of erroneous concepts. In short, we lack a generally accepted core term, although there is some evidence that such a term may be emerging.

2 Two classifications

To understand the advantages and disadvantages of particular terms and expressions for ethnic and planned languages, we can juxtapose them in two contrasting semantic groups.

First, we can classify them according in the *origin or genesis of a language*, thus: (1) artificial language, planned language, (2) natural language, popular language, ethnic language.

Second, we can classify them in terms of the *communicative function of a language*: (1) world language, auxiliary language, international language, universal language, (2) national language, language of the state. A few common expressions contain elements of both groups: natural world language, artificial auxiliary language.

It is important to *stress* that many of these expressions have in effect become technical terms (e.g. artificial language, international auxiliary language, world language) and can be found in catalogues and encyclopaedias. This does not mean that they lack ambiguity or are generally accepted. Other expressions (e.g. constructed language) cannot really be regarded as technical terms, though we consider them such for the sake of simplicity.

Because interlinguistics has only begun to emerge and gather international acceptance as a scientific discipline in recent years, interlinguistic terminology is still somewhat lacking in precision (on the term 'interlinguistics', see Blanke 1977). Alternatively, if specialists in interlinguistics consider certain expressions as adequately defined technical terms, these terms may not have achieved recognition in the discipline of linguistics. The shaping, definition, and diffusion of interlinguistic terminology accordingly depend upon the final general acceptance of the new scientific discipline of interlinguistics and also on a somewhat unified approach to interlinguistic terminology in itself. It is the purpose of this study to show that a unified terminology does not yet exist.

2.1 Terms according to origin or genesis

Let us turn to the first of our two categories: *classification according to the origin or genesis* of a language. The term 'artificial language' (*Kunstsprache, künstliche Sprache, artefarita lingvo, langue artificielle, iskusstvennyj jazyk*) is the term most widely used. Zamenhof himself used it. We can find it in library catalogues, bibliographies, encyclopaedias, and works on linguistics. In linguistics, at least as far as 'planned language' is concerned, it seems to have acquired the status of a technical term, but it is unsuitable for two reasons.

First, the term '***artificial language***' often carries a pejorative connotation, particularly in light of the linguistic Darwinism of August Schleicher (1873), the Young Grammarians, and other historically oriented linguists of the late nineteenth and early twentieth centuries. They maintained that languages develop naturally, like organisms that could not normally be created artificially; the result could only be, according to them, a kind of feeble homunculus.

Second, the expression 'artificial language' (*Kunstsprache, künstliche Sprache, etc.*), because of differences among linguistic schools and procedures, has several dissimilar meanings. We can distinguish the following:

> 1. Regularised and standardised literary language, as distinguished from dialects (Meyer 1901: 56; Baudouin de Courtenay 1908: 40; Vossler 1923: 259; Paul 1937: 411; Collinder 1938: 34; Tauli 1968: 22; Guchman 1973: 412; Akhmanova 1977: 37).

> 2. Ethnic languages, highly regularised to maintain them at a particular stage of development (Sanskrit, Church Latin) or to modernise them (Modern Hebrew, Bahasa Indonesia, Landsmål).

3. Consciously created languages to facilitate international communication (Schuchardt 1888; Jespersen 1928a: 1), that is, planned languages.

4. Nonredundant, formulaic, or symbolic languages to facilitate scientific thought (e.g., the symbol systems of logic, mathematics, chemistry). These are essentially idealised closed codes (Klaus 1972: 39; Motsch 1974: 23; Ljudskanov 1975: 107).

5. Programming languages for computers, for example, Algol, Cobol, PL/1 (Spitzhardt 1973: 640; Ljudskanov 1975: 107).

6. Machine languages for automatic translation.

Some authors limit the term to one of these groups, others use it for several. Denissow and Kostomarow (1977: 73) mix several matters together when they describe 'artificial languages' as 'Esperanto or the symbols of mathematics, chemistry or chess, or traffic signs, or the pragmatic systems of advertising, art and sport.' Broadly speaking, by 'artificial languages' some scholars understand all linguistic systems, elements, or phenomena that are in any way characterised by human consciousness. The most extensive, though early, study on this subject is Meyer (1901).

The term '*constructed language*' (*konstruierte Sprache; konstruita lingvo; langue construite*) is preferred by Jespersen (1928b). Others follow his lead (Holmström 1958: 189; Pei 1958/1968: 233; Hagler 1970: 38; Janton 1973: 7). The term is also used in Romanian (*limbi internationale construite*, Vraciu 1980: 273). Even this seemingly balanced term suggests the pejorative connotation of a colourless technology.

Relatively infrequently we find '*synthetic language*' (*synthetische Sprache, sinteza lingvo*). According to the International Auxiliary Language Association (IALA 1927: 8), a synthetic language is a type of auxiliary language based on national languages, modern or classical or both. Here, too, there is some negative connotation.

The term *'planned language'* (*Plansprache, planlingvo, langue planifiée, planovyj jazyk*) was created by Eugen Wüster (1931), who was seeking a suitable German equivalent for Jespersen's 'constructed language'. We will return to this term.

Occasionally we find terms consisting of several elements indicating origin or genesis in different ways, for example, *künstliche konstruierte Sprache*, **artificial constructed language** (Bink 1977).

2.2 Terms describing communicative function

Let us move to our second category: ***terms describing communicative function***. Primarily in the seventeenth, eighteenth, and nineteenth centuries, but also in our own day, we find the term 'universal language' (*Universalsprache, universelle Sprache, universala lingvo, langue universelle*) in the titles of works on international language (e.g. Will 1755; Jones 1769; Busch 1787) or in the names of projects ('langue musicale universelle,' Sudre 1866; 'système de langue universelle,' Grosselin 1836; 'Universalsprache,' Pirro 1868), Schleyer (1881) called Volapük 'Universalsprache für alle gebildeten Erdbewohner.' Several important specialists in interlinguistics use the term 'universal languages' in the titles of their works (Berger 1946; Rónai 1969; Bausani 1970; Knowlson 1975; Couturat & Leau 1979; Slaughter 1982).

The term *'universal language'* has two basic meanings:

> (1) the only language of a future humankind, described occasionally in utopian social models in the Renaissance and in more recent works of utopian socialism (Rátkai 1978: 13) or modern interlinguistics (Guérard 1934: 260);

(2) a consciously created language for international communication. The latter meaning is unsuitable because it gives the impression that the purpose of such a language is to push aside and replace national languages.

The term '*world language*' (*Weltsprache, mond(o)lingvo, monda lingvo, langue mondiale, vsemirnyj jazyk, mirovoj jazyk*) is used rather too freely among linguists and interlinguists, though it is firmly established as a sociolinguistic term and is used in linguistics generally with the additional attributes 'artificial' or 'auxiliary', especially in German: *Welthilfssprache*. The term has several meanings.

1. A language with worldwide or regional significance (Greek, Latin).

2. A language with 'a visible tendency to fulfil as many social functions as possible on an international level' (Denissow & Kostomarow 1977: 57). According to Frohne (1976) and Häusler (1981), English, French, Russian, Spanish, and German form a kind of 'world language club'. In this sense, all 'world languages' are 'international languages,' but all international languages are not necessarily 'world languages'.

3. The single language for all humanity, which, according to Stalin (1951), will develop from the merging of regional languages.

4. A consciously created language for international communication (Einstein 1885; Lott 1888; Drezen 1931/1991; Bodmer 1955).

Several projects for planned language are called 'world language' (e.g., 'Weltsprache' of Volk & Fuchs [1883], 'Mondolingvo' of Trischen [1906], 'Veltparl' of Armin [1896], 'Mundolingua' of Starrenburg [1922], etc.).

The use of the term among non-specialists with several of the above connotations has caused, and continues to cause, much confusion.

The use of the term '*auxiliary language*' (*Hilfssprache, Welthilfssprache, helplingvo, helpa lingvo, monda helplingvo, langue auxiliaire (mondiale), vspomogatel'nyj jazyk*) is as widespread as the use of the term 'artificial language'. Although Zamenhof used it, it originated with Le Hir (1867). Undoubtedly this term, which is widely used among Esperantists, is designed to reassure those people who, perhaps because of misunderstandings arising from such terms as 'universal language' or 'world language', fear that some created language aims to replace or displace national languages if only in those instances where they are insufficient as means of understanding: 'It is not our intention that a new language should take the place of existing languages.'

Occasionally the term 'auxiliary language' also carries pejorative overtones, because it seems to imply a supplementary facilitating device of less value or capability than the principal device, an ethnic language. Its two primary meanings are as follows:

1. A consciously created language intended as an additional aid for communication for an international context.

2. Occasionally ethnic languages like English, Spanish, or Pidgin English are called 'auxiliary languages' (Schneider 1979: 412), when they serve as supplementary means of communication alongside native languages.

The meaning of the term '*common language*' (*Allgemeinsprache, Gemeinsprache, komuna lingvo, obščij jazyk, vseobščij jazyk*) is very general and hence it is unsuitable as an interlinguistic term for 'planned language.' It has four major meanings.

1. The superdialectal form of a standardised national language (literary language, *Hochsprache*).

2. An international means of communication in a multinational state (*mežnacional'nyj jazyk*).

3. A language used for international communication, either ethnic or planned (Liptay 1892; Jacob 1946; Svadost 1968; Grimm 1976).

4. The common, single language for all humanity (Marr 1928).

'Unified language' (*Einheitssprache, einheitliche Sprache, langue unifiée, obščečelovečeskij jazyk*) is generally used as a synonym for 'single language for all humanity', but it also sometime means 'international language', either ethnic or planned (Jordan, in *Actes* 1933). The term is accordingly confusing.

The term **'lingua franca'**, named after the hybrid trade language used in the Middle Ages in the Mediterranean area, consisting of elements of Italian, Greek, and Arabic, is used widely in popular literature but seldom in the specialised literature of interlinguistics. The term carries several meanings; Samarin (1970) distinguishes three:

1. An ethnic language used for international contacts (Koine, Latin, French, Arabic, Hausa, Chinese, Hindi, Swahili).

2. Planned languages (Esperanto, Ido).

3. Pidgins (Pidgin English).

Samarin also notes as synonyms **'trade language'** (*komerca lingvo, Handelssprache, langue de traité*), **'contact language'** (*kontakta lingvo, Kontaktsprache*), 'vehicular language' (*langue vehiculaire, trafika lingvo,*

Verkehrssprache), 'international (universal) language', 'auxiliary language'.

The term '***vehicular language***' (*trafika lingvo, (Welt-)Verkehrssprache, langue véhiculaire, jazyk posrednik* i.e. carrier language) is particularly common in German and Russian as a synonym for 'international auxiliary language'. Again we can identify three meanings:

> 1. Consciously created languages (planned languages). The project of Fieweger (1893) is called internationale Verkehrssprache.
>
> 2. Generally, however, the term is reserved for ethnic languages used by two or several national groups for whom the language is not native (Černyšev 1968: 208). This is equivalent to the Russian *mežnacional'nyj jazyk*.
>
> 3. The international (ethnic) language used in international communication (Haarmann 1973: 122).

Given the multiplicity of its meanings, this term is unsuitable for our purposes.

The word '***interlanguage***' (*interlingua, Zwischensprache, Intersprache, interlingvo, interlangue*) is quite widely used but is not entirely suitable, for several reasons. The English term is in fact a compacted form of 'international language' (Holmström 1958: 94; Pei 1958/1968; Jespersen 1930-1931: 31; Gold 1982: 34). In the German literature we find the Latin form *interlingua* (Ölberg 1954) in the sense of 'international language' or *Intersprache* (Blaschke 1950: 18). The term has four meanings:

> 1. An international language (ethnic or planned).
>
> 2. The title of two planned language systems, namely a variant of Peano's (1903) Latino sine flexione and the naturalistic system of Alexander Gode (1971b).

3. A rudimentary language structure used in foreign language learning, standing between native language and target language and consisting of very simple syntactic structures and lexical material (Selinker 1972). This meaning is not widespread.

4. An artificial (often mathematical) machine language, used in machine translation, into which the original language is coded and from which the target language is derived (*MNL* 1973: 600).

Although the term 'interlinguistics' is linked to the Latin *interlingua*, the polysemantic nature of the latter makes its use inappropriate. Advocates of Interlingua sometimes see the term 'interlinguistics' as meaning 'the science of Interlingua', though others might see it as the science of 'interlinguae', or international languages.

The widely used term '***international language***' (*internationale Sprache, internacia lingvo, langue internationale, meždunarodnyj jazyk*) indicates with greatest clarity and simplicity the function of promoting communication between and among nations. It has two meanings (Sack 1951: 5) namely:

(1) ethnic languages functioning as world or regional languages

or

(2) consciously created languages for international communication (planned languages).

Rátkai (1980) understands by 'international language' only an interethnic means of communication that is the language of no particular people. Only Esperanto qualifies in this regard. He calls ethnic languages serving as languages of wider communication '***transnational languages***'.

Additional terms include *Verständigungssprache*, or '*language of understanding*' (Behrmann 1975), an unnecessary tautology; '*bridge language*' (*ponto-lingvo, Brückensprache*: Hagler 1970: 30); and, very rarely, '*global language*' (*globa lingvo, global'nyj jazyk*: Kuznecov 1982: 39).

We also sometimes find **compound terms** that describe parallel functions more than once: *langue auxiliaire commune* in Couturat and Leau (1903: x), 'international auxiliary language' in Bodmer (1955: 464), *universelle Hilfssprache* in Bausani (1970: 146), and so on. Other compound terms describe both genesis and function: *künstliche Weltsprache* (Haarmann 1973: 131), *künstliche Welthilfssprache* (Brugmann 1913-1914; Mayrhofer & Dressler 1969), *künstliche internationale Hilfssprache* (Trubetzkoy 1939), 'planned auxiliary language' (Jacob 1947), *künstliche allgemeine Sprache, internationale Kunstsprache, konstruierte Hilfssprache*, 'international planned language' (see below).

3 Planned language

We are left with the term '*planned language*,' or *Plansprache*. The internal structure of the German term allows at least the following interpretations:

(a) the language of a plan (e.g., in architecture), or 'plan language,'

or

(b) a language characterised by a plan, or 'planned language.'

Wüster (1931) of course had the second meaning in mind. The expression itself does not necessarily require that we understand it to mean 'consciously created non-ethnic language'. Occasionally we do in fact see Bahasa Indonesia or Modern Hebrew described as 'planned languages'. Certainly there is a planned element present in these languages, and this somewhat literal understanding of the term would seem to be supported by the fact that the branch of sociolinguistics called 'language planning' (*lingvoplanado, Sprachplanung, jazykovoe stroitel'stvo*) deals with the general phenomenon of conscious, planned human intervention in the sphere of language. However, if we consider certain ethnic languages as planned languages, one of the most important reasons for creating the term in the first place is accordingly negated, namely, replacement of the misleading contrast between 'natural' language and 'artificial' language. If Bahasa Indonesia is a planned language, it is a 'natural ethnic planned language', and Esperanto is an 'unnatural (artificial?) non-ethnic planned language'. So once again we find ourselves in the familiar dilemma. An expression becomes a term only if it is properly defined.

Wüster (1931) clearly created the notion of a 'planned language' not for any language planned to one degree or another but specifically to denote a language consciously created by human beings explicitly to serve as a means of international linguistic communication. Hence we can define a 'planned language' as *a language consciously created by an individual or group of people, in accordance with defined criteria, with the goal of facilitating international linguistic communication.*

In a similar way, for Jouko Lindstedt (1981), the first editor of the new periodical *Planlingvistiko,* planned languages are 'all languages born through conscious human creation.'

Given the above, we cannot agree with Helmar Frank, who broadens the meaning of 'planned language' unnecessarily. For him a planned language is 'a written or aural code consciously developed and agreed upon by one person or several people, required to serve only the goal of comprehensible transfer of data or instructions from or to a person' (Frank 1975: 18). He distinguishes between: (a) interlinguistic planned languages (e.g., Interlingue, Ido, Esperanto, Volapük) and (b) algorithmic planned languages, that is, programming languages. Influenced by Frank, for Thiele (1977) the language of chemistry is also a planned language. Given the history of the term 'planned language', the term 'interlinguistic planned language' may be regarded as a tautology.

István Szerdahelyi (1981: 4) argues that the term 'planned language' is preferred by German speakers but in most languages cannot be translated by a single word. It is true that the term was born in German and has become firmly established there (see Blanke 1985; Haupenthal 1976). But it need not be translated using a single word, since 'planned language' is a perfect synonym. A compound or participial construction is presumably possible, as in German or Esperanto, and such a compound should be used. In English we have found 'planlanguage' (Manders 1953-1954: 153) as well as 'planned language' (Jacob 1947), though the former is used by a non-native speaker of English. French has *langue planifiée* and Italian, less commonly, *lingua pianificata*. In Danish we find *plansprog* (Bagger 1980: 37), in Icelandic *planmal* (Böðvarsson 1963), in Dutch *plantaal* (de Wit 1981: 52), in Finnish *suunitelmakielet* (*Enzyklopaedia fennica*, vol. 8), in Russian *planovyj jazyk* (Kolker 1978: 11; Kuznecov 1982: 61), in Polish *język planowy* (Ejsmont 1981), in Serbo-Croatian *planski jezik* (Gajić 1980), in Czech *plánovaný jazyk*, and so on. So the claim that the term cannot be adequately translated seems unproven.

There are several advantages to the term 'planned language'. First, it alludes to the familiar fact that human beings consciously try, in planned fashion, to change their natural and social surroundings, often with considerable success. Second, since at least in the twentieth century the phenomenon of language planning, with its own sociolinguistic subdiscipline, is well known, the term 'planned language' seems perfectly natural. After all, the element of consciousness and planning in international relations through linguistic communication is of fundamental importance for interlinguistics.

II: The Term 'Planned Language'

Where, then, does Esperanto fit? Going back to my initial distinction (origin and genesis versus communicative function), we should avoid naming Esperanto artificial, auxiliary, universal, world language, and so on. It is *international* in its communicative function and *planned* in its *origin*.

I have stated elsewhere (Blanke 1981b, 1986a) my opposition to Frank's (1975) attempt to eliminate the name 'Esperanto' as the title of Zamenhof's language, calling it simply 'the International Language', or 'ILo'. Frank argues that the name 'Esperanto' is compromised in scholarly circles because of certain sect-like tendencies in parts of the Esperanto movement (an authentic problem). But one does not make something respectable by changing its name, but by changing its nature. Through serious work in and on the phenomenon itself we can raise its reputation. Furthermore, intentional hiding of the fact that we are dealing, when we speak of the 'Ilo', with the 'notorious' language Esperanto simply serves to deceive those people from whom Esperanto speakers most need to win cooperation. We might add that the term 'Ilo' has other meanings (abbreviation of International Labour Organisation, a suffix in Esperanto, for a while the name of the project Ido).

And, finally, it is important to distinguish among a project (a sign system that has not become a language), a project that has partially gained the status of language (we might describe Volapük, Ido, Latino sine flexione, Occidental-Interlingue, and Interlingua as 'incipient planned languages'), and the only fully developed system and so far the only complete international language, namely, Esperanto.

III

Is scholarly communication possible in a so-called 'artificial' language?[22]

1 Scholarly language

'Scholarly language', understood as the totality of linguistic elements used in individual fields and branches of science, is an integral part of a given language.

According to the prestigious German specialist in scientific language, Lothar Hoffmann (1984: 53), such scholarly language (variously known as specialised language, scientific language, or language for special purposes) is 'the sum of all linguistic resources used in a communicative field limited to a specific scientific field of inquiry, in order to guarantee communication among people in that field'.[23]

So defined, a 'scholarly language' is an abstraction. In practice, there exist in various languages what we might call *sublanguages* (lects) for various kinds of scholarly discourse, for industrial and technical areas of production, and for other special activities. But there also exist certain characteristics common to all such scholarly and specialised languages.

When we speak of such 'languages', we often have in mind specialised vocabulary, the 'terminology' of given fields. But in reality such specialised language includes syntactic rules, specific stylistic resources, phra-

---

[22] The co-author of this study is Wera Blanke. The text first appeared in the journal *Interdisciplinary Description of Complex Systems (INDECS)* in the special issue *The Phenomenon of Esperanto* edited by Humphrey Tonkin and Veronika Poór, vol. 13 (2015), no. 2 (see D. Blanke & W. Blanke 2015). Translated by Humphrey Tonkin.

[23] '...die Gesamtheit aller sprachlichen Mittel, die in einem fachlich begrenzbaren Kommunikationsbereich verwendet werden, um die Verständigung zwischen den in diesem Bereich tätigen Menschen zu gewährleisten.'

seologies, and mechanisms for the organisation of texts to create the various types that such texts assume.

The application of specialised language is particularly significant for at least three principal functions of language:

(a) *Communication*: Specialised communication allows for more effective and more precise linguistic communication than would be possible through the general resources of the language.

(b) *Discovery of new knowledge*: The discovery of new facts and connections in nature and society, and their cognitive appropriation, is made significantly easier through application of specialised language.

(c) *Recording, conserving and conveying new knowledge:* By applying adequate specialised linguistic resources to various phenomena and channels of communication, we can record facts, actions and connections in nature and society, thereby conserving their existence and transferring them to current and future users.

Given the increasing growth of human knowledge, the influence of science and technology is expanding in ordinary life. Accordingly, our understanding of specialised language plays a larger and larger role in everyday communication.

2 Planned languages, language planning, and research on scholarly language

Planned languages (other terms include: 'artificial' or 'constructed' international languages, international auxiliary languages, universal languages)[24] are the result of conscious and goal-oriented creation and can

---

24 On planned languages, see, among others, the monographs of Drezen 1931/1991, D. Blanke 1985 and Sakaguchi 1998 and the literature to which they refer, and also the edited collections by Schubert 2001, Tonkin 1997, and D. Blanke 2006.

therefore be regarded as products of *language planning*. This idea is particularly emphasised by the Estonian language planning expert Valter Tauli. He describes language planning as

> ... the methodical activity of regulating and improving existing languages or creating new common regional, national or international languages. (Tauli 1968: 27)

In this sense planned languages are both products of and devices for language planning. This is so at least of Esperanto (Tonkin 2011).

For the study of specialised language, planned languages are of interest for at least the following reasons:

(1) Planned languages are often results of the search for rational and more precise linguistic resources than can be found in ethnic languages. In this sense, they perform a similar role to that of efforts to regularise and adapt ethnic languages to the needs of specialised and automated communication (see Schubert 2011).

(2) Planned languages have historically provided an impulse for the development of specialised languages (including nomenclatures) and the emergence of terminology science.

(3) Language planning plays a significant role in the creation and development of specialised vocabulary in both ethnic and planned languages.

(4) Planned languages have played a role as means of international scholarly communication and continue to do so.

(5) Ethnic languages and planned languages, if they have developed specialised languages, have a common need for quality standards for the formation and expansion of terminology, for terminological standardisation and planning, and for the practical organisation of these activities.

(6) In addition – though to a different degree in various ethnic languages and a lesser degree in planned languages – we can observe efforts to collect and document terminology, to explore the development of theory, to examine knowledge transfer and research methods, and to exploit modern electronic resources and data-processing systems (among them, electronic terminology banks).

Because planned languages have been applied to communication needs only to a very limited extent, most of the results in the field of specialised communication in planned languages have been achieved (almost always in Esperanto) not by state-supported or institutionally supported efforts, but through private initiatives. The lack of professional grounding has led to considerable variability in the quality of individual specialised terminologies.

Given the varying extent and development of the application of given fields in planned languages, some parts of the specialised vocabulary should be regarded in the first instance as mere proposals, because they relate to a field not yet fully active in the medium of a planned language.

Description of the problems of scholarly communication in Esperanto has up to now been largely limited to the development of terminology.

3 Languages without linguistic specialisation?

3.1 Ethnic languages

A language that lacks specialised fields of communication faces the threat of decline and finally the withering away of its social significance. Such limited communicative functionality may lead to a kind of folkloric marginalisation and the use of the language only as a family language.

Even the ethnic languages of Europe may be threatened by such a development, given the hegemonic role of English and the pressure on other languages that such hegemony produces. Robert Phillipson (1992, 2009) has rightly drawn attention to the phenomenon of linguistic imperialism and its negative consequences. The gradual loss of specialised function will become evident in, among other considerations, the fact that important scholarly and specialised texts will cease to be produced in a given language, and specialised terminology will not be taught. Furthermore, there is a danger that important specialised texts written in the past will be ignored. This shift is beginning to concern even speakers of 'major' languages, like German and others, in which important scholarly texts have been produced for centuries. In bibliographies of current scholarly works, doctoral dissertations, and other forms of research, works in other languages are already barely mentioned, thus ignoring important discoveries (on the Anglicisation of economics, for example, see Sandelin 2001).

3.2 Planned languages

In addressing planned languages, we must distinguish among:

a) *projects* with no practical application,

b) some *planned-language systems with limited practical application* (particularly Volapük, Ido, Latino sine flexione, Occidental-Interlingue, Basic English and Interlingua), and

c) a planned *language* – i.e. a language in the full sense of the notion, with well-developed and *various* communicative functions – a status so far achieved only by Esperanto.

Furthermore, it would be a mistake to assume that all Esperanto speakers share the ideals of the language's creator, Zamenhof, or that they see the language as first and foremost an embodiment of the ideals of peace. Adepts of Esperanto may see the language as, variously,

a) a hobby

b) a language game

c) a means of artistic expression (for creative literature)

d) an instrument of practical communication

e) an idealistic or alternative means of identity, primarily, though not exclusively, in line with the ideas of Zamenhof

f) a language policy alternative.

Among these six there are variations and commonalities. Probably all Esperantists share some common values, but such commonality varies enormously from one speaker to another.

A certain proportion of the adepts of planned languages (particularly those in categories d, e, and f) are politically engaged (see D. Blanke 2007a). They are interested in language rights and are critical of the hegemonic position of a few major languages in international communication, particularly English. They argue for non-discriminatory communication through a politically neutral language and they draw appropriate attention to the phenomenon of linguistic imperialism and its negative consequences. Their attention is particularly focused on European language problems, which have proved especially complicated and multi-faceted within the European Union.

As for the development of Esperanto and its communicative potential, attention is often drawn to the abundant creative literature in the language, both original and translated. Such literature exists in considerable quantity and quality (on original literature, see Sutton 2008 and Gubbins 2012). There is no doubt that creative literature is of great significance in the development and stabilisation of the means of expression in a planned language and serves to prove its independent cultural function. However, it is insufficient if the language is ever to function in a given context as an *official*, even if limited, means of international communication on a par with other languages

Accordingly, the specialised-language function is indispensable, not least because in international cooperation in official contexts (organisations, institutions, etc.), most communication is on specialised topics. Such topics also play a growing role in everyday communication.

The German Romanist Karl Voßler (1872-1949) once put it like this: 'A purely poetic literature, without scholarly works, is a written dialect, but not a fully rounded literature' (Vossler 1925: 236).[25]

In sum, the modern scholarly application of a planned language is one of the basic conditions for its eventual role as a language policy alternative.

What role is played by specialised-language communication in planned languages, particularly Esperanto? We will attempt a brief summary.

4 The scholarly application of planned languages

Outside Esperanto, the application of scholarly language in the context of planned languages has been very limited:

In *Volapük* (1879, the work of the German Catholic prelate Johann Martin Schleyer), a strictly agglutinative language with radically adapted (not to say distorted) morphemes derived from Latin and from Romance and Germanic languages, there exist only a few modest at-

---

[25] 'Eine lediglich poetische Literatur, ohne wissenschaftliches Schrifttum, ist geschriebener Dialekt, keine vollwertige Literatur.'

tempts at commercial correspondence (see Haupenthal 1982: 29, 41, 47).

In *Latino sine flexione* (initiated in 1903 by the well-known Italian mathematician Giuseppe Peano), based on the ideas of Gottfried Wilhelm Leibniz (1646-1716) for a simplified Latin, a few scientific texts were published, primarily in the periodical *Schola et Vita* (1926-1939),[26] among them Peano's work *Formulario mathematico* (Kennedy 1980: passim, especially 107, 118, 125).

In *Ido* (1907, published by the well-known French mathematician, logician, and Leibniz specialist Louis Couturat), which is to some degree a reformed version of Esperanto, especially in word-formation and lexis, a few scientific texts appeared. They include some eight specialised terminologies, on, among other fields, biology, chemistry, business, machine building, mathematics, and radio technology, and also philological, philosophical and religious texts (see D. Blanke 1985: 199-201; Carlevaro & Haupenthal 1999).[27]

In *Occidental* (published in 1922 by the German-Baltic mathematics teacher Edgar de Wahl and known after 1945 as *Interlingue*), a largely uninflected but Romance-based language, there appeared only a few scientific texts, in the fields of philosophy, philology, and – even more rarely – politics, economics, and pedagogy. Worthy of mention, however, is a sizable collection of specialised texts in mathematics and a mathematical dictionary (see D. Blanke 1985: 167; Stenström 1997).[28]

In *Interlingua* (1951, initiated by IALA, the International Auxiliary Language Association and completed by the German-American Roman-

---

26 Věra Barandovská-Frank (2002: 17-20) mentions the following fields in which Latino sine flexione texts have appeared: astronomy, biology, ethnology, interlinguistics, culture, linguistics, literature, mathematics, medicine, pedagogy, psychology, sociology, and technology.

27 www.en.ido.li (site visited on 22.06.2018)

28 interlingue.pbworks.com (site visited on 22.06.2018)

ist Alexander Gode), a planned language deeply indebted to Romance languages with reduced inflective characteristics, abstracts appeared in the 1950s and 1960s in a few medical periodicals and between 1952 and 1955 in two abstract compilations, *Spectroscopia Molecular* and *Scientia International* (see Sexton 1993: 7-8.). The Interlingua book catalogue (Bibliographia 2002)[29] mentions only a few specialised publications, in, among other fields, demography, art history, mathematics, philology, philosophy, plant diseases, and theology. There are also a few specialised dictionaries, in biology and botany, among others.

Also in *Basic English* (1929, by the British linguist and translator Charles K. Ogden), a variant of English with a lexis reduced semantically to 850 words and some systematisation in word-formation, there appeared several specialised texts, for example in electrotechnology, geology, and economics (Ogden 1968: 75-82).

In these various planned languages very few specialised texts have appeared in printed form. However, we can find a number of new texts of this kind in the various versions of Wikipedia and in newly-established websites. A common element in all these linguistic systems is the fact that in principle they are structurally well-adapted for the presentation of specialised texts and terminologies. Even so, the limited number of specialised texts and dictionaries that have appeared in these languages hardly responds to the real needs of international communication, given that there are so few of them and the number of users of these languages interested in their use is so limited.

---

29 The catalogue is now available at http://www.interlingua.com/libros/. [All sites were last accessed (and if necessary updated) by the editors on 24th May 2018 – SF]

5 Specialised texts in Esperanto

5.1 A general overview

The initiator of Esperanto, a physician well-grounded in the natural sciences, Ludwig Leyzer Zamenhof (1859-1917), put no particular emphasis on the scientific role of his language, unlike, for example, the initiators of Latino sine flexione, Ido and Interlingua. However, in the first collection of model texts, *Fundamenta Krestomatio* (Zamenhof 1903/1992), we find popular science texts, for example in medicine and astronomy.

It was primarily French intellectuals who, at the turn of the nineteenth and twentieth centuries, first grasped the significance of Esperanto as a scholarly language and engaged themselves in its development. The language was not yet two decades old when the first such journal, *Internacia Scienca Revuo*,[30] was launched. Between then and 1909 organisations were founded for *scientists, doctors, vegetarians* and *railway workers* (see Blanke, Haszpra & Felsö 1988), all contributing to the development of their specialised languages. In 1910 a further scientific journal, *Medicina Internacia Revuo*, began publication.

It is difficult to present a complete picture of the scientific and scholarly initiatives and applications in Esperanto, since so much depends, and has depended, on individual efforts. Journals appear and, in due course, disappear,[31] though the possibilities for scientific and specialised discourse have increased with the arrival of web-based opportunities.

Specialised texts exist in this planned language in considerable numbers. Today they appear in small journals and bulletins, and in web-based dis-

---

30 On its beginnings see W. Blanke 2013: 43-52.

31 The fullest bibliography of periodicals in Esperanto to have appeared so far covers the period from the beginning of the language to the year 2006 and contains 14,143 titles (Hernández Yzal, Máthé & Molera 2010).

III: Is scholarly communication possible in a so-called 'artificial' language?

cussion groups and publications – of varying quality – at least in the following fields:

Atheism, ecology, economics, ecumenism, Esperantology, railways, philately, philosophy, forestry, linguistics and interlinguistics, law, journalism, the construction industry, language policy, language minorities, medicine, music, homeopathy, ornithology, education, post and telecommunication, amateur radio, interdisciplinary science, theology and various religions, vegetarianism.

In addition to *Internacia Scienca Revuo*, a particularly important role in the publication of scientific texts has been played, or continues to be played, by the following periodicals:

- *Medicina Internacia Revuo* (1910-1911, 1923-36, 1952-)
- *Internacia Pedagogia Revuo* (1908-1922, 1927-1939, 1956-1959, 1970-)
- *Homo kaj Kosmo* (astronomy, 1963-1987)
- *Esperantologio* (1949-1955, 1959-1961, 1999-)
- *Internacia Geografia Revuo* (1956-1964)
- *Kemio Internacia* (1965-1968)
- *Internacia Komputado/Fokuso* (1983-1988)
- *Planlingvistiko* (1981-1986)
- *Scienca Mondo* (science policy, 1976-1989)
- *Sciencaj Komunikaĵoj* (1975-1986)
- *Tutmondaj Sciencoj kaj Teknikoj* (in Chinese and Esperanto, 1985-1995).

The most important journal in general science up to now is *(Internacia) Scienca Revuo*. Its genealogy is as follows:

- 1904-1911: *Internacia Scienca Revuo*
- 1912-1914: *Scienca Gazeto*

- 1918/19: *La Teknika Revuo* (subtitled *Sekvo de Internacia Scienca Revuo*, continuation of *Internacia Scienca Revuo*)
- 1922-1923: *Internacia Scienca Revuo*
- 1926-1939: *Bulteno de ISAE*
- As of 1949: *Scienca Revuo* (*Fondita en 1904 kiel Internacia Scienca Revuo*, founded in 1904 as *Internacia Scienca Revuo*).

Recently the complete run of *Scienca Revuo* from 1949 to 2014 (more than 2,000 articles in various fields) has become available in electronically scanned form.[32]

A few journals in ethnic languages occasionally include contributions and summaries in Esperanto, for example the language-policy journal *Language Problems & Language Planning* (*LPLP*, as of 1977),[33] and the journal of cybernetics and education *Grundlagenstudien aus Kybernetik und Geisteswissenschaft/Humankybernetik* (as of 1977).

The bibliographically and scientifically oriented bulletin *Informilo por Interlingvistoj* (*IpI*),[34] published by the Centre for Research and Documentation on World Language Problems (CED), attempts, among other things, to register the most important facts and information about scholarly communication in Esperanto. As of 1992, the bulletin *Interlinguistische Informationen* (IntI), organ of the *Gesellschaft für Interlinguistik e.V.* (Society for Interlinguistics), has done the same, with contents similar to those of IpI.[35]

---

32 See https://scienca-revuo.info/issue/archive.
33 The journal began publication as *La Monda Lingvo-Problemo* (*LMLP*, 1969-1977). On *LPLP* see: https://benjamins.com/#catalog/journals/lplp/main.
34 Edited from 1974 to 1977 by Ulrich Lins, from 1983 to 1990 by Ryszard Rokicki and from 1992 to 2016 by Detlev Blanke. The bulletin is also available on the Web: http://www.esperantic.org/eo/publikajoj/ipi/. [It is now also available in English: http://www.esperantic.org/en/publications/ifi-information-for-interlinguists/ – HT]
35 See http://www.interlinguistik-gil.de/wb/pages/bulletin-inti.php/.

III: Is scholarly communication possible in a so-called 'artificial' language?

In the most recently published book catalogue of the Universal Esperanto Association (Esperanto-Katalogo 2001) publications on the following subjects are listed as available:

> Archaeology, astronomy, bee-keeping, biology, botany, chemistry, culinary arts, cybernetics, ecology, economics, ethnography, geography, geology, historiography, hydraulic engineering, hygiene, informatics, interlinguistics and Esperantology, journalism, law, linguistics, mathematics, medicine, meteorology, pedagogy, philosophy, political science, psychology, sociology, sport, stenography, telecommunications, theology (and philosophy of religion), traffic engineering, and zoology.

Every year some twenty or thirty specialised monographs of various lengths appear.[36] The UEA catalogue, mentioned above, contains information on the following specialised publications (by topic and numbers):

Philosophy	141
Geography	114
History	82
Linguistics	463
Religion	264
Science and Technology	313
in total	1377 titles

The available literature is regularly updated in the web versions of the catalogues.

Esperanto-language material in monographs, anthologies and periodicals is collected by several specialised libraries and archives across the world. Over the past decade, efforts have intensified to coordinate such activity with a view to conserving the collections and creating a world catalogue and bibliography.

---

[36] New publications are mentioned in the new publications section of the journal *Esperanto*, organ of the Universal Esperanto Association, Rotterdam.

Discussion on the topic continues in conferences and Internet discussion groups.[37] A particularly important step is the web-based catalogue of the Planned Language Collection of the Austrian National Library.[38] In addition, for almost fifty years scholarly materials and contributions on interlinguistics and Esperantology have been systematically recorded in the web-based bibliography of the Modern Language Association of America, where a search for 'Esperanto terminology' will yield numerous titles on problems of specialised terminology in Esperanto.[39]

5.2 Specialised texts in the Internet

We can probably not expect the emergence of many new scientific journals in printed form, given that the Internet has largely assumed the role of communication channel in the various fields. Several web-based journals have begun publication, however:

- *Teleskopo* (edited in Brazil) publishes scientific texts on various topics.[40]

Interlinguistic and Esperantological contributions have been published as of 1999 in

- *Esperantologio – Esperanto Studies*, which also exists in paper form.[41]
- As of 2006, the Swedish interlinguist Bertil Wennergren has edited the web-based journal on Esperanto studies *Lingva Kritiko*.[42]

---

[37] See Blanke 2009a. The 2014 KAEST Conference, for example, had as its principal topic 'Libraries and Archives: How to Protect Our Heritage?'. Discussion is ongoing at bibliotekoj@googlegroups.com.

[38] Trovanto: http://search.obvsg.at/primo_library/libweb/action/search.do?dscnt=0&scp.scps=scope%3A%28ONB_aleph_esperanto%29&tab=onb_sondersammlungen&mode=Basic&vid=ONB.

[39] https://www.mla.org/bibliography. On the MLA Bibliography see Tonkin 2010.

[40] http://www.teleskopo.com/index.htm/. [See https://web.archive.org/web/20160802013438/http://www.teleskopo.com/eldonoj.htm – SF]

[41] http://www.cb.uu.se/esperanto/.

[42] http://lingvakritiko.com/.

- From 2010 to 2012 *Inkoj: Interlingvistikaj Kajeroj*[43] was published by scholars in Italy.

A particular role in the creation of specialised texts has been played recently by *Vikipedio* (the Esperanto-language Wikipedia), and the various 'wikis' linked to it. The creation of articles, often with specialised content, has accelerated in recent years, and this has had a significant influence on the development of specialised language. The speed and sometimes hasty creation of such texts allows little time for competent discussion of the terms employed.

Here is how the major planned languages appear in Wikipedia:

Esperanto (to 12 January 2015)[44]	208,299 articles[45]
Ido[46]	26,229
Interlingua[47]	14,352
Interlingue/Occidental[48]	2,640

We should also mention the *WikiTrans* project of Eckhard Bick (2011), which automatically translates large numbers of English-language articles into Esperanto. As of mid-2014, more than four million articles had been translated into Esperanto.[49] These articles, being automatically translated, need to be edited for, among other things, specialised terminology.

---

43 'An Academic Journal on Planned and Artificial Languages' http://riviste.unimi.it/index.php/inkoj/index/. Texts appear in Italian, English or Esperanto.
44 http://eo.wikipedia.org/wiki/Vikipedio:%C4%88efpa%C4%9Do/.
45 At the end of 2014 a DVD was published with the complete Esperanto-Vikipedio (27 October 2014), containing 204,259 articles and with links to the current Vikipedio (www.ikso.net).
46 http://io.wikipedia.org/wiki/Frontispico/.
47 http://ia.wikipedia.org/wiki/Pagina_principal/.
48 http://ie.wikipedia.org/wiki/Principal_p%C3%A1gine/.
49 http://epo.wikitrans.net/.

There are several Esperanto-language branches of the Wiki family that include specialised texts:

- *Meta-Vikio*: website of the Vikimedio Foundation[50]
- *Vikilibroj* a project for the construction of open-source handbooks and textbooks[51]
- *Vikicitaro*: an open-source web-based dictionary of quotations[52]
- *Vikispecioj*: a project to register all living species[53]
- *Vikivortaro*: a general dictionary[54]
- *Vikinovajoj* an open source news agency.[55]

This abundance of already existing and steadily expanding texts naturally raises the question of the consistency and quality of the specialised language used and, particularly with WikiTrans, the influence of the English language.

5.3 Types of specialised texts

Many specialised texts are also available in the Esperanto Library of Science and Technology (STEB).[56] The growing number of specialised texts in Esperanto leads us to consider the characteristics of the phenomenon of 'specialised text' if we are to distinguish it from other texts, such as literary texts or general texts.

In the 1980s and 1990s the definition of *specialised text* has become the focus of linguistic attention. What, then, is a 'specialised text'? Lothar Hoffmann defines it as follows:

---

50 http://eo.wikipedia.org/wiki/Meta-Vikio/.
51 http://eo.wikibooks.org/wiki/%C4%88efpa%C4%9Do/
52 http://eo.wikiquote.org/wiki/%C4%88efpa%C4%9Do/
53 http://species.wikimedia.org/wiki/%C4%88efpa%C4%9Do.
54 http://eo.wiktionary.org/wiki/%C4%88efpa%C4%9Do/.
55 http://eo.wikinews.org/wiki/%C4%88efpa%C4%9Do/.
56 See Scienc-Teknika Esperanto-Biblioteko, STEB, at www.eventoj.hu/steb/.

III: Is scholarly communication possible in a so-called 'artificial' language?

> *Specialised text* is an instrument and a result of an act of linguistic communication occurring in connection with productive activity within specialised social contexts. It consists of a limited and ordered quantity of sentence or sentence-like units that are coherent with respect to logic, semantics and syntax. These units are complex signs corresponding to complex propositions in the human mind and to complex facts in objective reality. (Hoffmann 1985: 233-234)

Such specialised texts come in many types with varied characteristics and communicative functions. They can be either written or spoken. However, it is important to emphasise that it is not always possible to make a clear distinction between a scientific text for a colleague in the field and a popular science text for a wider audience.

We can distinguish a few major forms of specialised texts, such as:

- **scientific and scholarly texts.** *Treatise, scientific survey, conference intervention, examination material* (all four exist in Esperanto),

- **technical texts.** *Patent application, instruction manual for a machine* (such texts do not yet exist in Esperanto),

- **institutional texts.** *Law, decree, contract, birth certificate.* Translations of laws exist (in legal publications in Esperanto), likewise decrees and regulations (for example in offices), and contracts (for example agreements for cooperation among organisations), though not birth certificates.

- **field-dependent texts.** *Weather forecast (meteorology), prescription (medicine), recipe (culinary arts), instructions to patients (medicine, pharmacology).* There are abundant examples of recipes, and Esperanto-language radio and television programs involve weather forecasts, but the other forms are lacking.

To date, no detailed study of specialised texts in Esperanto (their typology, characteristics, and occurrence in linguistic practice) has been undertaken.

6 Organisational structures and spoken communication

Although Esperanto is in the first instance a written language, spoken use is expanding. This is so of specialised-language communication, which takes place in varying degrees of intensity, in *specialised organisations* and other fora, not least in online discussion groups. The following is a selection of specialised organisations (by year of foundation, according to Veuthey 2014: 61-75):

Science. Internacia Scienca Asocio Esperantista (ISAE, 1906, interdisciplinary)

Medicine. Universala Medicina Esperanto-Asocio (UMEA, 1908)

Vegetarianism. Tutmonda Esperantista Vegetarana Asocio (TEVA, 1908)

Railways. Internacia Fervojista Esperanto-Federacio (IFEF, 1909)

Catholics. Internacia Katolika Unuiĝo Esperantista (IKUE, 1910)

Christians (Protestants). Kristana Esperantista Ligo Internacia (KELI, 1911)

Teachers. Internacia Ligo de Esperantistaj Instruistoj (ILEI, 1949)

Post and Telecommunication. Internacia Poŝtista kaj Telekomunikista Esperanto-Asocio (IPTEA, 1966)

Amateur radio. Internacia Ligo de Esperantistaj Radioamatoroj (ILERA, 1970)

Mathematics. Internacia Asocio de Esperantistaj Matematikistoj (IAdEM, 1974)

Ethnography. Internacia Komitato por Etnaj Liberecoj (IKEL, 1978)

Forestry. Internacia Forstista Rondo Esperantista (IFRE, 1981)

Philosophy. Filozofia Asocio Tutmonda (FAT, 1983)

Cybernetics. Tutmonda Asocio pri Kibernetiko, Informadiko kaj Sistemiko (TAKIS, 1983)

Business. Internacia Komerca kaj Ekonomia Fakgrupo (IKEF, 1985)

Homeopathy. Internacia Naturkuraca Asocio (INA, 1986)

Law. Esperanta Jura Asocio (EJA, 1989)

Spiritualism. Asocio de Studado Internacia pri Spiritaj kaj Teologiaj Instruoj (ASISTI, 1989)

Building trades. Tutmonda Asocio de Konstruistoj Esperantistaj (TAKE, 1993)

Agriculture. Internacia Agrikultura Esperanto-Asocio (IAEA, 1996)

Education. Edukado kaj Interreto (E@I, 2001)

Social issues. Monda Asembleo Socia (MAS, 2005)

Islam. Islama Esperanto-Asocio (2007)

Numismatics. Esperanto Numismatika Asocio (ENA, 2012)

A high proportion of these and other specialised organisations include a web presence.[57]

There exist numbers of academic institutions whose goal is the promotion of interdisciplinary exchange. Among them are the *Akademio Internacia de Sciencoj San Marino* (AIS 1985: see Frank 1993: 910) and the *Internacia Scienca Akademio Comenius* (Neergaard & Kiselman 1992: III). International professional contacts are also aided by handbooks for scientists publishing in Esperanto or active as Esperantists (e.g. Darbellay 1981, Fössmeier & Tuhvatullina 2005).

These and other specialised organisations, institutions and informal groupings commonly organise their meetings in the context of the World Congress of Esperanto, an annual event that convenes anywhere from 1,000 to 3,000 (and even as many as 6,000 – in Esperanto's centennial year 1987) speakers from some sixty or seventy countries.

---
57 See http://www.esperanto.net/veb/org.html, which mentions more than 40 organisations.

Some organisations have their own conferences and other events. Railway specialists hold an annual congress, doctors a biennial congress, and interlinguists and Esperantologists several annual national and international events. Specialists in information sciences, computer science, and cybernetics – and also religious groups – organise events less regularly.

Popular scientific events also contribute to the development of specialised texts and the establishment of specialised vocabulary. As of 1948, for example, sessions of the so-called International Congress University take place during the World Congress (Wandel 2010). Also prominent have been various 'Summer Universities' (e.g. 1963-1990 in Gyula, Hungary; 1980 and following years in Veliko Trnovo, Bulgaria), and the University Summer Courses in Liège, Belgium, from 1972 to 1980, which produced some 30 published papers, on such topics as anatomy, biology, chemistry, literary studies, mathematics, pharmacology, psychology, sociology, linguistics, and zoology (D. Blanke 1986b: 82-87).

Particularly important was the series known as Application of Esperanto in Science and Technology (AEST) held in Czechoslovakia between 1978 and 1989. Individual conferences were devoted to selected topics (always with a secondary theme of 'Esperanto as a scientific language' and 'Esperanto and terminology'). The six volumes of this first series of events contains 156 separate papers. As of 1998 the series was continued by the Czech Esperanto Association under the title Conference on the Application of Esperanto in Science and Technology (KAEST). The proceedings of these conferences were also published.[58] A third series of biennial KAEST conferences has been organised since 2010 in Modra Harmónia, Slovakia, by a group of young specialists in Internet applications, computers and other electronic devices, (papers in Nosková/Baláž 2011; 2013).[59] Similar conferences etc. have been arranged from time to time in Bulgaria, China, and Cuba.

---

58 See Malovec 1999 and Pluhař 2001, 2003, 2005, 2007, 2009.
59 See http://kaest.ikso.net/.

III: Is scholarly communication possible in a so-called 'artificial' language?

Scholarly exchange in Esperanto has been particularly active in Japan. A series of six largely language-policy-orientated symposia have been recently organised by the Japanese Esperanto Institute (Raporto 2013: 83-85). Japanese scholars are particularly active in medicine, contributing frequently to *Medicina Internacia Revuo*, and have made important contributions to Esperantology.

Itô Kanzi (1918-2005, under the pseudonym Ludovikito) provided a fundamental basis for the scholarly study of Esperanto and of Zamenhof by editing 58 volumes of the work of Zamenhof and of journals, dictionaries and textbooks influenced by him (see the list in Privat 2007). In the Republic of Korea university-based activity has included publication of the journal *Mondo de Universitato* (Seoul, Dankook University, 1987-1994).

In several non-Esperanto specialised conferences, Esperanto is occasionally used as a conference language in parallel with other languages, for example as of 1968 by geologists (10 volumes of conference proceedings so far), and in the 1980s by specialists in cybernetics in Namur, Belgium. The international conference *Interkomputo* took place entirely in Esperanto in Budapest in 1982, attracting 200 computer scientists from nineteen countries. The conference produced over 100 papers, published in six volumes. In the international informatics conference in Budapest in 1985, seventeen out of 45 papers were given in Esperanto. The proceedings were subsequently published.

We should not underestimate the important role in the development of specialised communication played by informal correspondence among specialists, now much facilitated by the Internet. There exist discussion groups and innumerable individual contacts. The Universal Esperanto Association's Yearbook contains 1,700 addresses of variously oriented speakers of Esperanto in 100 countries, exchanging and promoting contacts on some 800 different topics (Veuthey 2014: 99-259).

7 Specialised vocabulary and specialised dictionaries

The structural characteristics of the Esperanto language make it particularly suitable for scientific communication, as the founder of terminology science Eugen Wüster (1889-1977) established long ago in his foundational work on language standardisation (Wüster 1931/1970: 294-323). Among these characteristics are the easy linkage of morphemes (a consequence of, for example, the convenient morpho-phonological syllabic structure, the lack of morpheme changes, etc.), the fully productive affix system and the flexible application of word-formation rules.[60] This system was initially analysed by René de Saussure (1910a, 2010b), brother of the linguist Ferdinand de Saussure.

Such characteristics facilitate the adaptation of the language to new communicative needs and render it suitable for automatic documentation of specialised language, as has been shown for example in the planned-language research and dialogue system PREDIS (Stoppoloni 1982) and in machine processing. The semiautomatic translation system Distributed Language Translation (DLT), initiated by Toon Witkam in 1983, in which a slightly modified Esperanto served as a bridge language (black-box language), was developed as far as a fully functioning prototype (Sadler 1991, Schubert 1999, Witkam 1983) before funding ran out. In recent years new initiatives have been published to develop software for machine translation into and out of Esperanto (see for example several contributions by Nosková & Baláž 2011). Also worthy of mention are the phonetic and phonological qualities of Esperanto, which favour high-quality speech recognition and speech synthesis (Koutny 2001).

Specialised vocabulary is recorded in specialised dictionaries.[61] Estimates of their numbers vary. Edward Ockey lists 200 specialised dictionaries of differing extent and quality up to the year 1980 (Ockey 1982). Ockey's list

---
60 On word formation in Esperanto see also D. Blanke 1981a.
61 On the earliest efforts see Haferkorn 1954, 1962, 1966.

has been updated to the year 2002 by Geoffrey Sutton, who mentions 280 dictionaries for some 70 fields (Ockey & Sutton 2002).[62] Some 140 specialised dictionaries are available on line.[63] Another web-based bibliography for 1980-2000 lists 188 specialised dictionaries for 88 fields.[64] Also the largest Esperanto-Esperanto dictionary, *La Nova Plena Ilustrita Vortaro de Esperanto*, includes specialised vocabulary for 73 fields (Waringhien & Duc Goninaz 2005: 36-37). Krause's *Granda Vortaro Esperanto-Germana* seems even richer, with specialised vocabulary for 86 fields (Krause 1999). A similar number of fields is covered in the German-Esperanto volume (Krause 2007).

Active development of specialised terminology has been particularly systematic and purposeful in the fields of forestry (D. Blanke & Panka 2010), railway terminology (Gulyás 2010), and medicine (Ferenczy 2010). Also the field of computer science is relatively well developed (Pokrovskij 1995, Nevelsteen 2012, Schweder 1999). Many dictionaries are no longer published in printed form, but regularly updated in web-based versions, for example a list of terminology related to international organisations, particularly the United Nations.[65]

8 Formation of specialised terms

For the formation of specialised terms, following responsible systematisation of the field and definition of its ideas, the following procedures are available:

- Creation of terms from already existing general words by modification of their definition, for example *funkcio* (function), which doubles as a part of the general vocabulary and as a mathematical term;

---

[62] See also the first such overview by Haupenthal 1991.
[63] http://www.eventoj.hu/steb/.
[64] www.uea.org/dokumentoj/terminaroj_ekde_1980.html/. 12th edition.
[65] https://sites.google.com/site/esperantoporun/dokumentoj/generalaj-dokumentoj/rekomendita-terminaro.

- Borrowing from other languages: *softvaro, sputniko*;
- Calques: *sin-mort-igo* (from the Latin *sui/cid/um*, or the German *Selbst/töt/ung*);
- Use of metaphorical terms: *elektra kampo*;
- Use of metonymy: the transfer of a proper name to a notion: *doplera efiko*,[66] *leĝo de Ohm*.

The most common procedures in the formation of neologisms are calquing and the borrowing of compoundable morphemes from other languages. This sometimes leads to the creation of synonyms: *rul/ŝtup/ar/o* and *eskalator/o* for German 'Rolltreppe' and English 'escalator.' For a while the terms *komput/il/o, komputer/o* and *komputor/o* competed for acceptance. The compound 'komput/il/o' emerged as the dominant term.

Given Esperanto's extremely flexible word-formation system, it is possible to form specialised terms through the use of this system, independently of the methods mentioned above. But up to now Esperanto has tended to follow ethnic-language models, particularly in the natural sciences.

The various requirements imposed on terms by their creators either reinforce or undermine their applicability.[67] Such requirements include:
- an idea as the basis of a term
- link to a field
- link to systems within the field
- precision to be applied as needed
- (reversible) disambiguation[68]
- transparency of meaning
- concision (linguistic economy)
- internationality
- ease of pronunciation.

---

66 See Maradan 2010.
67 See D. Blanke 1986c: 51-55; W. Blanke 2013: 101-150.
68 Reversible disambiguation = one idea should correspond with one term, and one term with one idea.

Additional requirements, specific to Esperanto, include *internationality* and *conformity to system*, i.e. conformity to the *Fundamento de Esperanto*, Zamenhof's description of the grammar of Esperanto, established in 1905 (see Zamenhof 1903/1992). Selection of criteria for terminology formation should conform to the norms of Technical Committee 37 (ISO/TC 37).[69]

Terms in Esperanto are almost always based on individual proposals published in texts or dictionaries, discussed, tried out in practice, and finally accepted into the language and its specialised dictionaries, where they may stabilise or, in due course, be eliminated from use.

Various methods for the discussion of new proposals for specialised vocabulary have been applied. From 1968 to 1981, Rüdiger Eichholz stimulated discussion through his *Slipara Vortaro*.[70] On small slips of paper (A-7 format) he presented specialised terms in German, English and French. He also added the Decimal Classification number and, where possible, a line drawing. On the basis of the received reactions from his readers across the world, he published an Esperanto translation of the German dictionary *Bilder-Duden*, known as *Esperanta Bildvortaro* (Eichholz 1988), based on the second edition of the *Bilder-Duden* of 1958 (Mannheim: Dudenverlag). In 2012 there appeared a much enlarged and newly edited edition of the *Bildvortaro*. One third of it was derived from the material compiled by Eichholz, while two thirds were newly edited and added by Petro De Smet and Jozefo Horvath.[71] This new Esperanto edition was based on the sixth German edition, *Duden – das Bildwörterbuch* (Mannheim: Bibliographisches Institut & F.A. Brockhaus AG, 2005).

---

69 http://www.iso.org/iso/iso_technical_committee.html?commid=48104/ (Terminology and other language and content resources).

70 In his introductory work to general terminology science and terminological lexicography, Wüster alludes to examples in the *Slipara Vortaro*: Wüster 1991: 206.

71 http://eo.wikipedia.org/wiki/Bildvortaro/; Desmet & Horvath 2012.

In the early 1990s, Eichholz went over to a new computer-based mode of discussion, publishing his extensive *Pekoteko* (Eichholz 1992), a work that recorded the international discussion of individual terms through the exchange of diskettes. This method was later replaced by the more convenient and effective mode of web-based discussion.

9 Efforts to coordinate terminology work

It was in 1911 that the first principles were developed for the creation of specialised vocabulary in Esperanto (Rollet de l' Isle 1911; Verax 1911/1912). In the 1950s the terminology centres of the *Internacia Scienca Asocio Esperantista* and the Esperanto Academy, the principal language-cultivation institution for Esperanto, attempted to advance and expand terminological work, but not to a degree that we could rightly call standardisation of the kind undertaken by national standardisation institutions.

In an effort to achieve better results, UEA founded its Esperanto Terminology Centre in 1987 (TEC/UEA Rotterdam).[72] The centre collaborated with *Infoterm*[73] and *TermNet*,[74] the principal worldwide terminological agencies. With the direct or indirect support of TEC, conferences and training seminars were organised and instructional material was published, for example the *Terminologia Kurso* and essay collection of Jan Werner (Werner 1986; 2004) and a handbook for the creation of terms, *Terminologia Gvidilo* (Suonuuti 1998). Recently, efforts have again been made to improve the quality of terminology work through the Internet.[75] Thus, UEA in 2010

---

[72] On TEC's operations and achievements, the problems associated with it, and prospects for the future, see W. Blanke 2013: 151-219.

[73] Internationales Informationszentrum für Terminologie / International Information Centre for Terminology, Wien. / Internacia Informcentro pri terminologio: http://www.infoterm.info/.

[74] Terminology Network, Wien (international network of terminology institutions): http://www.termnet.org/.

[75] See, for example, http://esperanto.net/tec/.

renewed its contact with *Infoterm* (Vienna) and joined the *ISO/Technical Committee 37*.[76]

Specialised bibliographies, libraries and archives record theoretical studies and current and former practice in Esperanto (D. Blanke 2004).

10 Planned-language impulses for terminology work

Efforts originating in the sixteenth and seventeenth centuries to create a-priori (philosophical) universal languages, based on the classification of all known knowledge, take their place in the search for the 'perfect language' which should in turn facilitate 'accurate' and 'precise' thought. From such efforts derived the impulse to, among other things, develop nomenclatures and classification systems (Hüllen 1984). Esperanto and other planned languages had a direct effect on the development of terminology science, particularly in the work of Eugen Wüster (1898-1977). We can regard his work in Esperanto and in lexicography as preparation for his founding of terminology science.[77]

Another example is the Soviet interlinguist, the Latvian Ernest K. Drezen (1982-1937), who was from 1921 to 1937 the leader of the Esperantist Union of the Soviet Republics (Sovetrespublikara Esperantista Unio). He led the team that translated Wüster's principal work into Russian (Wjuster 1935). He was also active in terminology science, among other things as a member of the terminology commission of the All-Soviet Committee on Standardisation (Kuznecov 1991: 16). Drezen developed the idea of introducing into ethnic languages an international terminological code (*terminologia ŝlosilo*), based on Esperanto (Drezen 1935/1983, 70ff.), which Wüster accepted and further developed, but never completed (Schremser-Seipelt 1990).

---

[76] On recent developments see the article by Mélanie Maradan, *Esperanto aktuell* 3 (2010): 15-16. Maradan, a specialist in translation and standardisation, serves as representative of the Universal Esperanto Association for its relations with Infoterm and ISO/TC 37. As of 2013 she is a member of Infoterm's board.

[77] On Wüster see W. Blanke 2008: 62-99; 2013: 59-97.

We should also mention the German engineer and Esperantist Alfred Warner (1931-), who collaborated with Haferkorn, maintained contact with Wüster in the period 1966-1997, and for several decades led the work of the German terminology-standardisation institute DIN[78] (see W. Blanke 2008: 84-99; 2013: 85-97).

11 Conclusion

If the speakers of an international planned language like Esperanto wish to aid in the exchange of knowledge and experience among speakers of different languages and play a significant role as promoters of their language as an official means of international communication, the language must possess the potential for specialised expression. The results up to now have shown the complete suitability of Esperanto for such expression and its clear utility in international specialised communication in a growing number of fields. If international political relations and economic forces ever bring about an objective need for just and rational linguistic communication, the experience of Esperanto shows that such communication is fully realisable even in specialised fields. Through systematic and end-directed language planning, particularly with regard to terminology, it is possible, given experience so far, to adapt the language to future needs for such expression.

---

[78] DIN = Deutsches Institut für Normung (German Institute for Standardisation).

IV

Terminology Science and Planned Languages[79]

Introduction

The reader is certainly familiar with the basic issues of terminology science and the main problems of terminological activities. However, what exactly are 'planned languages' and what relation do they have to terminology science? What role did the founder of terminology science, Eugen Wüster, play in this connection?[80]

The term 'planned language' itself (de *Plansprache*, fr *langue planifiée*, ru *planovyj jazyk*, Esp *planlingvo*) was coined by Wüster, who used it for the first time in his doctoral dissertation (Wüster 1931/1970).[81] It refers to a language that was created with the aim of facilitating international linguistic communication (see chapter 1, above). Today this term is common in specialist literature on interlinguistics. Outside this subject area the terms *international auxiliary language, world auxiliary language, artificial world language, universal language*[82] etc. are more common.

The terminologist and the adept of a planned language are connected in their effort to rationalise a linguistic message and to make it more effective: the terminologist strives for the exact description of a techni-

---

79 First published in Oeser & Galinski 1998: 133-168. See Blanke 1998b. Translated by Will Firth and Katrin Blanke. Edited and updated for this volume by Humphrey Tonkin.

80 [The original publication of this article marked the hundredth anniversary of Wüster's birth – HT]

81 See Wüster 1955/1976. The citations are to the 1976 reprint.

82 de: Internationale Hilfssprache, Welthilfssprache, künstliche (Welt)Sprache, Universalsprache; fr: langue internationale auxiliaire, langue mondiale auxiliaire, langue (mondiale) artificielle, langue universelle; ru: meždunarodnyj vspomogatel'nyj jazyk, mirovoj vspomogatel'nyj jazyk, iskusstvennyj (mirovoj) jazyk, vseobščij/vsemirnyj jazyk.

cal term – a description characterised by, for example, a well-balanced relation of linguistic comfort and accuracy, and contributing to precise and stable specialist communication, especially after standardisation has been achieved. Wüster considered this balance of comfort and accuracy an important feature in the linguistic quality of an expression (Wüster 1931/1970: 85).

Likewise, the author of a planned language attempts to reach the highest possible linguistic quality; in a way he looks for an ideal language for international communication, i.e. a fully grammatical system that should be easier to learn than ethnic languages, should permit more precise expressions, and should furthermore – as a neutral means of communication – facilitate equality in international communication.

This idea includes the requirement that such a language should be suited to use as language for special purposes, which means its suitability for the development of terminology.

The relation of effort and result in communication is an issue for both the terminologist and the adept of a planned language.

In this respect we should state that relations between universal languages and technical systematic representations are no new phenomenon. The philosophical (a-priori) universal languages created since the 16th and 17th centuries – based on the classification of the knowledge available at the time – were constructed to facilitate 'right thinking' and to give completely new insights into the fundamental principles of the 'right philosophy' (Descartes). They influenced the development of nomenclature and classification systems (such as decimal classification), as well as concept systems used as the basis of lexicographic works, e.g. in Roget's *Thesaurus of English Words and Phrases* of 1852 and in newer indices of concepts (see Hallig & Wartburg 1952).[83]

---

83 See Slaughter 1982, Hüllen 1984.

IV: Terminology Science and Planned Languages

If we strive for rational and effective specialised communication, we need quality criteria for terms and terminologies both for ethnic and planned languages, as well as the standardisation and planning of terminology and their effective practical organisation.

In his work Wüster dealt with all these aspects, especially in the 1920s and 1930s.[84] It is not coincidental that his main work deals with national linguistic standardisation and its generalisation, i.e. international linguistic standardisation, the 'highest stage' of which would be the 'introduction of a complete auxiliary language' (Wüster 1931/1970: 411). Although he later regarded the possibilities of international acceptance of a planned language more sceptically, he never lost his connections with this issue.

There is abundant evidence for the assumption that Wüster's intensive treatment of planned languages contributed significantly to gradually developing the principles of his general theory of terminology science. This appears to have been the heuristic effect of the study of planned languages in Wüster's own work as well as that of other terminologists, an aspect that has still not received the attention it deserves (but see W. Blanke 1989, 1997).

In the following section, the phenomenon of 'planned languages', especially planned languages in their role as specialised languages, will be addressed first. Esperanto plays a distinctive role here. This is followed by a description of the role of planned languages in the development of Wüster's terminological thought, and then by some comments on current efforts to apply the findings of terminology science in the field of planned languages.

---

84 See the author's study of Wüster's attitude to planned languages (in Esperanto) written as an introduction to the microfiche edition of the Encyclopaedic Dictionary (Blanke 1994).

1 Planned languages

From the sixteenth century until the present there have been around a thousand attempts to create international linguistic means of communication (Blanke 1985: 66-98; Duličenko 1990: 13ff.). These attempts are the subject of interlinguistics, a scientific discipline that – as some authors see it – deals only with planned languages ('special interlinguistics' or 'interlinguistics in the narrower sense'). Others consider the main subject of this discipline to be international linguistic communication in all its forms and with all its means ('general interlinguistics'). For Wüster, interlinguistics was the science of planned languages (Wüster 1955/1976).[85]

Phenomenologically, planned languages are a facet of the human invention of languages which at the graphemic level includes pasigraphics (universal sign systems), systems of stenography, secret sign languages (codes), international alphabets, and also sign languages.

As systems of communication that have a phonemic level instead of, or in addition to, the graphemic level, the area of invented human languages[86] can be considered to include invented children's languages, secret languages, magical and sacral languages, or also the imaginary languages of social utopias and modern science-fiction literature which exist in partial form in filmed versions, like the Klingon language from the recent series *Star Trek*.

Planned languages can also be regarded as the product of language planning if this is understood as 'the methodical activity of regulating and improving existing languages or creating new common regional, national or international languages' (Tauli 1968: 27).

---

[85] Regarding the different views on the subject of interlinguistics see the surveys by Blanke 1977, 1998d, and Schubert 1989b.

[86] See in particular Bausani 1970, Blanke 1985: 18-65, Albani & Buonarroti 1994, Mannewitz 1997.

IV: Terminology Science and Planned Languages

If we examine the creation of planned languages, which has been going on for centuries and continues into the present,[87] and if we wish to understand this phenomenon properly, we need to make a distinction between a project and a language – a distinction often not made in the linguistic literature. Numerous factors must act in combination to lead a language from project stage to a functioning international language. Here a certain linguistic quality of the project is definitely a prerequisite, but is not in itself sufficient to explain a degree of practical success. It is especially factors other than linguistic ones that lead to the acceptance of a project in practice and ensure that, in several stages, it becomes a language.

Only a few of the existing planned languages have functioned for any length of time and enabled a certain level of communication. These are Volapük, Esperanto, Latine sine flexione, Ido, Occidental-Interlingue, Basic English, and Interlingua.

Volapük was relatively well-known until the end of the nineteenth century. Latino sine flexione (called 'Interlingua' in the 1920s, but not to be confused with Interlingua-Gode) had adepts until World War II, especially in Europe. The same was true for Basic English. Occidental-Interlingue had a small speech community until the beginning of the 1980s but today is considered dead. Besides Esperanto, only Ido and Interlingua continue to play a role. Ido still has several hundred adepts who arrange small international meetings. They are organised in a small association and publish two or three journals. Also Interlingua has several hundred adepts, in around twenty countries. They arrange international meetings (with 30-50 participants) and publish some 10-20 new titles in their language annually (see Bibliographia 1990-1998).

---

87 Projects are constantly being created. Some of them are presented on the Internet (see Becker 1996a). [On Slavic constructed languages on the Internet see Meyer 2016 – SF]

The planned languages mentioned above were used for certain special-language applications (see D. Blanke & W. Blanke 1998). In Volapük (1879, Johann Martin Schleyer), a strictly agglutinative language with considerably changed morphemes of Latin, Romance, and Germanic origin, there were modest attempts to develop commercial correspondence.

In Latino sine flexione (1903, Giuseppe Peano), which is based on Leibniz' idea of a simplified Latin for scientific purposes, some texts on mathematics and astronomy as well as on philological issues were published, especially in the journal *Schola et Vita* (1926-1939).

In Ido (1907, Louis Couturat), a reformed Esperanto in terms of word formation and lexical stock, a number of technical texts and dictionaries were published in biology, chemistry, commerce, photography, mechanical engineering, mathematics, radio technology, as well as texts dealing with philological, philosophical and religious issues.[88]

Occidental (1922, Edgar v. Wahl, renamed 'Interlingue' in 1949), a kind of New Romance with reduced inflections, has only a few special-language texts of mainly philosophical and philological content, to a lesser extent on politics, economics and pedagogy. Furthermore, there are a number of mathematical texts and a mathematical dictionary.

Interlingua (1951, Alexander Gode/International Auxiliary Language Association) is also a planned language with a large proportion of Romance roots and a simplified inflection. Abstracts in several medical journals were published in the 1950s and 1960s and the two scientific journals *Spectroscopia Molecular* and *Scientia International* from 1952 to 1955 (Sexton 1993). The Interlingua Book Catalogue (Bibliographia 1998) contains publications on demography, art history, mathematics, philology, philosophy, phytopathology and theology.

---

[88] [On the use of Ido and other planned languages in science, see Gordin 2015, esp. pp. 135-158 – HT]

Also in Basic English (1929, Charles K. Ogden), a simplified English of 850 basic words which were chosen according to their semantic aspects, texts were published on electrical engineering, geology and economics.

Except for Esperanto, all systems mentioned here have in common that in principle their linguistic structure makes them quite suitable for the expression of specialised issues and terminologies. However, even the few published special-language texts and dictionaries have not served real international communicative needs as the numbers of speakers were – and still are – too small.

For this reason there have been no organisations cultivating special-language application in any planned language with the exception of Esperanto.

2 Esperanto

Esperanto, founded in 1887 by Ludwig L. Zamenhof, developed from the rough outline of a project into a language with distinct communication achievements. Esperanto is an agglutinative language with predominantly Romance lexical stock and an efficient system of word formation. The broad practice of this planned language has been relatively well documented.[89] As already predicted by Ferdinand de Saussure (1967: 90), this planned language entered its 'semiologic life' on the grounds of its practical usage and has been subject to the laws of language change (Philippe 1991).

The sources, structure, functions, development, and communication capacity in Esperanto and also the speech community of this language are the subject of the field of Esperantology. Esperantology is the only philological-linguistic discipline dealing with a single planned language

---
[89] See, among others, Kökény & Bleier 1933-34/1979; Lapenna, Lins & Carlevaro 1974.

to have developed and boasts a comprehensive specialist literature (see Blanke 1996).

The term Esperantology (Esp: *esperantologio*) was introduced in 1921 by Wüster, who – in contrast to the definition of interlinguistics mentioned above – saw in it only the linguistics of Esperanto (Wüster 1955/1976).

The special-language usage of Esperanto started at a relatively early stage. For example, short popular science texts (in astronomy, biology, mathematics, medicine, and other fields) were included in one of the first collections of model texts that contributed to set standards in the language (*Fundamenta Krestomatio*: see Zamenhof 1903/1992). In 1904 the first scientific journal, *Internacia Scienca Revuo*, was launched, and in 1906 the first scientific association, *Internacia Scienca Asocio Esperantista* (ISAE), was founded.[90]

Today there is no doubt about the suitability of Esperanto as a language for special purposes. The catalogue of the Universala Esperanto-Asocio for 1994, for example, lists publications in monographs and anthologies on the following topics:

> archaeology, astronomy, biology, biochemistry, botany, chemistry, computer science, ecology, economy, energetics, ethnography, genetics, geology, information technology-cybernetics, interlinguistics/Esperantology, law, linguistics, mathematics, medicine, meteorology, pedagogy, physics, psychology, sociology, telecommunications, theology (and various religious philosophies), transport, zoology (see UEA 1994).

Some 30-40 specialised titles are added to the catalogue every year. A considerable volume of material in special language can also be found in journals and bulletins.

---

90 [See Gordin 2015, esp. pp. 124-128 – HT]

IV: Terminology Science and Planned Languages

Some specialist journals in ethnic languages occasionally contain contributions or abstracts in the planned language, e.g. the journal *Language Problems & Language Planning* and the cybernetically-pedagogically oriented *Grundlagenstudien aus Kybernetik und Geisteswissenschaft/ Humankybernetik* (Basic Studies in Cybernetics and the Arts/Human Cybernetics) both launched in their present form in 1977.

The specialised vocabularies of Esperanto are indexed in around 300 special dictionaries for more than eighty areas, which differ greatly in volume and quality (Ockey 1982, Haupenthal 1991). The following fields merit emphasis: botany, chemistry, computer science, electrical engineering, engineering, forestry, geology, mathematics, medicine, radio technology, railroads, religion(s), trade.[91] Also, the largest monolingual dictionary for Esperanto definitions contains relevant terms from various subject fields (Waringhien & Duc Goninaz 2005: 18-20).

International specialised communication in the planned language Esperanto is realised especially within the framework of various specialist organisations and other bodies.

Academic institutions like the *Akademio Internacia de Sciencoj*, founded in 1985 (see H. Frank 1993), and *Internacia Scienca Akademio Comenius*, founded in 1986 (see Neergaard & Kiselman 1992), promote interdisciplinary exchange in Esperanto. Also, bibliographies of scientists who publish in Esperanto or are active in other respects serve this purpose (Darbellay 1981, T. Frank 1996).

These and other scientifically-oriented organisations, institutions and groups usually arrange their meetings within the world congresses that are held annually (generally with 1,500-6,000 Esperanto speakers from 50-80 countries). However, they organise their own international scien-

---

[91] See also the contributions of Heinz Hoffmann on railroad terminology and Karl-Hermann Simon on the *Lexicon silvestre*, published in the conference proceedings of ProCom '98 (Blanke 2003b).

tific meetings, conferences and seminars as well. Examples of these are the Summer Courses at the University of Liège/B held from 1972-1980 with more than 30 volumes of lecture notes in anatomy, biology, chemistry, comparative literature, linguistics, mathematics, pharmacology, psychology, sociology, and zoology (Blanke 1986c: 82), and the series of lectures on the application of Esperanto in science and technology (*Apliko de Esperanto en Scienco kaj Tekniko*) held in Czechoslovakia (1978-1989). The total of 156 contributions was published in six volumes. A similar series of lectures started in China in 1987.[92]

Esperanto has been accepted as conference language also at some non-Esperanto expert meetings, for example since the 1980s at the cybernetics conferences in Namur, and since 1968 at conferences of geologists, leading to eight conference volumes up to now. The international scientific meeting *Interkomputo* (Budapest 1982) in which Esperanto was the sole conference language brought together 200 computer experts from nineteen countries whose 100 seminar papers were published in six volumes.

As Wüster (1931/1970: 294ff.) already outlined in his standard work, Esperanto is a suitable means of scientific communication due to the unique properties of its linguistic structure.

The most significant of these properties are, for example, the fact that morphemes can be combined very easily (because of the convenient morpho-phonological syllabic structure, the lack of allomorphs, etc.), an efficient affix system, and highly productive rules for word formation (Blanke 1981a, Blanke 1985, Schubert 1993). Furthermore, these properties enable the language to adapt to new needs in communication and make it suitable for the requirements of automatic technical documentation. A slightly modified Esperanto serves as intermediate language

---

[92] [Such conferences and lecture series continue to be held in various settings, often under the auspices of the *Internacia Akademio de Sciencoj* or as part of the annual World Congress of Esperanto – HT]

in the semiautomatic translation system DLT (Distributed Language Translation). This system reached prototype stage (Sadler 1991).[93]

The methods for coining new terms in Esperanto include the usage of words from the common language (*funkci/o* – function), the usage of words found in other languages (*softvar/o* – software, *sputnik/o* – Sputnik), loan-translations (*dur/disk/o* – hard disk), metaphorical constructions (*elektr/a kamp/o* – electrical field), and so on.

The two main methods for forming neologisms are the use of morphological neologisms and the borrowing of basic words that may be transformed (e.g. *rul/ŝtup/ar/o* vs *eskalator/o* for escalator). Besides *komput/il/o*, the words *komputer/o* and *komputor/o* are still in some competition for 'computer'.[94]

Requirements for a term in a planned language (Dehler 1985), which can – from case to case – complement or exclude one another, are the same criteria that apply to ethnic languages: relation to the subject, relation to the system, and (as the case may be) precision, lack of ambiguity, self-explanatoriness, conciseness, etc. Additional requirements specific to Esperanto are the internationality of an expression and loyalty to the established structure (i.e. corresponding to the basic norm of Esperanto, the *Fundamento de Esperanto*, standardised and codified in 1905).

Terms in Esperanto almost always originate from individual suggestions presented in texts and dictionaries that are discussed, examined in practice, and eventually incorporated into the lexical stock.

Among other approaches, the computer-aided terminological indexing and discussion system *Pekoteko* (= *perkomputora terminkolekto*, Eichholz 1992) serves indexing purposes and international discussion.

---
93 [A commercial venture, the project was later discontinued for financial reasons – HT]
94 [*Komputilo* is now (2018) generally accepted – HT]

In archives for planned languages (see Gjivoje 1980, Veuthey 2014: 80-83), among others the Austrian National Library (Planned Languages Collection) and the *Centre de documentation et d' étude sur la langue internationale* in La Chaux-de-Fonds (Switzerland), as well as specialised libraries (Blanke 1985: 302 ff.), the historical documentation of the practice of planned languages (also their use for special-language communication) is being documented and researched.

3 The role of planned languages in the work of Eugen Wüster

In 1913 the 15-year-old Eugen Wüster became acquainted with Ludwig Zamenhof's language. He taught it to himself and progressed so quickly to such a high level that just two years later he began to translate intensively from his native German into Esperanto. He even ventured into poetry and translated parts of Dante's *Divine Comedy* in 1918. However, his main interest was increasingly aimed at the specialist use of the planned language and related problems. Part 8 of his bibliography, 'Planned languages – Esperanto', contains 128 entries in total, of which 82 are in Esperanto (see Lang, Lang & Reiter 1979).

Four works in particular show the close interconnection between planned languages on the one hand and the emergence of terminology science on the other hand:

- the encyclopaedic dictionary,
- Wüster's doctoral dissertation,
- the international electrotechnical vocabulary
- the international key to terminology.

IV: Terminology Science and Planned Languages

3.1 The encyclopaedic dictionary

Wüster's most significant works for the development of Esperantology are in the fields of lexicology and lexicography.[95] These works are closely connected with his main lexicographic contribution, the *Enzyklopädisches Wörterbuch Esperanto-Deutsch / Enciklopedia vortaro esperanta-germana* (EV, Wüster 1923-1929)[96] which was of preparatory significance for his later works. It was based on Zamenhof's idea of a 'Provisional Comprehensive Dictionary' that indexes the current lexical material of Esperanto as exactly and comprehensively as possible, serving as basis for an 'Official Comprehensive Dictionary'. Young Wüster adopted this idea and announced in 1921 – at the age of 23 – that after three years' work he had created a manuscript that might serve as basis for such a dictionary (Wüster 1921).

This dictionary was scheduled to be published in seven parts. However, only four appeared (1923, 1925, 1926, and 1929): the last published part ends at page 576 with the word *korn-o* (horn). By 1932 Wüster had completed work on a fifth part, but it was never printed.

In addition to the lexical material, the EV contains a foreword in which Wüster presents his ideas on language policy and discusses his principles of Esperantology.

The dictionary was not conceived solely for native speakers of German. It was meant to serve as a source of material and an example for Esperanto dictionaries in other ethnic languages. The published part contains

---

[95] These include
- *Maŝinfaka Esperanto-Vortaro prielementa* (Esperanto Dictionary on Machine Elements, 1923)
- *La Oficiala Radikaro* (a collection of Esperanto word roots officially recognised by the Language Academy of Esperanto, 1923)
- *Die Verhältniswörter des Esperanto* (the prepositions of Esperanto, 1924)
- *Zamenhof-radikaro* (word roots used by Ludwig Zamenhof, 1927).

[96] On the EV see Plehn 1985; Blanke 1994, 1998c.

some 35,000 entries. Had the dictionary been published in its entirety, it would presumably have contained 70,000-80,000 entries and would thus have come close to the scope of so-called academic dictionaries.[97]

In comparison with the compilers of other dictionaries, we can state that Wüster, in the 1920s, had indexed much more of the lexical material of Esperanto then in use than was later achieved by authors of more recent dictionaries, even if we consider that since then the language has developed and changed considerably. His source of material was his exceptionally rich library, which contained the complete relevant Esperanto writings of his time, which he analysed and catalogued lexicologically with the aid of collaborators in Austria and abroad.[98]

The second part of the EV – 2,161 pages of manuscript (to Zz) – was published as a microfilm edition by the Austrian National Library and thus was made accessible to Esperantologists. As a special feature it contains a reproduction of a section of the fifth part that Hans-Joachim Plehn (Wieselburg, Austria) prepared as a typed document on the basis of the original manuscript for '*korn/o – Ludovik/in-o*' (Wüster 1994).

The EV shows how in a short time a planned language project developed into a planned language. Alfred Schmitt (1936) emphasises this fact in *Indogermanische Forschungen*:

> Any evaluation of the significance of such a project depends, of course, on how the individual evaluates Esperanto or the issue of a planned language in general... I shall ... restrict myself to saying ... that the said work is significant to the scholar of linguistics even if he rejects planned languages or doubts their purpose. Because here we find all the lexical material of Esperanto that has been

---

97 See also the contributions by Otto Back, Sabine Fiedler and Wim de Smet in the conference proceedings of ProCom '98 (Blanke 2003b).

98 This comprehensive card index containing more than 100,000 cards is now in the Department of Planned Languages in the Austrian National Library (International Esperanto Museum).

elaborated to date; it has been collected with amazing diligence, and organised and presented very elegantly. With these properties, Wüster's book offers – if we may say so – a detailed record of an experiment conducted for fifty years with much effort and astuteness. Such a protocol retains its value even if the experiment in question fails or does not find practical use. Therefore, we can only strongly encourage the publication of the missing sections in order to avoid the danger of the book remaining a torso for all time.

3.2 The dissertation

The lexicological and lexicographic issues that Wüster addressed in the EV and that raised problems or opened new perspectives for research can be regarded as the groundwork for his doctoral dissertation (Wüster 1931/1970) which in turn is considered a standard work of terminology science. A glance at the introductory chapter of the EV, titled 'Esperantological Principles', makes this clear.[99] Here we find the first treatment of concepts that are of central significance for terminological standardisation.

Chapters A 'Correctness and Quality of a Term', B 'Centripetal and Centrifugal Development of Language', and C 'The Linguo-Economic Principle of Lexical Material', discuss, for example, the concepts of 'correct and erroneous naming', 'linguistic quality' (degree of quality, quality factor), 'quality of the system' (functional quality of the system), the requirements of a 'good term' (conciseness, exactness, comfort), questions of 'linguistic economy' and 'economy of lexical material'. Chapter D adds 'Problems of Transcription'. Chapter E, 'On the Names of Animals and Plants', contains rules for the assimilation of zoological and botanical expressions in Esperanto. Chapters A-C are written bilingually. Wüster

---

99 Written in 1923, bilingual (German and Esperanto). In: Wüster 1923-1929: [26]-[66]. The Esperanto version was reprinted in Wüster 1978: 71-115.

also describes the stages from the coining of a term by individuals up to its acceptance and registration (1. initiation, 2. registration of proposals, 3. decision, 4. registration of the decision). While it is true that the principles relate to Esperanto and are illustrated with examples from the planned language, Wüster also considers them fundamentally applicable to ethnic languages.

Much of this material is to be found, in adapted and further developed form, in Wüster's dissertation, and later in recommendations and standards of the committee ISA 37 'Terminology' (after World War II ISO/TC 37 'Terminology [Principles and Co-ordination]').

A third of Wüster's dissertation[100] is devoted to the chapter 'Fully Grammatical International Systems of Terminology (International Language)'. Wüster's analysis is not restricted to Esperanto but also includes other systems such as Volapük, Ido, Occidental, Latino sine flexione, and Novial. At the time, it was the best and most comprehensive scientific work on the issue of planned languages.[101]

The book was translated into Russian on recommendation of the leading Soviet interlinguist and esperantologist Ernest K. Drezen. Not only was Drezen a pioneer of interlinguistics[102] but his works also contributed significantly to language standardisation and terminology science in the USSR. In 1992, an international scientific conference on terminology was devoted to him and his co-operation with Wüster in the 1930s (see Draskau & Picht 1994).

In his dissertation, Wüster describes technical language (*Zwecksprache* [language for special purposes]) seen from the perspective of the engineer and technician. As Felber and Lang (1979: 21) describe it,

---

100 There is an abridged version both in German (Wüster 1934) and in Esperanto (Wüster 1936a).

101 This book was my first encounter with the scientific aspects of the issue of planned languages.

102 His main work on interlinguistics *Historio de la Mondolingvo* was published in its fourth edition in 1991 (Drezen 1931/1991), edited and annotated by Sergej N. Kuznecov.

He examines the present state of the tool of linguistic communication and contemplates the desired stage. He thus gives a scientific basis to technical language standardisation.

The interlinguist, examining the book, finds his opinion confirmed: Wüster's analysis of the present stage of a specialist language and his thoughts about the desired stage clearly bear the mark of his experiences with planned languages. The rationality of planned languages – as a basis for comparison – is an important part of his research.

In a letter to the author (October 18, 1971), Wüster confirmed this impression. Replying to a question regarding possible examples for a comparative linguistic study on word formation that the author was planning, he wrote:

> I do not recall if there are already similar works... If you want it to gain the attention of people who are not interested in Esperanto itself, you should present and use Esperanto as a grammatical model language in a similar way to what I did in my book *Internationale Sprachnormung*.

3.3 The International Electrotechnical Vocabulary

After World War I there was a steady growth in interest in the idea of an international planned language. The terminological usage of the language had already developed a solid footing before the war and continued to develop positively afterwards. Scientific texts and special dictionaries appeared in various areas. Prominent members of intellectual life, including leading figures from the field of science and technology, expressed their sympathy with the idea of an auxiliary language. They trusted that Esperanto would play an appropriate role and called for it to be promoted.

This was particularly true of the field of electrical engineering which boasted adepts and active speakers of Esperanto in several European countries (especially France), but also in the USA, Japan, and China, who called for it to be promoted in their specialist field.

One of these in Germany was Georg Klingenberg, managing director of AEG (Allgemeine Elektrizitäts-Gesellschaft) and active adept of Esperanto, to whom Wüster dedicated his dissertation. Also the two international professional organisations, the *Société Internationale des Électriciens* (founded in 1886) and the International Electrotechnical Commission (IEC, founded in 1906) had a positive attitude toward Esperanto. Both organisations maintained active relations with the *Internacia Scienca Asocio Esperantista* (ISAE, also founded in 1906).

From the beginning the IEC considered special-language standardisation one of its most important tasks. The aims of the ISAE seemed to the IEC to be similar to their own. Especially in radio broadcasting Esperanto played an active role in the 1920s. Between 1922 and 1927 there were at times 150 radio stations broadcasting programmes in Esperanto. From 1924 to 1926 nine specialised dictionaries on radio broadcasting were published in Esperanto. Wüster gives numerous precise facts and figures of this kind in his dissertation (Wüster 1931/1970: 371-381).[103]

He thus saw a chance to introduce Esperanto in the area of electrical engineering, an important area of technology. At the World Electricity Congress in Paris in 1932, he gave a report on the issue of terminology, which triggered a vivid discussion that proved to be positive for Esperanto. Furthermore, after the congress prominent electrical engineers from various countries gave their support, especially from Austria, France, Germany, Spain, Holland, and the Soviet Union. The president of IEC was eventually willing to include Esperanto terms into the *Vocabulaire electrotechnique international*, which was in preparation.

---

[103] The dissertation includes the following subchapters: General electrical engineering and power engineering, lighting engineering, general electrical telecommunications, telegraphy, telephony, radio.

In the end, the first edition of the IEC dictionary (1938) contained definitions and terms in French and English, and their equivalents in German, Italian, Spanish and Esperanto, which were listed in six corresponding indexes at the end of the book. Wüster elaborated the Esperanto equivalents, which was not stated in the dictionary but is obvious from his correspondence. In 1950 an unabridged reprint appeared (see IEC 1938/1950). In the second, considerably extended, edition published from 1954-1970 in single issues, Esperanto is not included.

3.4 The international key to terminology

3.4.1 From idea to project

In his dissertation Wüster considered neither English nor Latin suitable as a fully grammatical system for international specialist communication. He was of the opinion that

> ... the only neutral solution is ... to select standardised terms for international exchange from the national languages and to combine them in a fully grammatical system of its own. The new standardised word constructions are to be formed from word elements that should – if possible – be known to all technicians of all nations; the method of word combination has to be standardised. These word combinations will then possess – in contrast to the old, etymologically combined foreign words – their own inherent mnemonic device... After standardisation of comparatively few word elements, technology is capable of standardising terms and their meanings purely as needs require and of expressing terms in the simplest possible phonetic form. Then international technical standardisation is more a standardisation of script forms than of sound forms. We need to distinguish between two steps in the construction of such a planned language:[104] firstly, all concepts need to be named that have names in national

---
104 It seems that in the German text Wüster used the expression 'Plansprache' (planned language) for the first time.

languages; in a second step the newly emerged concepts need to be named in the auxiliary language and in the national language. The task of the first step can be solved in the following way: for basic concepts, word elements (sound elements) with the largest possible degree of internationality are standardised. The concepts expressed by connection or application of these word elements should also be internationally recognisable. The word elements and a large part of the terms are thus chosen according to the degree of their international mnemonic effect. (Wüster 1931/1970: 294-295)

If international terms are lacking, they should be created by process of word formation.

Here the idea of an 'international key to terminology', although not yet termed as such, was suggested for the first time. Furthermore, Wüster pleaded for a complete international auxiliary language for technical communication and found Esperanto to be most suitable for this task. Also this idea was taken up in the Soviet Union.[105]

Impressed by the translation of Wüster's dissertation into Russian (Wjuster 1935),[106] the Soviet Committee for Standardisation applied to the International Federation of National Standardising Associations (ISA) in 1934 for the appointment of a commission on terminology to look into the development of an 'international terminological code'.[107] The Soviet side also gave a first report on possible concrete steps, elaborated by Ernest Drezen.[108] As a result, the ISA instructed the Soviet

---

[105] See the report on the history of the first draft in Wüster 1936b.

[106] Ernest K. Drezen, leading Soviet esperantist, terminologist and interlinguist, supervised its completion (see Kuznecov 1991 on Drezen). [On Drezen's terminological work, see also Lins 2016/2017: esp. 6-8 – HT]

[107] Different names were used in the relevant discussion: *Internationaler technisch-wissenschaftlicher Schrift- und Lautcode* (international technical-scientific script and sound code), *ISA-Code, Terminologie-Code* (terminology code), *Wortstammschlüssel* (word-root key), *Terminologieschlüssel* (terminology key), *Weltwörterschlüssel* (world word key) (see Schremser-Seipelt 1990: 22ff.).

[108] This report was translated into Esperanto: Drezen 1935/1983.

Committee for Standardisation to present a concrete project. The draft, presented in 1935, was mainly based on Esperanto word roots and was discussed vigorously within the ISA, in particular with the background of the critique by proponents of Occidental who pleaded that, if possible, natural Romance word forms should be given preference for inclusion in the code. In this respect they criticised Esperanto roots and word formation. In 1938, the code draft in its present form was rejected after repeated discussion.

Wüster continued intensive work on this project but modified his attitude towards Esperanto in the course of time and increasingly included naturalist planned languages in his considerations. He was increasingly inclined to the 'more natural' Romance forms. The reasons he stated for this were that, with its Romance roots, the Romance derivative system was much more regular than he had previously supposed, and that it would result in the development of a 'sub-language of foreign words' (Wüster 1970: 421), which could be taught and studied.

Another factor – which, however, he never mentioned – was presumably the situation in Germany and the German sphere of influence, which became increasingly unfavourable for Esperanto after Hitler's takeover in the 1930s. Eventually, in 1936, all activities for the language were completely prohibited (see Lins 1988, 2016/2017). At this time, German engineers held leading positions at the ISA. An additional fact is that Drezen, the motor of the code project, fell victim to Stalin's purges in 1937. Thus there was no support left from the Soviet side. Wüster's intensive study of the planned language Occidental, his collaboration in the International Auxiliary Language Association (IALA), and his knowledge of its later product, Interlingua (1951), made this more 'naturalist' type of planned language seem to him more suitable for a code than Esperanto (see Wüster 1970: 421 ff.).[109]

109 Planned languages of the naturalistic type are aimed at people with a prior knowledge of Romance languages. They are based on the efforts of their founders to create a planned language using the Romance word stock found in the European languages without changing it much. This

For the terminology key, Wüster elaborated in several stages various word root lists (*Radicarium*) and affix lists (*Affixarium*) of different length in the 1930s and after World War II.[110] Both in ISA 37 and in its successor, Technical Committee 37 (TC 37) of the International Organisation for Standardisation (ISO), the project met with interest and was discussed and revised. Its essential ideas found their way into the international recommendation ISO-R 860-1968, 'International Unification of Concepts and Terms'. In his supplementary report to the first edition of his dissertation entitled '35 years later' (Wüster 1970), Wüster clearly outlined the planned structure of the terminological code:

(1) The code consists of two parts. One part comprises the word roots, and the other one the derivative elements (affixes).

(2) Each of the two parts is ordered firstly in concepts, and secondly in alphabetical order.

---

language was intended to look as 'natural' as one of its Romance source languages. This property can be bought at the price of lesser autonomy in word formation because it has to follow its Romance examples to a great extent (or even exclusively, e.g. in Interlingua). Esperanto (and also Ido) are planned languages of the 'schematic' or 'autonomous' type: they use predominantly Romance word material but are not necessarily restricted to this source. Additionally, they have a system of word formation that is predominantly regular ('schematic') and independent of its source languages ('autonomous'). See Blanke 1985: 157-201 [and the present volume] on these two main groups of planned languages. Word constructions are therefore not easily decoded. In his various drafts Wüster offers numerous examples of word roots, affixes and derivatives, illustrating this issue: e.g. Esperanto: *eduk/i – eduk/o – eduk/a – eduk/ist/o*; Occidental and Interlingua: *educa/r – educa/t/ion – educa/t/ion/al (educa/t/iv[e]) – educa/t/or.*

110 See the manuscript 'Dezimal-Radikarium (Stamm-Wörterbuch, nach Dezimalklassifikation geordnet) der europäisch-naturalistischen Mittelformen und des Esperanto, ergänzt durch die Sprachen Französisch, Italienisch, Spanisch, Englisch, Deutsch und Russisch. Ableitungen: 621.8 Maschinenelemente und 621.9 mechanische Bearbeitung (Werkzeuge, Werkzeugmaschinen). Dem Technischen Komitee ISA 37 eingereicht von ÖNA im Mai 1938 als eine der Entscheidungsunterlagen für den Code, zugleich als Entwurf eines etymologischen Stamm-Wörterbuches für diesen.' The manuscript includes a collection of affixes and various appendices. In this material Wüster specifically refers to the authors of planned languages Julius Lott (author of the project 'Mundolingue' 1899), Woldemar Rosenberger (Idiom Neutral 1912), and 'especially von Wahl' (i.e. Edgar de Wahl, Occidental 1922). See also word lists in the appendix of Schremser-Seipelt 1990.

(3) When forming the part that is ordered in concept groups, the commonness of word elements needs to be considered and made transparent. With that, synonyms may be assessed. That means that a selective application of the code is possible. Only this way the terminological code may be teachable, and teachable step by step.

(4) The word elements are spelled the same way as Latin is today. This spelling has remained most complete in French and English.

(5) Suffixes and word endings are spelled in a normal form that does not show any national peculiarities. The so-called Romance 'prototype form'[111] has proved suitable for this purpose.

(6) The internationalised terminologies consist of word roots of the terminological code and their combinations (mostly derivatives, less often word compounds).

(7) The individual prototype elements get an internationally standardised pronunciation to facilitate the learning of the terminological code and exercise with it.

(8) International words that are not Romance are allowed into the code as 'foreign words'. Their pronunciation is the same as in their original language.

(9) Only a minor addition to the terminological code is needed in order to create a complete 'terminological language'. (Wüster 1970: 424-425)

This addition consists of rules which would largely coincide with those of Interlingua.

Wüster devoted himself to the development of the terminological code until the end of his life. As late as September 1976 he presented a report on the code at a discussion of the ISO/TC 37 secretariat in Moscow (see Nedobity 1982).

A few months later Wüster passed away. In further documents of ISO/TC 37 the essential ideas of the terminological code were increasingly

---
111 Here he means more or less the form that can be seen in Interlingua.

abandoned, and currently this project is not a subject of discussion. Schremser-Seipelt (1990: 82ff.) in her doctoral dissertation gives various reasons for the growing opposition to the project of a terminological code, naming, among others,

- nationalist and purist tendencies regarding language in several countries,
- developing countries striving for more equality and independence in international scientific-technological exchange,
- criticism of the Eurocentrist basis of the code,
- problems with the choice of a suitable system of concepts,
- linguistically motivated doubts.

The material on the terminological code that was elaborated by Wüster in several stages and differing degrees of detail can be found in the 'Wüster archive' of Infoterm and has yet to be further evaluated and used.[112]

3.4.2 The key and Esperanto

With regard to English and Esperanto in their role as auxiliary languages in relation to the terminological code, Wüster repeatedly emphasised their different tasks: 'There cannot be the question "Terminological or auxiliary language?", because the terminological code is an end in itself. It serves as a basis for understanding and is necessary for the extension of the Romance sub-language within all complete languages, most particularly with regard to Esperanto and English' (Wüster 1970: 430).

On Esperanto, Wüster explains elsewhere:

> Esperanto as an oral and written means of communication between people who have studied it is much more effective than naturalist systems of planned languages and the language of ter-

---
[112] A microfiche edition is available from Infoterm.

minology. An exception to this might be special-language purposes in subject fields that have Romance nomenclature. Given these limitations, Esperanto is even incomparably more effective than English, if this is not the partner's native language... Esperanto is full of life... The terminological language in contrast cannot be anything else than austere... Unfortunately, in comparison with the terminological language Esperanto has a decisive disadvantage: because of its autonomous system of derivatives it is understood only by the people who have studied it, and this is only a very small fraction of humanity. (Wüster 1970, 432)

Wüster is pessimistic about the chances for the further spread of Esperanto. An important reason for the relatively modest acceptance of Esperanto is to be found, in his view, in 'some properties of the external form of the language, which do not affect the practical usability of the language in any way but in most cases repel speakers of European languages' (Wüster 1970: 433).[113]

In his critique of the external form of Esperanto – which is more often heard in Europe than in Asia, for example – Wüster bases his arguments on Eurocentrist positions. In reality, however, hardly any subject-field or terminological activities could be observed among naturalist systems. These activities have basically been limited to Esperanto.

---

[113] After World War II Wüster continued his relations with Esperanto uninterruptedly: he published contributions in *Scienca Revuo*, maintained an extensive correspondence with Esperantologists from all over the world, was named honorary member of the Universal Esperanto Association (UEA), and chaired the 23rd session of the *Esperanto Internacia Somera Universitato* at the 55th World Esperanto Congress in Vienna (1970). His opening address in Esperanto was titled 'Internacia terminologio en la servo de la informatiko' (see Wüster 1971). Additionally, he maintained contacts with adepts of Interlingua. He bequeathed his comprehensive special library on planned languages to the International Esperanto Museum/Planned Languages Collection (IEMW) in Vienna, a department of the Austrian National Library. See the contribution by Herbert Mayer in the conference proceedings of ProCom '98 (in Blanke 2003b).

4 Terminology work in the planned language today[114]

As early as 1911, Esperanto-speaking scientists elaborated terminological principles for the first time (Verax 1911/12, Rollet de l'Isle 1911). In the 1950s and beyond, the joint terminology centre of ISAE and the *Akademio de Esperanto* – the Esperanto Language Academy – tried to structure and develop their terminology work on the basis of the results of terminology science. In this period, continual contact was maintained with Wüster. As of 1982 a Terminology Esperanto Centre (TEC)[115] (see W. Blanke 1988) attempted to continue this tradition. Later it established contacts with Infoterm and TermNet (Vienna). These contacts stimulated the organisation of conferences,[116] training seminars, and the development of teaching materials. Several ISO recommendations were translated into Esperanto in the 1970s for internal use and have been revised and adapted to current developments (see also Eichholz 1986).

An important basis for future terminology work is the translation into Esperanto of the *Guide to Terminology* by Heidi Suonuuti (see Suonuuti 1997, 1998). And, last but not least, it is thanks to the efforts of TEC/UEA that Eugen Wüster's work on terminology and on interlinguistics and Esperantology has recently found more attention in the Esperanto language community and that significant new impetus is also being devoted to terminological activities.[117]

---

114 See the contribution of Wera Blanke in the conference proceedings of ProCom '98 (Blanke 2003b).

115 Terminologia Esperanto-Centro de Universala Esperanto-Asocio, located, as of 1987, in Rotterdam (Nieuwe Binnenweg 176, NL-3015 BJ Rotterdam).

116 For example, Gerhard Budin spoke about problems of international cooperation in the area of terminological planning at the TEC Conference during the 77th World Esperanto Congress 1992 in Vienna (see Galinski, Budin, Krommer-Benz & Manu 1994).

117 [Several of Wüster's studies in Esperantology were later collected in an Esperanto edition: see Wüster 1978 – HT]

V

Causes of the relative success of Esperanto[118]

In order that a language be worldwide, it is not enough to call it so.

(L.L. Zamenhof 1887)[119]

Did Esperanto succeed? No and yes!

To understand the linguistically interesting phenomenon of how a project for a universal language[120] could become a living language, we would do best to look at the language initiated in 1887 by Lazar Ludvik Zamenhof (1859-1917) under the pseudonym Dr. Esperanto. The pseudonym became the name of the language. The frequently expressed assertion that Esperanto 'did not succeed' is both right and wrong, depending on how one looks at it.

Esperanto was not a success on Zamenhof's terms. Zamenhof hoped that the world would officially adopt his language as a means of intercommunication alongside the various mother tongues, thereby facilitating contact among people of differing languages and reducing interethnic conflicts.

On the other hand, Esperanto has succeeded in two ways. First, it has shown that a language project can be transformed into a living language,

---

118 The original text was first published in *Language Problems & Language Planning*. See Blanke 2009b. Translated by Humphrey Tonkin.
119 Slogan on the cover of the first brochure (*Unua libro*), published in Russian (Dr Esperanto 1887).
120 Languages deliberately created for international communication are given a variety of designations: *universal language, world auxiliary language, (international) artificial language.* The preferred scholarly term is '(international) planned language.' On terminology see the present volume, especially Chapters 1 and 2.

— 99 —

fully functioning and evolving with all the functions that any human language has. This fact, which is easy to verify in practice, throws a new light on various linguistic laws and suppositions (cf. Duličenko 1997). In this sense, certain indications of the reliability of the ancient human dream of a universal language can be found also in other systems, particularly Volapük (Johann Martin Schleyer, 1879), Latino sine flexione (Giuseppe Peano, 1903), Ido (Louis Couturat, 1907), Occidental-Interlingue (Edgar de Wahl, 1922) and Interlingua (IALA[121]/Alexander Gode, 1951).[122]

Second, Esperanto has outlived its competitors. Before 1887 various projects had been published and after that time several hundred additional ones were added. In fact, up to the present day we can probably count more than a thousand projects for invented languages, of various types and quality, many of which have recently appeared or will appear in the Internet.[123] Despite these developments, Esperanto is, at least up to now, the only planned language with a significant language community, in terms both of numbers and of quality, who employ the language for their various aims and needs.

A misunderstanding frequently found in the literature of linguistics and in the mass media is a failure to distinguish between a language project and a language,[124] leading to the assertion that Esperanto 'has no culture'.

121 IALA: International Auxiliary Language Association (1924-1953), an international linguistics society that addressed the problem of an international auxiliary language and in 1951 launched Interlingua, primarily on the basis of the work of Alexander Gode (Blanke 1985: 167-183).

122 On the various efforts to create and disseminate an international planned language, see, among others, Bausani 1970; Blanke 1985; Couturat & Leau 1903+1907/2001; Drezen 1931/1991, 2004; Duličenko 1990; Isaev 1976, 1991; Kuznecov 1982a, 1982b, 1984, 1987; Pei 1958/1968.

123 Until 1970, the date at which he completed editorial work on the book that he published years later, Aleksandr Duličenko collected information on 917 projects (Duličenko 1990). New projects continue to appear, particularly on the Internet: see Becker 2001, Fettes 1997, Okrent 2009. [On Slavic constructed languages on the Internet see Meyer 2016 – SF]

124 On the difference between a *project* for a planned language and an actual planned language, see Blanke 1991 and Blanke 2006: 49-98; also Schubert 2001.

A language project lacks a language community, but a functioning language has such a language community. It is difficult to assert of the Esperanto language community that it has no culture. We might add that the specificities and characteristics of this language community, with its structures, traditions, activities, important people, and in fact with its entire history, are reflected and preserved in the language, particularly in the lexis, as has been shown by, among others, Aleksandr Mel'nikov (1992; 2004) and Sabine Fiedler (1999; 2002) – and these characteristics are passed on from generation to generation.

Various factors have negatively or positively affected the situation and position of Esperanto. Conscious of the fact that there have been many attempts to create an international 'artificial' language, or an international writing system,[125] we have to ask ourselves how to explain the relative success of Esperanto and the fact that the language developed and adapted itself to the changing communication needs of its speakers.[126]

In the history of the efforts, extending over several centuries, to create a universal language or writing system, the predominant subject of discussion has been the linguistic details of individual projects, particularly in the twentieth century. Raised less often is the issue of the social dimensions of the language. It is evident, however, that the historical situation has up to now been unfavourable to the idea and dissemination of a planned language. Among the negative influences in the twentieth century have been two world wars, revolutions, persecution under the regimes of Hitler and Stalin (Lins 1988, 2016/2017), dismissals and misinterpretations, hegemonic ambitions of major powers with respect to their languages, and so on.

Undoubtedly the relative success of Esperanto is due also to its structural characteristics, but probably only to a secondary degree. One could cer-

---

125 'World writing system' or 'pasigraphy': Blanke 1976.
126 Several studies have attempted to raise the question 'Why did Esperanto win?' among them Jirkov 1931, Blanke 1975.

tainly hypothesise that the structural qualities of other projects were not inferior to those of Esperanto, although it is difficult to arrive at objective criteria for such a measurement. The relative success of Esperanto is therefore due to the interaction of various factors, primarily having to do with linguistic structures and with non-linguistic conditions.

Linguistic factors[127]

Several specific structural factors have undoubtedly helped Esperanto to succeed. We have identified seven of them.

First, lexical sources are easily recognisable for many. The lexical roots used in planned languages, particularly in the twentieth century, tend to be drawn from Romance languages, although in varying quantities from project to project. This overwhelming Romance element can be explained historically by reference to the wide international distribution of Latin-derived languages and language elements. This is so of Esperanto as well, whose lexical roots are for the most part of Romance derivation. According to Janton (1993: 51) about 75% of Esperanto morphemes are derived from Romance languages, 20% from Germanic languages, and 5% from other languages. Other studies indicate a higher level of Romance elements, as high as 90% (Corsetti, La Torre & Vessella 1980). The numbers of course depend on the nature of the text (everyday language, literary language, technical language) and on the quantity of texts examined.

Second, Esperanto has an easily grasped phonology. We have already noted that the lexical structure, being Latinate, is relatively easily grasped by many. The same is true of the phonology – and particularly so for speakers of European languages (although less so for Asians).

---

[127] I will omit linguistic examples to avoid getting lost in details. On the structure of Esperanto see the numerous grammars (particularly Wennergren 2005) and textbooks, and also the linguistic studies of Gledhill 2000, Isaev 1981, Janton 1993, and Wells 1978/1989.

The simple vowel system (five vowels), compared to French or English, permits relatively easy acquisition of pronunciation for non-Europeans as well. The consonant system presents greater difficulties. However, the sound system is in general relatively acceptable – and this holds true also for Africans of various linguistic backgrounds, as the phonetician Max Mangold (1979) has established

Third, Esperanto has a phonological alphabet and simple orthography. The Latin alphabet, with a few diacritics, allows for a phonological (phonemic) orthography, which is accordingly particularly simple. Each separate letter (grapheme) represents only one separate sound (phoneme). The phonemes allow some allophonic variety and therefore do not limit the pronunciation norm too strictly. The spoken use of the language internationally has, over the years, led to relatively unified pronunciation – a characteristic strengthened by more frequent personal contacts, meetings and other forms of programming, and modern acoustical communication such as radio, recordings, telephony, the acoustic possibilities of the Internet, compact discs and other forms of electronic storage and dissemination.

Fourth, Esperanto lacks morphemic variants. In Esperanto all morphemes, both free and bound, are invariant. Thus there are no allomorphs as in ethnic languages, where such phenomena appear for reasons often explainable only in historical terms and arising from the effects of morpheme combination, or because of semantic distinctions, or changes of accent, or various other causes (the only exception occurs in nicknames).

Fifth, Esperanto allows for easy combinability of morphemes through productive word formation. According to Maria Stepanova (1971) the ability to combine morphemes to create morpheme structures (words) is guided by internal valency factors occurring between morphemes. One can distinguish between morphophonological internal valency and semantic internal valency. Because of Esperanto's relatively simple morpheme-structure, its lack of allomorphs, its lack of historically determined infixing at the junction of morphemes, and other factors, word formation can more readily follow semantic principles than undergo limitation through morphophonological factors. However, other factors influenced by ethnic languages do on occasion intervene, for example analogy, factors resulting from language economy, and so on. Word formation, which constitutes an open system, is autonomous and does not depend on outside linguistic models, as is the case for example with Interlingua. For these reasons, word formation in Esperanto is very elastic and productive.[128]

Sixth, Esperanto is open to the assimilation of new international lexical elements. An important factor in the enrichment of the language is the relatively easy assimilation of current international lexical elements in the form of basic morphemes (i.e. lexical roots).

Seventh, Esperanto is characterised by unambiguous marking of the principal classes of words and grammatical categories. The principal classes of words, at least in European parlance, namely verb, noun, adjective and derived adverb, have unambiguous markers (word-category suffixes). This is also so for grammatical categories as well (tenses, moods, cases, participles). This makes the grammatical structure of sentences relatively transparent.

---

[128] Blanke 1981a, in a comparative study of German and Esperanto word-formation, establishes the superiority of Esperanto to the, in this respect, relatively creative German language. For this reason the language is particularly suitable for machine translation projects, as Schubert (1992, 1993) has demonstrated.

Non-linguistic factors

The various structural characteristics mentioned above account for the relative ease of learning[129] and application – important advantages for a language proposed as a means of international communication, especially one that lacks a strong economic or political lobby. However, the non-linguistic factors are more important than those related to linguistic structure. Let us begin with a brief history.

The final third of the nineteenth century was marked by increasing rapidity of capitalist development, greater internationalisation of commerce, politics and culture, and a deepening of spiritual and scientific exchanges. During this period of history, at least in Europe, there was a certain openness to the idea of an international language, which helped the spread of Volapük (1879). Also important was the recruitment potential of Catholic circles by the author of Volapük, the priest Johann Martin Schleyer. Volapük was the first planned language to achieve a degree of dissemination, though it quickly disappeared with the onset of the twentieth century (Schmidt 1986, Haupenthal 1982). Its early success is surprising, because Volapük had serious linguistic defects, such as a complicated word-formation system, and a morpheme system derived chiefly from Latin, English and German, but much transformed and accordingly having low recognisability and insufficient redundancy.

Despite its linguistic failings, Volapük soon had its clubs in many countries, where one could not only learn the language but also put it to practical use, particularly in printed texts and in correspondence. Volapük is proof of the fact that non-linguistic rather than structural characteristics are decisive in producing a certain level of success. According

---

129 It is difficult to decide which aspects of a language learned as a foreign language are easy or difficult, since everything depends on the learner's original language. For this reason 'ease of learning' is always relative. Otto Back, however, has formulated some criteria for judging whether a language is 'easy' or 'difficult' (Back 1972, 1979; and see also Mangold 1979).

to the Volapükist Johann Schmidt, at the end of the nineteenth and beginning of the twentieth centuries there existed some 400 clubs and 18 national associations totalling 30,000–40,000 members (Schmidt 2005). Although these numbers are probably exaggerated, it is clear that for a certain period Volapük was linked with the idea of a neutral international means of communication. The evident linguistic failings of Volapük and the collapse of its movement led many Volapükists to move over to the new language of Doctor Esperanto.[130]

Of special significance for the success of Esperanto was the politically wise attitude of its initiator Zamenhof. He intuitively understood the essential problems of the structure and functioning of a language, among them the relation between the linguistic system (*langue*) and its concrete application (*parole*), the importance of the language community, the relationship between stability and evolution, and the problem of norms and their codification. Although we should really mention other people besides Zamenhof whose role was very important, for reasons of space we will limit ourselves to the role of Zamenhof, which was particularly decisive. We have singled out ten non-linguistic factors decisive to the development of the Esperanto language community.

First, Esperanto constitutes a language scheme open to further development. Zamenhof did not present a language project elaborated in any great detail, with many texts and an extensive dictionary, as did, for example, Alfandari (1961), author of Neo. In his first brochure, he simply presented sixteen basic grammatical rules, 929 morphemes and a few model texts. In short, he published a sketch of a language project. This sketch, however, contained enough information to allow those interested to learn the project and apply it, initially for correspondence, but, as of 1889, in a journal (*La Esperantisto*, 1889-1895).[131] By creating texts and engaging in correspondence, the early users applied the

---
130 [Garvía suggests that this transfer of loyalties may have been less widespread than commonly assumed: see Garvía 2015 – HT]

131 A reprint of the journal with an afterword by Reinhard Haupenthal appeared in 1988 (Hildesheim, Zürich, New York: Olms).

language and created the *parole*, which in turn reflected back on the language system, the *langue*. The subscribers to the journal formed the first Esperanto language community, which actively participated in the further construction of the language. Although Zamenhof himself created many texts, they would have been without value were it not for the other users of the language.

Second, the Esperanto language is linked to a humanistic ideal. In his language Zamenhof saw not only a technical device to facilitate international communication, but above all an instrument for reducing inter-ethnic conflicts and wars between nations. He saw the language as helping the brotherhood of humanity. It was precisely this idea, the 'internal idea' of Esperanto (Blanke 1978), rather than its relative ease of learning, that for many people constituted a stronger reason to learn the language. This ideology of brotherhood also influenced Zamenhof in his attempts to found a cosmopolitan religion, the 'Hillelism' (hilelismo) or 'Humanitism' (homaranismo) that received less attention than the language itself (see Zamenhof 1972). We find a similar ideology of brotherhood in Schleyer's Volapük, but for the most part not in the other projects mentioned above.

Third, Zamenhof saw language as a social phenomenon. At the First World Congress of Esperanto in 1905 in Boulogne-sur-Mer (France), where the language was widely spoken for the first time, Zamenhof formally relinquished all rights to 'his' language. He understood that a language cannot depend on the desires of a single person, but is rather a social phenomenon. This realisation distinguished him from Schleyer, who saw Volapük as his personal invention, over whose development he wished to retain a deciding influence.

Fourth, Esperanto was intended for universal application. As with Schleyer and Volapük, but in contrast to the founders of Latino sine flexione, Ido, Occidental-Interlingue and Interlingua, Zamenhof proposed for his language universal application that would include its use for artistic purposes. He understood that literary translations, many of which he himself produced[132] and original literary production (Sutton 2008) can have great significance for the development and expansion of the language.

Fifth, Zamenhof saw his language as a language for all levels of society. In contrast to the authors of Ido, Occidental-Interlingue, Interlingua and other projects, Zamenhof's relation to his language community was not elitist but democratic. His language was intended to serve all classes and levels of humanity. Writing in 1910 to the editor of the German periodical *Der Arbeiter-Esperantist*, Zamenhof observed: 'Perhaps for no one in the world does our democratic language have such significance as for workers' (Zamenhof 1948: 263). And in fact in the years before and following World War I there emerged a relatively strong workers' Esperanto movement – which, among other things, proved the social usefulness of the language as a politically practical instrument (Noltenius 1993).

Sixth, Esperanto was intended to protect ethnic languages. The uninformed sometimes suppose that Esperanto stands in opposition to ethnic languages and that it is designed to push them aside or even take their place. Although the idea of a single worldwide language does appear on occasion in social utopias (Mannewitz 1997), in the Esperanto movement it has never gained much traction. To the contrary, Zamenhof stated quite clearly as follows:

> An international language not only aims to give to people from different ethnicities ... the capability of understanding one another, but it also in no way intends to interfere with the internal life of these ethnicities... An 'international language' and

---

[132] Zamenhof translated, among other titles, the plays *Hamlet* (Shakespeare, 1894), *The Government Inspector* (Gogol, 1906), *Iphigenia in Tauris* (Goethe, 1908), *The Robbers* (Schiller, 1908), and *Georges Dandin* (Molière, 1908), and most of Andersen's Fables. He also translated the complete Hebrew Old Testament (1907-1917): see Blanke 2006: 315-330.

a 'global language' are two quite different things, and in no way should one confuse the two. (Zamenhof 1929: 281)

Today's Esperanto language community shows interest in, and awareness of, the dominant influence of English and the situation of other languages. The disequilibrium in national and international means of communication has political, economic, and cultural-policy effects, not all of them positive. Phillipson, among others (2003, and see the review in *LPLP* 27/1 [2003]), has analysed these issues, particularly in the European context. The users of Esperanto propose their language as a neutral international language whose effect would be to reduce and finally neutralise the position of English as a device for interlingual understanding and thus free the various ethnic languages from the often suffocating pressure that English exerts on them.

Seventh, Esperanto was envisioned by Zamenhof as a practical instrument. Zamenhof hoped that the linguistic characteristics (see above) that he had given to his language would rapidly allow it to function in practice. He succeeded in this regard. The widespread practical application of the language, removed from disputes over linguistic details, constituted a major stabilising factor and was one of the decisive elements in Esperanto's success.

Eighth, from an early stage, Esperanto possessed stabilising textual models. For those newly learning and applying Esperanto, it was important to have textual models that would help orient them to the lexis, grammar and style. For this reason Zamenhof's enormous production of translated and original text had a major effect in providing models.[133] This was particularly significant also because, very soon after the publication of the first brochure, proposals began to surface for various reforms.

---

133 Between 1973 and 2004, the Japanese publisher and Zamenhof scholar Itô Kanzi, under the pseudonym Ludovikito, edited and published all of Zamenhof's works in 34 volumes and, in a further 22 volumes, the materials, journals, textbooks, and dictionaries that appeared in Zamenhof's time and under his editorship, or with his advice or approval.

Ninth, Zamenhof was careful to allow democratic decisions on reforms. Zamenhof collected the various proposals for reforms and recast them in the form of a new language project, in fact a variant of his original project. He submitted them to a decision by the first small language community, the subscribers to *La Esperantisto*. By a democratic written ballot the subscribers in 1894 refused the reform proposals. This was an important step in the further stabilisation of the language.

Tenth, and finally, the problem of dealing with reforms was partly responsible for the early establishment and codification of standard Esperanto. Since discussion of reforms did not end with the vote, and several variants of Esperanto appeared, it became important to set limits to distinguish the normal development of the language from the creation of an essentially new project. For this reason, at the first World Esperanto Congress in Boulogne-sur-Mer on August 9, 1905, Zamenhof and those close to him proposed the acceptance of an 'untouchable' basic standard, the so-called *Fundamentals of Esperanto* (Zamenhof 1991). This basic norm continues to serve as a compulsory unifying platform for the language, though it defines only the essence of the language (alphabet, basic grammar, basic morphemes, and model texts) and does not hinder its lexical and stylistic development.

Ensuring stability and building community

The publication of the competing reform project Ido in 1907, whose author was the French scholar Louis Couturat,[134] seemed a direct threat to Esperanto and presented a challenge for the adepts of Zamenhof's language. Zamenhof, for his part, redoubled his translation work. The practitioners of the language continued as usual, without expressing much interest in language disputes. But significant numbers of intellec-

---

134 Philosopher and logician, publisher of the manuscripts of Gottfried Wilhelm Leibniz, co-author of the fundamental study *La Langue universelle* (Couturat & Leau 1903+1907/2001).

tuals from the Esperanto language community went over to Ido, while others worked to defend Esperanto. The pressure to attack or defend Esperanto motivated them to subject it to closer analysis and to describe its principal characteristics in theoretical terms. This was particularly true of word-formation in Esperanto, in which Ido followed a different path and criticised the Esperanto approach (Couturat 1910, 1911).

The mathematician René de Saussure, brother of the linguist Ferdinand de Saussure, was among those who came to Esperanto's defence. Because of his studies of the theory of word formation in Esperanto (R. de Saussure 1910a; 1910b), he is regarded as one of the founders of Esperantology (Esperanto studies).

To monitor observance of the Fundamentals, and the evolution of the language, a Language Committee was established at the first congress in Boulogne in 1905. In due course the Language Committee became the Esperanto Academy, the principal language-cultivation body for Esperanto. The conservative role played by the Language Committee and its successor helped stabilise the language and played a role in defending it against reforms deemed unnecessary.

From the start, Zamenhof worked at building the structure of the language community. He collected addresses of learners of Esperanto and published them in *La Esperantisto*, whose first volume recorded one thousand such individuals. They formed the kernel of the future language community. Little by little, local clubs came into being, along with a few national associations and various periodicals with their subscribers. To allow for more effective and diversified international use of the language, the need developed for tighter coordination and development of the language community, not least to defend the language against competing proposals. Hence the founding of the Universal Esperanto Association (UEA) in 1908, and of other more specifically focused organisations, such as the International Esperantist Science Association in 1907, and organisations for Catholics (1910) and Protestants (1911). These organisations, along with national associations and their journals, permitted the further construction of the base of the language community, in which were reflected a wide diversity of political and religious tendencies. Little by little this community became a social factor with practical outcomes. Common ideals (the internal idea, mentioned above), strengthening of the organisational base of the community, defence of the language against its critics – all these factors strengthened the sense of common identity.

Over the years the distinction between the organisational base on the one hand and the language community on the other has grown clearer. A wide range of organisations has emerged at the international, regional, national and local levels, along with institutions of various kinds – facilitating agencies, learning centres, publishers of books and journals, cultural centres, libraries and archives, radio stations, various forms of electronic contact, networks of globally active representatives, and a wide range of conferences, meetings, festivals, and the like. This language community, with its ideals and traumas (the Ido crisis, international disputes, political persecutions), indeed its whole history, its leaders, and its remarkable activities, has created what Alexander Mel'nikov (1992; 2004) calls a 'quasi-ethnicity', a living quasi-diaspora.[135]

Esperanto studies today: Descriptive and research-based scholarship

The present and future position of Esperanto depends on relatively broad scholarly analysis and description of the language. The field of Esperanto studies (or Esperantology) explores the sources, structure, development, function, communicative domains and the language

---

[135] On the social make-up of the Esperanto movement see Forster 1982 and Rašić 1994; on current issues in the Esperanto movement see Tonkin 2006 (in Esperanto), 2009 (in Italian).

community as a whole. Esperanto is the only planned language that is researched on an ongoing and systematic basis.

The results enter – though still in insufficient quantity – the multilingual research literature. But the larger part, perhaps sixty percent of the work in Esperanto studies, is published in Esperanto itself – which presents something of a barrier to linguists who do not know Esperanto. These materials are collected in special libraries and archives and the publications are recorded in bibliographies.[136]

To understand the phenomenon of Esperanto fully, it is not enough to study the scholarly literature: it is essential to observe and experience the language in practice. It is, after all, practice that reveals the truth.

---

[136] See the following chapter. Scholarship in Esperanto is particularly well represented in the *MLA International Bibliography*.

VI

Paths to the scholarly literature on interlinguistics and Esperanto studies[137]

Scholarly literature in interlinguistics and Esperanto studies is steadily expanding. Finding one's way around it is increasingly difficult even for experienced researchers, especially if the goal is a literature search on specific issues. For those new to the field, the situation is particularly complicated if the goal is to produce something original. As a result, even in newer publications important earlier studies sometimes go unnoticed.

Accordingly, a rather broad introduction to the sources of material seems useful. The primary purpose of the study is to help guide the researcher to those mainly scholarly materials, and also to places and instruments offering the most up-to-date bibliographical information

---

[137] The original text was first published in *Language Problems & Language Planning*, translated by Humphrey Tonkin. See Blanke 2003a. It was subsequently reissued as as an *Esperanto Document* (Blanke 2004). An abbreviated adaptation appeared as 'How not to reinvent the wheel: The essential scholarly literature in interlinguistics and Esperantology' in *INDECS: Interdisciplinary Description of Complex Systems*. 13/2: 200-215. The present text has been corrected, expanded, and updated by the author and edited by Humphrey Tonkin. The original English-language version appeared in four additional languages, as follows:
- *Esperanto*: Interlingvistiko kaj esperantologio: vojoj al la faka literaturo. (*Esperanto-Dokumentoj* 39E). Rotterdam: Universala Esperanto-Asocio, 2003, 40 pp.
- *German*: Interlinguistik und Esperantologie: Wege zur Fachliteratur. (*Esperanto-Dokumente* 7). Bamberg: Deutsches Esperanto-Institut 2003, 58 pp.
- *Czech*: Interlingvistika. Cesty k odborné literatuře. (Translated and with a complementary chapter on interlinguistics in the Czech Republic by Miroslav Malovec). Dobřichovice: KAVA-PECH, 2003, 69 pp.
- *Chinese*: Guojiyuxue he shijieyuxue: tongxiang zhuanye wenxian zhi lu. Interlinguistics and Esperanto studies: Paths to the scholarly literature. Translated from Esperanto with an additional chapter on interlinguistics in China by LIU Haitao: *Interlinguistische Informationen* 13 (2004), Sonderheft (special edition). Berlin: Gesellschaft für Interlinguistik, 49 pp.

and other material. In the present text the author often refers to the interlinguistics newsletters *IntI* and *IpI* (*Interlinguistische Informationen* and *Informilo por Interlingvistoj*) because a knowledge of their contents is very helpful in locating and evaluating the literature.

To make the study adequately international and to avoid the danger of ignoring important items, I have shared the draft of the study with several competent specialists, who provided numerous useful corrections and additions.[138]

1 Interlinguistics and Esperanto studies (Esperantology)

1.1 Definitions

For the limited purposes of the present study I will apply the most commonly accepted definition, namely that *interlinguistics* is the study of planned languages or interlanguages,[139] in theory and practice. However, for more and more researchers interlinguistics also includes other aspects of language invention, language planning and language policy and further aspects (including economic, legal, cultural theory, IT and others). Sometimes the term interlinguistics refers to the study of interlinguistic contact and interlinguistic relations and interferences (e.g. Wandruszka 1971). Although these aspects of the topic can play a role

---

138 For helpful corrections and suggestions the author thanks Věra Barandovská-Frank, Wera Blanke, Osmo Buller, Renato Corsetti, Sabine Fiedler, Martin Haase, Wim Jansen, Kim Uson, Ino Kolbe, Ilona Koutny, Andreas Künzli, Sergej Kuznecov, Jouko Lindstedt, Ulrich Lins, Liu Haitao, Miroslav Malovec, Cornelia Mannewitz, Geraldo Mattos, Aleksandr Mel'nikov, Carlo Minnaja, Ursula Niesert, Marc van Oostendorp, Otto Prytz, Árpád Rátkai, Humphrey Tonkin, Usui Hiroyuki, Balázs Wacha, and Yamasaki Seikô.

139 In using the term 'interlanguages' to describe systems of international communication, we should note that in literature on foreign language acquisition, by contrast, the term 'interlanguage' normally refers to a language formed in the mind of the learner (see Selinker 1972).

VI: Paths to the scholarly literature on interlinguistics and Esperanto studies

in interlinguistic research, they do not constitute the traditional understanding of the objectives of interlinguistics.[140]

A *planned language*[141] (also *universal language, artificial language, world [auxiliary] language, international constructed language*) is a language consciously created to facilitate international linguistic communication.

For *Esperanto*, so far the most successful planned language, an independent linguistic and philological discipline has emerged, known as *Esperanto studies* or *Esperantology*. Esperanto studies, understood broadly, is a branch of interlinguistics which examines the sources, principles of construction, structure, development, function and practical communicative capabilities of this planned language. It is also concerned with research on the Esperanto-speaking community, which exists in a kind of diaspora, and its history. It includes studies of the language community because, unlike ethnic languages, the language 'created' its community.

Interlinguistics includes Esperanto studies, though we sometimes treat Esperanto studies separately. Although all Esperanto studies are interlinguistic studies, the reverse is not always so. And consequently not all interlinguists are scholars of Esperanto. Comparable independent 'philologies' have not emerged for other systems of planned language, though their investigation is of potential scholarly interest. This abstemiousness is in my view unfortunate, and a loss for the growth of knowledge in linguistics.

---

140 On the currently differing parameters of the definition of interlinguistics see the surveys by Schubert (1989b: 7-44), D. Blanke (2006: 19-35) and Sakaguchi (1998: 309-323). The term is normally either (a) limited to the study of planned languages, systems of international communication, or interlanguages, or (b) inclusive of other, e.g. politico-linguistic aspects.

141 The expression *planned language* (Esp *planlingvo*, de *Plansprache*, en *planned language*, fr *langue planifiée*, it *lingua pianificata*, ru *planovyj jazyk* etc.) was introduced by the founder of the field of terminological science, Eugen Wüster (1898-1977), and has established itself as an interlinguistic term in various languages (Wüster 1955/1976; Blanke 1997a, b). See our earlier chapter on Wüster.

1.2 Scholarly and scientific value

Examination of problems in interlinguistics and Esperanto studies can in fact contribute significantly to an audit of a whole string of basic linguistic concepts, because, looked at through this particular prism, they assume additional properties. Interlinguistic viewpoints can also inspire research in adjacent disciplines – not only the fundamental question of the capabilities of consciously created languages to function and develop (a topic that should be of interest to general linguistics), but also basic questions in specific problem areas, among them the following.

Comparative linguistics. Comparison of languages can more clearly show the particular characteristics of the individual languages being compared. This is true for both planned languages and ethnic languages. Particularly important in this respect is that research on an ethnic language from a planned language perspective can contribute to a better understanding of the *relationship between thought and language*. The American linguist Edward Sapir draws attention to this truth (1931: 13):

> It is, therefore, highly desirable that along with the practical labour of getting wider recognition of the international language idea, there go hand in hand comparative researches which aim to lay bare the logical structures that are inadequately symbolised in our present-day languages, in order that we may see more clearly than we have yet been able to see just how much of psychological insight and logical rigour have been and can be expressed in linguistic form. One of the most ambitious and important tasks that can be undertaken is the attempt to work out the relation between logic and usage in a number of national and constructed languages, in order that the eventual problem of adequately symbolising thought may be seen as the problem it still is.

On occasion, other linguists who have studied planned languages point to the stimulating value in general of interlinguistic studies for linguistics – among them the Danish English-language specialist Otto Jespersen who studied *inter alia* Ido and himself created the Novial project. Furthermore the French linguist and phonologist André Martinet was active in the planned-language movement and for a time served as linguistic director of the International Auxiliary Language Association (IALA). In an interview in 1987 he remarked as follows:

> Undoubtedly, my contact with Ido, though very superficial, was very important for my later linguistic thought, because it allowed me to realise that it is not morphological complications that constitute the richness of a language... The contact with a language like Ido immediately convinced me that there was something crucial in the language: its phonological, grammatical structure ... never mind, and that all these morphological complications, which are imposed by tradition, are useless and only make communication between users of the language more difficult.[142]

The theory of language planning. Valter Tauli clearly indicates the connections between language planning and planned language by including interlinguistics among the target areas of language planning: 'Interlinguistics can be defined as the science of IL [international language] planning, or more precisely, the branch of TLP [theory of language planning] which investigates the principles, methods and tactics of IL planning' (Tauli 1968: 167). Tonkin (2015) addresses the relationship between language planning and planned languages. It is certainly no accident that the journal *Language Problems & Language Planning* (its predecessor had the Esperanto title *La Monda Lingvo-Problemo* 1969-

---

[142] Incontestablement, mon contact, très superficiel d'ailleurs, avec l'ido, a été très important pour ma pensée linguistique ultérieure, car il m'a permis de prendre conscience que ce ne sont pas les complications morphologiques qui font la richesse d'une langue... Le contact avec une langue comme l'ido m'a immédiatement convaincu qu'il y avait quelque chose de central dans la langue: sa *structure* phonologique, grammaticale ... peu importe, et que toutes ces complications morphologiques, qui sont imposées par la tradition, sont inutiles et ne font que rendre plus difficile la communication entre les gens qui utilisent la langue' (Martinet 1991: 676). On Martinet, see Klare 2012.

1977), an internationally recognised scholarly journal, was founded and is currently edited by interlinguists.

Language change. In an earlier chapter, we described nineteen stages in the development of a fully functioning planned language. In the case of Esperanto, the only planned-language project to complete these nineteen stages, it would be particularly worth exploring what kinds of language change have taken place between the stage of 'publication and projection' (1887) and the emergence, particularly since the Second World War, of Esperanto as 'family language' (on linguistic change in Esperanto see Blanke 2010).

The study of specialised language use. Elsewhere in this volume we address the subject of Esperanto as a language of scholarship and the heuristic role of Esperanto in the work of Eugen Wüster, founder of the science of terminology (see also the surveys in Wera Blanke 2008, 2013).

Computational linguistics (including machine translation). In this regard the role of Esperanto as an internal computer language in the semi-automatic project 'Distributed Language Translation' (DLT, see Schubert's surveys of 1988, 1996, 1999 and Liu 2001) is worthy of mention. A few systems of machine translation that include Esperanto have recently appeared (see Nosková & Baláž 2011), and particularly the Esperanto translation of the English Wikipedia through the WikiTrans system (Bick 2011).[143]

The theory of foreign-language instruction. On the propaedeutic effect of the teaching of a planned language in the learning of other foreign languages, see Lobin (2002) and the overview in Corsetti and La Torre (1995, 2001) of the various experiments along these lines (see also Fantini & Reagan 1992).

---

[143] [On the current state of Esperanto and machine translation, see Gobbo 2015b – HT]

Language policy. The issue of equal rights to non-discriminatory international communication and the problems of intercultural communication have particularly engaged the interest of interlinguists.[144]

A particular perspective is provided by the connections between **Asian language-reform movements** (Chinese and Japanese) and Esperanto, addressed in the years 1933-1936 in the Japanese journal *Kokusaigo kenkyu* (Studies in the International Language), published in Tokyo under the editorship of Oosima Yosio (see Usui 2008: 186-187; Lins 2008).

2 Misunderstandings

The quality of a study on a given topic is heavily dependent on, among other things, the scholarly literature consulted or neglected. Although it is essential to acquaint oneself with the relevant publications before expressing oneself on a given topic, this often does not occur.

Opinions expressed on planned languages, particularly Esperanto, by authors of studies of linguistics and language policy, in various languages, are often superficial or are not based on fact or rooted in the disciplines in question (see, for example, Haselhuber 2012: 383-384; Van Parijs 2011: 39-46; Dorren 2014: 240-243). Fiedler (2015a) analyses such attitudes to planned languages in a broad range of language policy texts. Among common errors are the following.

(a) No distinction is made between, on the one hand, planned language *projects* that never became *languages*, and, on the other hand, authentically functioning planned languages. There are hundreds of projects,

---
[144] See, for example, Fettes & Bolduc (1998), Fiedler (2010), Hübler (1985), Müller (1992), Mattusch (1999), Phillipson (1992, 2003), Piron (1994), Skutnabb-Kangas (2000), and Tonkin (2012), who include interlinguistic viewpoints in their publications. An overview of planned languages and language policy is provided by Blanke (2007a).

and new ones are constantly appearing, particularly on the Internet.[145] The principal representative of planned language systems that achieved the status of full-fledged language is *Esperanto*, proposed in 1887 by L.L. Zamenhof (1859-1917) as a preliminary project. From this preliminary document, the users – as a result of the interplay of various factors (see Chapter 5 in the present volume) – created over a period of decades a richly expressive means of communication with the principal characteristics of a developing language. Other systems that achieved the status of languages include *Ido* (primarily the work of Louis Couturat 1907) and *Interlingua* (developed chiefly by Alexander Gode 1951), which still have small language communities.

(b) Not infrequently, writers (e.g. Okrent 2009) present *different manifestations of language invention* equally, in a single context, so that Esperanto appears next to Klingon and other recent 'cult languages', 'literary constructed languages', or 'Hollywood planned languages' (Gobbo 2015a), created for films or television series (Adams 2011) which – unlike traditional planned languages – were not constructed to facilitate international communication.

(c) This failure to distinguish among invented languages leads to one of the chief arguments against planned languages, namely their alleged *'lack of culture'*. Authors seem unaware that in the case of Esperanto there exists a language community which for almost 130 years has used and therefore developed the planned language. This community is the creator, carrier, and conserver of a specific culture containing elements of world culture and also unique elements linked specifically to characteristics of the language community itself, with its institutions, activities, history, traditions, and literature.[146] Two recent encyclopaedic volumes in English, by Sutton (2008) and

---

145 Duličenko (1990) lists over 900 systems (up to the date of completion of the book in 1970). On the lively language invention on the Internet, see, for example, Barandovská-Frank (2009).

146 [See Mel'nikov 2015 – HT]

Gubbins (2012), and in Esperanto by Minnaja and Silfer (2015), describe original literature in Esperanto. Books on the extensive translated literature in Esperanto have yet to be compiled, however.

(d) We sometimes hear arguments to the effect that the lack of *'scientific planning'* in planned languages means that they cannot work, cannot be accepted. This is both true and false. If one considers the aims which authors of planned languages link to their languages (such as general global use as a second language, the peacemaking role of a neutral language in international conflicts, etc.), their planned languages have indeed fallen short. In another respect, however, some of them did not fail: they showed that it is possible to initiate a language that can be learned, used and promoted by human beings, thus creating a language community with particular characteristics. This community ensures language development, causes certain forms of language change, and even creates and nurtures a culture, expressed in the language and influencing it, thus giving the planned language more and more of the features that characterise so-called natural languages.

3 Difficulties in approaching the phenomenon of planned languages

Inaccurate presentations of topics in interlinguistics and Esperantology are not automatically expressions of prejudice or intentional ignorance. We must concede that a planned language, functioning in practice, is an anomaly in the conceptual sphere of no small number of traditionally trained linguists.

Sometimes we also encounter a kind of psychic opposition to an 'artificial' language, which seems to constitute an absurd contrast, or even a threat, to a 'natural' language (Piron 1994).

Persecution of Esperanto under Hitler and Stalin (see Lins 1988, 2016, 2016/2017) may also have a deterrent effect in circles insufficiently knowledgeable politically and historically.

And, in addition, there is indeed a *specific language barrier* that inhibits access to the scholarly literature. For the non-specialist, the approach to the scholarly literature of interlinguistics and Esperanto studies is often very difficult. As we have already remarked, as much as sixty percent of this literature exists in planned languages (some ninety percent or more in Esperanto). As a consequence, linguists, if they say anything at all about interlinguistics, often base their remarks on randomly unearthed and not always up-to-date sources. As a result their pronouncements are often unsatisfactory or downright wrong.[147] As any scholar knows, any serious study has to begin with a literature search. The same is true for interlinguistics. This has to include review of the scholarly literature written in Esperanto.

Over the past decades it has become obvious that in some fields scholars rely, quite inadequately, primarily on literature in English, giving no consideration to publications in other languages. Such an approach could have fatal consequences for interlinguistics, because in this field many valuable and indispensable publications exist only in German, Russian, Italian, French, and Hungarian.

4 Separate bibliographies

Searches in separate, free-standing bibliographies offering a survey of interlinguistics can produce good results, and several bibliographies of linguistics also contain sections on interlinguistics.

---

[147] For example in Bußmann (2002). See the articles on *Ido, Interlingua, Welthilfssprache*. A separate article on *Esperanto*, which is mentioned in the other articles, is missing. In Glück (2005) interlinguistics is better represented. Haarmann (2001), although his sources are old, can also be cited as a positive example. [See also Lo Bianco 2004 – HT]

4.1 Bibliographical surveys in interlinguistics

To find one's way in the scholarly literature, it helps to know where to look for basic information and so develop an awareness of the sources. The most extensive historically oriented bibliography for works up to the mid-1920s, *Bibliografio de Internacia Lingvo,* was compiled by Petr E. Stojan (1929/1973)[148] with 6,333 entries. The bibliography was reprinted in 1973 (Stojan 1929/1973). A more up-to-date bibliography (and bibliography of bibliographies) appeared in 1985 (Blanke 1985: 296-381; with over two thousand titles). Haupenthal (1968), Tonkin (1977), Wood (1982) and Tonkin & Fettes (1996) provide a selection of more recent work.

To date the fullest chronologically ordered list of planned language systems (recorded up to 1973) is that of Duličenko (1990), who provides a brief commentary on each, along with specimen texts and basic bibliographical information.

The present author has compiled a bibliography of bibliographies in interlinguistics and Esperanto studies (including hidden bibliographies), and has also compiled a list of some 2000 titles covering the most important literature in interlinguistics and Esperanto studies up to the end of the 1970s (Blanke 1985: 296-381).

Many studies can be found in the often hard to find small journals and bulletins in or on planned languages, which are often short-lived (four or five years on average).

Periodicals are the sources of the most up-to-date information on the history and current activities of planned-language communities. The largest of such bibliographies lists 14,143 titles (Hernández Yzal, Máthé

---
148 The Olms website contains a bibliographical supplement up to the year 2007 by Reinhard Haupenthal: http://www.olmsonline.de/no_cache/en/dms/met/?IDDOC=8761.

& Molera 2010). The 2010 volume was based on Máthé (1993), a bibliography covering the period from 1880 to the mid-1990s and listing 11,393 titles, some 90 percent associated with Esperanto, as shown in Table 1. Máthé's publication can be seen as a continuation of the bibliography of periodicals in planned languages compiled by Rondo Takács (1934)[149], which recorded 1276 titles in Esperanto and 195 in other planned languages. The proportion of journals in the various languages remains little changed.

Máthé has identified 11,300 periodicals in and on planned languages.

Table 1. Periodicals by language project (Máthé 1992)

Journals in or about the language	Founding date of language	Number of journals	% of total
Esperanto	1887	10,440	91.63
Volapük	1879	297	2.61
Ido	1907	286	2.51
Occidental-Interlingue	1922	99	0.87
Interlingua (IALA/Gode)	1951	83	0.73
Other planned languages		188	1.65

The most recent summary bibliography of interlinguistics and Esperantology (in Esperanto and German), with more than 300 titles (mostly monographs and anthologies, with a few individual studies, however without information on web access) was compiled by Irmi and Reinhard Haupenthal (Haupenthal & Haupenthal 2013).

---

[149] See Máthé (1993) and the preview publication *Rondo Takács* (1992). In Budapest during a brief period following Máthé's bibliography, a total of eighteen issues of the bibliographic bulletin *Periodaĵoj* appeared (1993-1994).

4.2 Bibliographies on individual planned languages

Few planned languages have reasonably complete bibliographies. One such is *Volapük*, in which no recent works have appeared (Haupenthal 1982). The beginnings of this first planned-language movement can also be reconstructed through a reprint of the first major Volapük journal.[150]

Another is *Ido*, in which occasional publications are still produced (Carlevaro/Haupenthal 1999); a third is *Occidental-Interlingue*[151], which has at its disposal today only a modest newsletter (Stenström 1997). Occasionally information on publications in *Interlingua* is posted on the Internet.[152] On the Internet there are also various lists of planned language projects, and the results of variously motivated language invention. Such lists, however, do more harm than good, because in general they deal with projects, presented at different levels of detail, and not with systems which have become fully-fledged languages in practice (see the note on Harrison and his *Journal of Planned Languages* in section 7.1).

4.3 Planned-language literature published in individual countries

There is a bibliography of all interlinguistics publications appearing in the German Democratic Republic between 1949 and 1990 (Blanke 1990). Similar national bibliographies of interlinguistics publications exist for Romania (Dominte & Nagy 2000) and the Soviet Union /Russia (Duličenko 1983, Gorecka & Korĵenkov 2005). Additional bibliographies of planned-language literature appearing in individual countries,

---

150 *Rund um die Welt. Zeitschrift für Volapükisten und solche, die es werden wollen.* vol. 1-4 (April 1888 – March 1892), reprint prepared by Reinhard Haupenthal (Hildesheim-Zürich-New York: Georg Olms, 2000).

151 After 1947 Occidental (created in 1922) was called Interlingue, not to be confused with Interlingua (published in 1951).

152 http://www.interlingua.com/libros.

include the Czech Republic, Japan, Yugoslavia, Lithuania, and the Netherlands (Haupenthal & Haupenthal 2013: 5).

4.4 National periodical bibliographies

Occasionally we find interlinguistics sections in *national* linguistics bibliographies. One such example was the annual publication *Sprachwissenschaftliche Informationen* (linguistic information), published by the Central Institute for Linguistics of the Academy of Sciences of the German Democratic Republic. From 1985 to 1991 it included a section entitled Plansprachen (planned languages).[153]

4.5 Bibliographies on single fields of linguistics

Bibliographies on single fields in linguistics generally do not have sections on interlinguistics. Among the exceptions, however, is *Kommentierte Bibliographie zur Slavischen Soziolinguistik* (Brang & Züllig 1981: 1143-1157), which contains 192 partly annotated items and particularly refers to the Slavic sphere of language-invention.[154]

4.6 Personal bibliographies

Personal bibliographies tend to be included in Festschriften, but are sometimes published separately. Such bibliographies exist for André Albault, Adolf Burkhardt, Louis Couturat, Ada Csiszár and Henri Vatré (Haupenthal & Haupenthal 2013: 5-6). There are particularly detailed

---

[153] See Jüttner (1990). The author of the present study also collaborated.

[154] For Slavic planned languages see Ana-Maria Meyer's thesis (2014) and similarly the studies by Lindstedt, Duličenko, van Steenbergen and Merunka / Heršak / Molhanec in *Grundlagenstudien aus Kybernetik und Geisteswissenschaft/Humankybernetik* (grkg), vol. 57 (2016), Nr. 2 (Juni), pp. 64-136.

bibliographies for Reinhard Haupenthal (Vallon 2015), Aleksandr Duličenko (Romančik 2006), Gaston Waringhien (Haupenthal 2009), Humphrey Tonkin (Blanke & Lins 2010) and Detlev Blanke (Becker 2011).

Bibliographies of the publications of more than seventy individuals have appeared in *Informilo por Interlingvistoj* (IpI) and *Interlinguistische Informationen* (IntI)[155] since 1992 (up to and including 2016), among them such prominent interlinguistics scholars as Otto Back (issue 57),[156] Věra Barandovská-Frank (81), Ignat F. Bociort (90), Dalibor Brozović (69), Tazio Carlevaro (73), André Cherpillod (82), Renato Corsetti (76), Till Dahlenburg (69), Michel Duc Goninaz (68), Aleksandr D. Duličenko (39, 42, 58-59), Sabine Fiedler (30, 68), Helmar Frank (84-85), Federico Gobbo (86), Hitosi Gotoo, Reinhard Haupenthal (92-93), Magomet I. Isaev (65), Wim Jansen (63), Goro Christoph Kimura (68, 84-85), Christer O. Kiselman (90), Ilona Koutny (70), Erich-Dieter Krause (92-93), Ulrich Lins (68), Aleksandr Mel'nikov (88-89), Carlo Minnaja (69), Hermann Ölberg (42), Seán Ó Riain (96-97), Claude Piron (65, 68), Alicja Sakaguchi (34) and Klaus Schubert (63).[157]

---

155 [All issues of *IntI*, from 1 (1/1992) to 100 (3-4/2016) are accessible online: www.interlinguistik-gil.de (→ Bulletin *IntI*). The last two issues (99 and 100) were edited by Sabine Fiedler and Cyril Brosch. *IntI* 99 is mainly dedicated to Detlev Blanke, 100 (I and II) contains an index compiled by Till Dahlenburg – SF]

156 The numbers refer to the issues of *IpI*.

157 The following is a complete list (**Ipi**//Inti): Otto Back (**57**//*59*), Věra Barandovská-Frank (**81**//*82*), Hermann Behrmann (**86**//*88*), Detlev Blanke (**76**), Ignat F. Bociort (**90**//*92*), Werner Bormann (**58-59**//*60-61*), Ed Borsboom (**77**//*78-79*), Ivo Bratanov (**61-62**), Dalibor Brozović (**69**//*72*), Oxana Burkina (*70-71*), Tazio Carlevaro (**73**//*75*), André Cherpillod (**82**), Renato Corsetti (**76**//*78-79*), Till Dahlenburg (**69**//*69*), Constantin Dominte (**57**), Michel Duc Goninaz (**68**), Aleksandr D. Duličenko (**39, 42, 58-59**//*40, 60-61, 62-63*), Heiner Eichner (*83*), Sabine Fiedler (**30, 68**//*30, 68*), Rudolf Joseph Fischer (*55-56*), Helmar Frank (**84-85**//*86-87*), Federico Gobbo (**86**//*89*), GOTOO Hitosi (*94-95*), Viktor Petrovič Grigorev (**61-62**//*62-63*), Reinhard Haupenthal (**92-93**//*94-95*), Magomet I. Isaev (**65**//*66-67*), Wim Jansen (**63**//*66-67*), KIMURA Goro Christoph (**68, 84-85**//*68, 85*), Christer O. Kiselman (**90**), Johannes Klare (*94-95*), Ilona Koutny (**70**//*70-71*), Bernd Krause (*91*), Erich-Dieter Krause (**92-93**//*94-95*), KURISU Kei (**76**//*76-77*), Andreas Kück (*70-71*), Mauro La Torre (**73**//*75*), Ulrich Lins (**68**//*68*), LIU, Haitao (**58-59**//*60-61*), Ronald Lötzsch (**58-59**//*60-61*), Wilhelmus J.A. Manders (**24**), Max Hans-Jürgen

We should perhaps also mention here the bibliographies on Jan Ámos Komenský (*IpI* 1+2-3, *IntI* 2 and 3-4) and Wilhelm Ostwald (*IpI* 37, *IntI* 46), both important from the perspective of interlinguistics.

4.7 University dissertations and final theses

Interlinguistics and Esperanto (or Esperantology) are official subjects of study in only a few universities. In this regard particularly worthy of mention is the work of István Szerdahelyi (1924-1987) at Eötvös Loránd University (ELTE) in Budapest, and his ten-or-so university textbooks (see Koutny 2009).[158] The holder of the chair in interlinguistics at the University of Amsterdam was, until recently, Wim Jansen (now succeeded by Federico Gobbo), also the author of textbooks (Jansen 2012/2013). The program in Interlinguistic Studies at Adam Mickiewicz University in Poznan, Poland, has been in operation since 1998 under the guidance of Professor Ilona Koutny.[159]

Over the past four decades, the number of university dissertations and various kinds of final theses has grown greatly. They have been listed by Symoens (1989, 1995) and, since 1995, in the bulletins *IntI* and *IpI* (see below). Information on university dissertations is also available on the Internet.[160]

Mattusch (**57//**59), James McElvenny (**89**), Georg Friedrich Meier (**5//***5*), Aleksandr Melnikov (**88-89//***90*), Carlo Minnaja (**69**), Hermann Ölberg (**42//***44*), Seán Ó Riain (**96-97//***98*), Wilhelm Ostwald (**37//***46*), Fabrizio A. Pennaccietti (**61-62//***62-63*), Claude Piron (**65, 68//***66-67*,*69*), Velimir Piškorec (**68**) Alicja Sakaguchi (**34//***35*), Jürgen Scharnhorst (*92*), Klaus Schubert (**63//***64-65*), Denis Silagi (**65//***66-67*), Karl-Hermann Simon (**77//***78-79*), Erich Spitz (**21//***23*), Petro Evstafjevič Stojan (**74**) TANAKA Katsuhiko (**70//***70-71*), Humphrey Tonkin (**50-51, 72//***52-53, 73*), Adomas Vaitilavičius (**20**), Luisa Calero Vaquera (**73//***74*), Balázs Wacha (**69//***68*), Gaston Waringhien (**1//***2*), Bengt-Arne Wickström (**66//***66-67*), Toon Witkam (**70//***72*), Fritz Wollenberg (**69//***68*), Eugen Wüster (*28*).

158 For a list of university degree studies and doctoral dissertations supervised by Szerdahelyi, compiled by Iván Bujdusó, see: *Informilo por Interlingvistoj* 98 (3/2016) 10-22, *Interlinguistische Informationen* 99 (2/2016) 8-17.

159 http://www.staff.amu.edu.pl/~interl/.

160 http://www.edukado.net/biblioteko/diplomlaborajhoj.

5 Serial bibliographies

5.1 Linguistics bibliographies

Several linguistics bibliographies contain sections on interlinguistic materials and Esperanto. Among them, the most important are the annual bibliography of the Permanent International Committee of Linguists, the *Bibliography of General Linguistics and of English, German, and Romance Linguistics*, the abstract service *Linguistics and Language Behavior Abstracts*, and, above all, the *International Bibliography* of the Modern Language Association.

5.1.1 BL-CIP

The *Linguistic bibliography for the year ... and supplements for previous years*, published by the Permanent International Committee of Linguists under the auspices of the International Council for Philosophy and Humanistic Studies, is edited by Mark Janse and Sijmen Tol, with the assistance of Inge Angevaare and Theo Horstman.[161] The *Linguistic bibliography* (BL-CIP) has appeared regularly since 1939 and is the largest linguistics bibliography in the world.

The volume for 1998 (published in 2000) covers 2700 periodicals and contains 20,743 items. Since 1948 the interlinguistics section has had various names:

(1) Langues auxiliaires – auxiliary languages,

(2) Interlinguistique (langues planifiées) – Interlinguistics (planned languages) and, as of 1989,

(3) Interlinguistique – Interlinguistics.

---

161 https://brill.com/linguistic-bibliography-year-2012-bibliographie-linguistique-de-l-annee-2012/

The quantity of titles registered in this section is very small and in no sense representative of the nonetheless significant literature produced. Over the fifty years from 1948 to 1998 it has added up to 496 titles, so an average of 9 or 10 a year. Literature in planned languages is barely noticed at all.

5.1.2 BLL

The *Bibliography of General Linguistics and of English, German, and Romance Linguistics* is compiled by Elke Suchan, Heike Westermann and Marc-Oliver Vorköper Frankfurt/Main: Klostermann.[162] It records only a limited range of literature on linguistics. In addition to general linguistics, it concentrates on English, German and Romance studies. For the year 2001 it covered 1,300 periodicals. Its interlinguistics sections are Plansprachen (1971-1980) and, as of 1981, Plansprachen / Artificial languages. Criteria for inclusion of items, as with BL-CIP, are unclear. Occasional contributions in planned languages are listed. Recently the compilers have become aware of *Interlinguistische Informationen (IntI)* and the papers of the conferences of GIL (Supplements, *Beihefte*, to *IntI*). Between 1971 and 2001 a total of 353 titles with interlinguistics content have been recorded, so an average of 10-15 items per year.

5.1.3 LLBA

The U.S. abstract service *Linguistics and Language Behavior Abstracts (incorporating Reading Abstracts)*, formerly San Diego, now Ann Arbor, Michigan, began publication in 1965. It defines itself as a 'collection of nonevaluative abstracts which reflects the world's literature in language behavior, linguistics, and related disciplines and a comprehensive book review bibliography' (LLBA 29 [1995] 1: 19). The series appears five times a year in volumes totalling some 400-500 pages. Individual volumes contain concise summaries of articles in linguistics journals and monographs. In section 18, *International Languages*, a subdivision of *Descriptive Linguistics*, it is not uncommon to find English summaries of

---

162 http://www.blldb-online.de/.

interlinguistics materials published in various languages.[163] In 1998 some 73 abstracts appeared and in 1999 a total of 44, among them many contributions not necessarily attributable to interlinguistics.

5.1.4 The MLA Bibliography[164]

(1) Organisation of the bibliography
The largest quantity of interlinguistic studies is recorded in the huge volumes (now in the form of an online data base) of the MLA Bibliography. Before 1931 the bibliography formed part of the Association's journal, *PMLA* (then known as *Publications of the Modern Language Association of America*), and covered only U.S. publications, but since then its international coverage has steadily increased.

Since 1960, interlinguistics publications have been listed primarily under the following rubrics:

> 1960-1967: *International Languages* (under *General Language and Linguistics*)
>
> 1968-1973: *Interlinguistics* (under *Composite and Derivative Languages, Other Communicative Behavior*)
>
> 1974-1980: *International Languages*
>
> 1981-1982: *International Languages. Auxiliary Languages*
>
> As of 1983: *Auxiliary Languages. International Languages*[165].

In the period 1960-1968 only a few sporadic titles were listed, and very few from 1969 to 1978. Continuous and more systematic compilation began in 1979.

---

163 http://search.proquest.com/llba/.
164 On MLA see Tonkin (2010).
165 Bibliographers for the interlinguistics sections were Willem A. Verloren van Themaat (1979-1989), Humphrey Tonkin (1980-2011), Jane Edwards (1984-1998), Detlev Blanke (1992-2011). The current (2016) bibliographer, as of 2012, is Wim Jansen [soon to be succeeded by Natalia Dankova - HT].

Between 1960 and 1998 a total of 5,723 titles were listed; for the period 1999-2008 some 2,735 titles were added. So between 1960 and 2008 a total of 8,458 titles appeared, primarily on Esperanto. These numbers are, however, only minimal, because a further group of items must be added, from the rubric *Invented Languages* and (as of 2000) in the section *Teaching of Language* (dealing, among other things, with the methodology of teaching Esperanto). Further items can be found in the sections on literatures and literary theory, for example on national literary translations in Esperanto, literary criticism, and individual authors who write in Esperanto.

Until 2008, the MLA Bibliography was published annually in two large volumes, one of them a *Subject Index*, and the other containing *Classified Listings* and an *Author Index*. These volumes are generally available in national and university libraries and linguistic and literary institutions. The Subject Index recorded the items by topic and (in the case of literary entries) by author (e.g. articles on the work of the important original Esperanto writer William Auld, or on Esperanto translations of the works of Shakespeare). The items were referenced to the Classified Listings. The Classified Listings allowed the user to identify individual planned language systems, particularly Esperanto. The volume also contained a huge index of authors.

(2) General subsections in the opening chapter

I have made a somewhat systematic study of items registered in the ten most recent printed compilations, so for the period 1999-2008. In the introductory part of the chapter entitled 'Auxiliary Languages. International Languages' I found (though not in all years), the following subsections:

Bibliography, grammar (grammatical categories, pronoun), lexicology (lexicography, word borrowing), morphology, phonology (syllable), syntax (voice), translation (machine translation), writing systems (orthography).

VI: Paths to the scholarly literature on interlinguistics and Esperanto studies

Mentioned during this period are studies in various languages dealing with the following planned language projects, in addition to Esperanto: *Adjuvilo, Dilpok, Glosa, Ido* (bibliography, grammar, lexicology [etymology, phraseology], morphology, onomastics [toponymy]), *Interlingua* (bibliography, grammar, lexicology [lexicography], morphology [word formation], translation), *Ling, Solresol, Paraglot, Loglan/Lojban* (syntax), *Neo, Occidental* (bibliography, grammar, lexicology [etymology, word borrowing], morphology, phonetics [orthoepy], syntax [word order], writing systems [orthography], *Slovio* (lexicology), *Unish* (grammar, lexicology, syntax, writing system), *Volapük* (bibliography, lexicology [etymology, lexicography]), and *Zilengo*.[166]

(3) Subsections on Esperanto studies
The chapter 'Esperanto language' deals with studies largely focused on Esperanto, with the following divisions: bibliography, grammar (article, preposition, pronoun, verb), lexicology (etymology, lexicography, phraseology, slang, terminology, word borrowing), morphology (word formation), onomastics (anthroponymy, toponymy), phonetics (consonants, orthoepy, phonology, speech synthesis, syllable, vowels), pragmatics, prosody (intonation), semantics, stylistics (metrics, rhetoric), syntax (aspect, case, clause, negation, predicate, voice, word order), translation (machine translation), writing systems (alphabet, graphemics, orthography, punctuation).

Material recorded in the MLA Bibliography as of 1963 can also be consulted electronically. As of 2009, the entries can be accessed *only* in electronic form. Access to this material requires a password, generally available (as with the printed volumes) through universities and research institutes, national libraries, and similar institutions.

In short, there exists a diverse literature in Esperanto studies, of dimensions that cannot be ignored.

---
166 Of the systems mentioned, only *Ido*, *Interlingua* and (to some degree) *Occidental/Interlingue* have their own actually functioning small language communities. Volapük also still has a few followers, particularly in Britain.

(4) What languages are used in the scholarly literature?

Increasingly, scholars tend to cite literature in English, paying little attention to work in other languages (see, for example, Ammon 1998, Gazzola 2012, Sandelin 2001). This shortcoming prompted me to investigate the 'language application policy' of MLA's bibliographers. Do they tend to favour English-language literature, also in the fields of interlinguistics and Esperanto studies?

I carried out a detailed analysis of the languages of publication (main heading 'Linguistics', section on 'Auxiliary language. International language') in the volumes for 1999-2008 (MLA 1999-2008). All told, 2,735 bibliographical units were listed. Table 2 shows their languages of publication.

Table 2. Language of publication of interlinguistics articles in the volumes MLA 1999-2008[167]

Language of publication	quantity	quantity %
Esperanto	1,943	71.0
German	298	10.9
English	110	4.0
French	57	2.0
Italian	41	1.5
Russian	31	1.3
Dutch	29	1.0
Hungarian	28	1.0
Other planned languages[168]	81	3.0
Other languages	117	4.3

Table 2 shows that, at least in terms of quantity of publications, English is not the principal language of publication. The quantities, of course, say nothing about quality. They do indicate, however, that interlinguists, at least

---

[167] Fiedler (2011: 99) analysed the language used in MLA entries for the year 2006, on the basis of a list supplied by Tonkin (2007).
[168] *Interlingua*: 36, *Ido*: 30, *Occidental/Interlingue*: 13, *Glosa*: 1, *Loglan*: 1.

during the years in question, tended to publish their work in Esperanto, and that interlinguistic work was particularly active in Germany. But also in English-speaking countries and in such places as Estonia, France, Hungary, Italy, the Netherlands, and Russia there existed, and continues to exist, a certain research tradition on interlinguistic topics. Because scholars in these countries, and also in Germany, often publish their work in Esperanto, the figures do not give an entirely accurate picture of actual research activity.

The following table, although not current, nevertheless indicates the different intensity of the registration of items of interlinguistic bibliography in BL-CIP, BLL and MLA. The relationship between the bibliographies has presumably not changed much.

Table 3. BL-CIP, BLL and MLA compared

Bibliography	1993	1994	1995	1996	1997	1998	1999	2000	2001
BLCIP	11	10	13	24	20	12	*[169]	*	*
BLL	7	10	11	20	25	5	15	17	8
MLA	397	285	392	329	251	327	209	289	311

Of course, such quantitative indices in no sense reveal anything about the quality of the publications.

5.2 Interlinguistics newsletters with a bibliographical orientation

Interlinguistics newsletters provide information on new publications and events relatively rapidly and precisely.

(1) In this connection the newsletter *Fokuso* (1967-76), edited in Esperanto by Ebbe Vilborg, merits special attention. In all, it contains 1303 bibliographic items in the sections *ĝenerala kaj kompara interlingvistiko*

---
[169] Because of publication delays the most recent volume (2002) at the time of this comparison relates to 1998.

(general and comparative interlinguistics), *Esperanto, Ido, Interlingua, Interlingue, aliaj projektoj* (other projects).

(2) CED, the *Centre for Research and Documentation on World Language Problems* (Rotterdam and Hartford), under whose auspices *Language Problems & Language Planning* is published, has, since 1974 (in three series, with interruptions), produced in Esperanto an interlinguistics newsletter entitled *Informilo por Interlingvistoj, IpI*.[170] The newsletter provides information on new publications in interlinguistics and Esperanto studies, and on conferences and other events in the field of interlinguistics and Esperantology. By the end of 2016, a total of 99 issues (2,200 pages) had appeared in the third series.[171]

(3) Comparable to *IpI* is the German-language newsletter *Interlinguistische Informationen (IntI)*,[172] bulletin of the German Society for Interlinguistics (Gesellschaft für Interlinguistik e.V., GIL), published regularly from 1992 to 2016, when it reached its 100th issue (more than 1,600 pages in total). *IntI*, edited by the present author, is aimed at German-speaking linguists and people interested in linguistics and carries much of the same information as *IpI*.[173]

Both *IpI* and *IntI* are designed to follow as closely as possible new developments on planned languages, including publications. The issues contain chapters on current bibliography which are constantly updated.

---

170 http://esperantic.org/en/communications/ipi/archive/. From 1974 to 1977 *IpI* was edited by Ulrich Lins, Köln (first series: 1-4), from 1983 to 1990 by Ryszard Rokicki, Warsaw (second series: 1-21) and as of 1992 by Detlev Blanke, Berlin (third series:1-99). See the analysis of IpI in Blanke 2013.

171 [*Informilo por Interlingvistoj* is now published by the Esperantic Studies Foundation as an on-line publication under the editorship of Humphrey Tonkin and Yevgeniya Amis. It has been joined by a new parallel English-language publication, *Information for Interlinguists, IfI*, also published on line by the Esperantic Studies Foundation and with these same editors. – HT]

172 http://www.interlinguistik-gil.de/wb/pages/bulletin-inti.php/.

173 [The 100th and final issue of *Interlinguistische Informationen*, an index to the other 99 issues, appeared in 2017 (published in New York by Mondial). GIL continues to feature news and other information on its website. – HT]

They do not limit themselves to Esperanto but also include politico-linguistic and other aspects of international linguistic communication (especially the language policies of the European Union), though of course the contents are limited by the information reaching the editor. For all issues of *IpI* and *IntI* for the decade 1992-2002 there are indexes of persons compiled by Ino Kolbe (*IpI*: issues 40-41, *IntI*: issues 42-43), and now for issues 1-99 of *IpI*[174] and issues 1-99 of *IntI*.[175]

(4) From 1991 to 1996 *Flandra Esperanto-Ligo*, the Flemish Esperanto League, published the newsletter *Terminoteko* (ed. Bernhard Pabst)[176]. Its primary aim was to record publications in and on specialised language in Esperanto, particularly specialised terminology. A total of 14 issues appeared.

(5) In the United States from 1975 to 1985 there appeared nine issues of the newsletter *Esperanto Studies*, published by the *Esperanto Studies Association of America*. As of 1991, in effect continuing this earlier bulletin, for a number of years the Esperantic Studies Foundation published a newsletter entitled *Esperantic Studies* (between 1991 and 1999, 12 issues appeared). As of issue 13 (2002), the series appeared in electronic form for several years. It has now been succeeded by *Information for Interlinguists*.[177]

Finally we should mention that the Chinese interlinguist Liu Haitao has reproduced part of these materials in ten issues of his Chinese-language newsletter *Interlingvistika Kuriero*.[178]

---

[174] http://www.esperantic.org/wp-content/uploads/2015/09/IPI_Indekso_1-99.pdf.
[175] http://www.interlinguistik-gil.de/wb/media/inti/IntI_100.pdf.
[176] http://www.familienforschung-pabst.de/EspBiographien/PPLeitS.htm.
[177] http://www.esperantic.org/en/publications/ifi-information-for-interlinguists/.
[178] http://www.lingviko.net/ikmalnova.htm.

5.3 Periodical indexes

Finding important journal articles is particularly difficult. This is so both of journals in planned languages and, in some measure, journals in other languages. But there are some useful aids.

5.3.1 Periodicals in linguistics

Often only by chance a researcher becomes aware of a given interlinguistic study written by someone outside the field in a linguistics journal. It is indeed difficult to search the large quantity of linguistics journals in the average university library for significant material in interlinguistics. Some help is provided by international bibliographies of studies in the scholarly periodical literature, whose indexes can yield lesser-known material. The same is true of reviews. The German scholar Felix Dietrich was the founder of such a bibliography.[179] But as of 1972 this process can take place at one's own desk.

The city and university library of Frankfurt/Main (DFG-Sondersammelgebiet Linguistik[180]) publishes *Current Contents Linguistik* (sic!): *Inhaltsverzeichnisse linguistischer Fachzeitschriften. Tables of Contents of Linguistic Journals (CCL)*. Annually, four issues are published (each with some 300 or 400 pages). CCL reproduces the contents pages of some 250[181] linguistics periodicals, among them *Language Problems & Language Planning (LPLP)*. The publication, however, only covers languages with Latin or Cyrillic alphabets.

---

179 *Internationale Bibliographie der Zeitschriftenliteratur*, begründet von Felix Dietrich (Osnabrück 1897-). As of 1965 the bibliography is published in three sections: A. *Bibliographie der deutschen Zeitschriftenliteratur*, B. *Bibliographie der fremdsprachigen Zeitschriftenliteratur / Répertoire bibliographique international des revues / International Index to Periodicals*, C: *Bibliographie der Rezensionen und Referate*.
http://www.degruyter.com/databasecontent?dbid=ibz&dbsource=%2Fdb%2Fibz.

180 DFG = Deutsche Forschungsgemeinschaft/ German Research Association, special collection in linguistics.

181 The edition of CCL 30 (2002), No. 1-2, lists 260 titles. The bibliography is now online:
https://www.ub.uni-frankfurt.de/ssg/ling_contents.html.

5.3.2 Esperanto periodicals

Many minor studies, contributions to discussion, or other expressions of special problems in Esperanto studies are scattered among various Esperanto journals. There is a danger that they will be forgotten. Yearly indexes or tables of contents for a few journals give some help, particularly if the researcher is examining the Esperanto language community. *Esperanto*, the organ of the Universal Esperanto Association publishes such an index. However, so far, selected bibliographies or listings exist only for a very few journals, for example *Literatura Mondo* (M. Benczik 1976), *Nica Literatura Revuo* (Vatré 1988), *Scienca Revuo* (Bednarz 1984), *der esperantist* (Knöschke & Kolbe 1997, Kolbe 1998)[182] and *Paco*.[183] Reprints of Esperanto magazines are also helpful for the historian. For example, there exists a reprint of the first periodical in Esperanto, *La Esperantisto* 1889-1895.[184]

Also valuable is the bibliography of Esperanto magazine articles (*Esperanto-Gazetartikoloj*), compiled by Bernhard Pabst. As of the end of January 2003, the bibliography, which exists only as an electronic data bank, contained 6,500 entries, partly annotated.[185]

5.4 Catalogues of books in and on planned languages

Commercial book catalogues of literature in planned languages are currently published online regularly only by the *Universala Esperanto-Asocio* (UEA, Rotterdam).

---

[182] See also the selected bibliography in *der esperantist* 26 (1990), 5 (163): 97-109.

[183] Only GDR publications (Berlin) 1966-1989; on this, see the selected bibliography in *der esperantist* 26 (1990), 4 (162): 90-93.

[184] *La Esperantisto. Gazeto por la amikoj de la lingvo Esperanto. 1889-1895.* Afterword by Reinhard Haupenthal. Hildesheim-Zürich-New York: Olms, 1988.

[185] http://www.esperantoland.org/ebea/. See also Pabst 2003.

UEA's catalogue for 2001[186] contains over 3,500 titles, among them textbooks and dictionaries in 47 languages. Sections on *Language, Esperantology, Interlinguistics, Language Problems* and *Esperanto Movement and History* offer some 500 titles. The bibliographical section contains 49 titles. Annually some 200-250 new titles are published in Esperanto in various genres. The primary source of information on these new publications is the journal Esperanto in its '*Laste aperis...*' (recently appeared) section.

The book list for Interlingua for the year 2000[187] contains around 250 titles, primarily learning materials in 22 languages. An analysis of the new publications in the catalogue reveals that annually somewhere between five and ten new titles are published. Materials on interlinguistics are rare.

It is also useful to search Internet lists of second-hand books.[188]

6 Basic works

In the past, initial information on planned languages was customarily drawn from national encyclopaedias, such as the *Encyclopedia Britannica* and the *Brockhaus-Enzyklopädie*, or dictionaries of linguistics, though, of late, information from the Internet (Wikipedia) has been gaining influence. Occasionally such sources also include references to the scholarly literature. But in general the information to be found in these sources is unsatisfactory, is seldom sufficiently current, and con-

---

[186] See Libroservo de UEA, 2001. *Esperanto-Katalogo*. Rotterdam: Universala Esperanto-Asocio, 190 pp. The catalogue is regularly updated on line at http://katalogo.uea.org/.

[187] See *Bibliographia de Interlingua. Catalogo de publicationes in e pro Interlingua*. Beekbergen: Servicio de libros U.M.I., edition januario 2000, (numero 27), 28 pp. The most recent editions may be consulted on line at www.interlingua.com.

[188] A search of the large German network of used bookstores at www.zvab.com yielded 300 titles (April 20, 2003).

tains errors, sometimes even perpetuating widely-credited myths and prejudices.

6.1 Surveys

Among basic works on interlinguistics and Esperanto studies are historically significant items by Couturat and Leau (1903+1907/2001) and Drezen (1931/1991). More recent volumes include those by Albani and Buonarroti (1994, 2010), Barandovská-Frank (1995), Bausani (1970), Blanke (1985, 2006), Duličenko (2003, 2006), Gobbo (2009), Guérard (1922), Jansen (2004), Kuznecov (1982a, 1987), Large (1985), Monnerot-Dumaine (1960), Pei (1958/1968), Sakaguchi (1998), and Szerdahelyi (1977).

The earliest rigorous analyses of planned languages in terms of their communicative potential were carried out by Wüster (1931/1970: 277-407). Other more recent overviews can be found in Pei (1958/1968), Monnerot-Dumaine (1960), Bausani (1970), Szerdahelyi (1977), Blanke (1985), Large (1985), Kuznecov (1987), Sakaguchi (1998), Duličenko (2003; 2006), and Gobbo (2009).

In addition, numerous monographs have appeared on universal languages in particular historical periods (especially the seventeenth and eighteenth centuries: Knowlson 1975, Slaughter 1982, Maat 1999, Stillman 1995, Strasser 1988, and others), and on authors and regions (see additional items in Haupenthal & Haupenthal 2013: 7). Künzli (2006) describes the particularly rich interlinguistic tradition of Switzerland. Sutton (2008) records the most important original literary works written in Esperanto. See also the English-language anthology of Esperanto literature by Gubbins (2012). Abundant material on planned languages is included in the encyclopaedic work of Albani and Buonarotti (2010).

6.2 Handbooks of linguistics

To date, interlinguistics has played only a small role in scholarly discourse in linguistics, as is evident from a review of surveys and handbooks of linguistics, only a few of which mention interlinguistic topics. Positive exceptions are the extensive Hungarian handbook on languages by Fodor (2000) and the bilingual (German-English) multi-volume series of detailed handbooks on linguistics known as *HSK*.[189]

The new series *Wörterbücher zur Sprach- und Kommunikationswissenschaft*, edited by Stefan J. Schierholz and Herbert Ernst Wiegand, also published by Gruyter (Berlin), contains short articles (in German) by Cyril Brosch on Esperanto, Ido, Interlingua, natürliche Sprache, Novial, Occidental-Interlingue, Plansprache, Universalsprache, and Volapük.[190]

---

[189] Several of the volumes in the series of Handbooks on linguistics and communication science (*Handbücher zur Sprach- und Kommunikationswissenschaft, HSK/ Handbooks of Linguistics and Communication Science*), published by de Gruyter (Berlin-New York), contain chapters on interlinguistics: see the following:
- Vol. 3 (*Soziolinguistik/ Sociolinguistics*), Part 1(1987): Alicja Sakaguchi, Welthilfssprachen, pp. 365-370; Part 2 (1988): Pierre Janton, Plans for an International Language, pp. 1679-1687;
- Vol. 5 (*Wörterbücher/Dictionaries*), Part 3 (1991): Reinhard Haupenthal, Lexikographie der Plansprachen, pp. 3120-3137;
- Vol. 7 (*Sprachphilosophie/ Philosophy of Language*), Part 2 (1996): Vivian Salmon, The Universal Language Problem, pp. 916-928;
- Vol. 12 (*Kontaktlinguistik/Contact Linguistics*), Part 1(1996): Otto Back, Plansprachen, pp. 881-887;
- Vol. 13 (*Semiotik/Semiotics*), Part 4 (2004): Peter Mühlhäusler, Universal Languages and Language Planning, pp.3614-3634.
- Vol. 14 (*Fachsprachen/Languages for Special Purposes*), Part 1 (1998): Detlev Blanke/Wera Blanke, Plansprachen als Fachsprachen, pp. 875-880;
- Vol. 17 (*Morphologie/Morphology*), Part 2 (2004): Detlev Blanke, Plansprachen, pp. 1563-1573.
- Vol. 18 (*Geschichte der Sprachwissenschaften/History of the Language Sciences*), Part 1 (2000): Jaap Maat/David Cram, Universal Language Schemes in the 17th Century, pp. 1030-1043;
- Vol. 20 (*Sprachtypologie und sprachliche Universalien/ Language Typology and Language Universals*), Part 1 (2001): Heiner Böhmer, Künstliche Sprachen und Universalsprachen, pp. 85-94.
- Vol. 21 (*Lexikologie/Lexicology*), Part 2 (2005): Detlev Blanke, Wortschatzbesonderheiten in Plansprachen, pp. 1101-1107.
- [Vol. 28 (*Phraseologie/Phraseology*), Part 2 (2007: Sabine Fiedler, Phraseology in Planned Languages, pp. 779-788. – SF]
- Vol. 40 (*Word formation*), Part 3 (2015): Klaus Schubert, Word Formation and Planned Languages, pp. 2210-2225.

[190] The series is currently available online only, at http://www.degruyter.com/view/WSK/wsk_id_wsk_artikel_artikel_15822.

6.3 Anthologies

Relatively up-to-date information can also be found in various anthologies and multiple-author publications: Haupenthal and Haupenthal (2013: 8) mention more than 30 titles. Historically important material has been reprinted by Haupenthal (1976) and more recent contributions by Tonkin (1997). Among anthologies, particularly worthy of mention are Duc Goninaz (1987), Szerdahelyi (1980), Mattos (1987), Chrdle (1995), Schubert with Maxwell (1989b), Isaev (1991), Kiselman and Mattos (2001), Schubert (2001), and Koutny (2009). See also Benczik (1999), Fiedler and Liu (2001), Haupenthal (1985; *Menade* 1998), Minnaja (2001), I. Haupenthal and R. Haupenthal 2000; 2003; 2004), Isaev (1976; 1991), Mattos (1987), Régulo Pérez (1987 = *Serta Gratulatoria*), Schubert (1989a, 2001), Szerdahelyi (1980).

6.4 Festschriften

From time to time, beginning in 1985, festschriften dedicated to outstanding interlinguists and esperantologists have appeared, along with books dedicated to non-Esperantist linguists and interlinguistic studies (Haupenthal & Haupenthal 2013: 9; Blanke 2011a).[191]

---

[191] The genre of Festschriften in Esperanto was founded by Reinhard Haupenthal with his volume for Waringhien (1985). Haupenthal & Haupenthal (2013) and Blanke (2011a) list Esperanto-language Festschriften for, in addition to Gaston Waringhien (1985), Juan Régulo Pérez (*Serta Gratulatoria* 1987), Reinhard Haupenthal (*Menade*, 1998), William Auld and Marjorie Boulton (ed. Benczik, 1999), André Albault (ed. I. and R. Haupenthal, 2000), Detlev Blanke (ed. Fiedler and Liu, 2001; 2011), Fernando de Diego (ed. I. and R. Haupenthal, 2003), Adolf Burkhardt (ed. R. Haupenthal, 2004), Humphrey Tonkin (ed. Blanke and Lins, 2010) and Claude Gacond (ed. I. and R. Haupenthal, 2011; ed. R. Haupenthal, 2014). Blanke (2011a) also mentions some 18 non-Esperanto Festschriften written for professional linguists in various languages that contain 37 studies by scholars in interlinguistics. We should also add a second Festschrift for Helmar Frank (2013, with 19 interlinguistically interesting contributions) (ed. V. Barandovská-Frank, 2013).

Among the *festschriften* the researcher can find lists of the publications of the individuals being honoured: for *André Albault* in I. Haupenthal and R. Haupenthal 2000, for *Detlev Blanke* in Fiedler and Liu 2001, for *Adolf Burkhardt* in I. Haupenthal and R. Haupenthal 2004, for *William Auld* and *Marjorie Boulton* in Benczik 1999, for *Fernando de Diego* in I. Haupenthal and R. Haupenthal 2003, for *Helmar Frank* in Barandovská-Frank 1993a, 1993b, and Pinter 1999,[192] for *Reinhard Haupenthal* in Menade...1998,[193] for *Gaston Waringhien* in Haupenthal 1985, and so on. In *IpI* and *IntI* lists of publications of interlinguistics scholars appear occasionally (see above).

The works of a few prominent interlinguists and Esperantologists have been collected from specialised planned-language periodicals and other difficult-to-find sources, and published, at least in part, in collected volumes. First among them is the initiator of Esperanto Ludwik Zamenhof,[194] but also included are Atanas D. Atanasov (1983), Kálmán Kalocsay,[195] Gaston Waringhien (e.g. Waringhien 1989), and Juan Régulo Pérez (1992).[196]

6.5 Conference proceedings

Several series of conferences on interlinguistics have resulted in the publication of *conference proceedings*. Particularly worthy of attention are the partly Russian-language and partly Esperanto-language series *Interlinguistica Tartuensis* (1982-2009, 9 volumes, ed. Aleksandr Duličenko)[197]

---

192 Titles of interest for interlinguistics are scattered among the lists of Frank's publications.

193 See the first list of Haupenthal's publications (Esther Haupenthal 1995).

194 Between 1973 and 1997 the Japanese editor Itô Kanzi, under the pseudonym Ludovikito, published in 58 volumes all the publications of Zamenhof and materials that came into being under the influence of Zamenhof (see Esperanto-katalogo 2001: 67-70).

195 Ada Csiszár had, as of the end of 2002, published eight volumes of the works of Kálmán Kalocsay, containing critiques, reviews, representative works, etc.

196 [Also Eugen Wüster 1978 – HT]

197 Between 1982 and 1990 Aleksandr D. Duličenko published seven volumes

and the German-language series of the Gesellschaft für Interlinguistik (GIL, the German Society for Interlinguistics),[198] whose conference proceedings had produced by the end of 2016 a total of 23 volumes (on GIL see Blanke 2011b).[199] Although annual Esperantology Conferences have had a place in the World Congresses of Esperanto since 1978, their proceedings have been published only since 2005.[200]

Also worthy of mention are the papers of the colloquia on interlinguistics held at the University of Łódź (Poland),[201] and the proceedings of the interlinguistics symposia organised by the Association of Polish Students (Związek Polskich Studentów) in the 1970s and 1980s.[202] In the 1980s and 1990s the Centre for Research and Documentation on World Language Problems (CED) organised a series of policy-oriented conferences, several of them in co-operation with the language services at the United Nations, whose proceedings appeared in mimeograph form.[203]

Also the German Gesellschaft für Interlinguistik e.V., GIL (Society for Interlinguistics), as of its fifth conference (1995) publishes its proceedings as supplements to *Interlinguistische Informationen* (IntI, see section 5.6).[204]

---

in the series *Interlinguistica Tartuensis* (for more precise information see *IntI* 40, *IpI* 42).

198 www.interlinguistik-gil.de/.

199 [From 2017 onwards, the papers presented at the annual GIL conferences are published in *Jahrbuch der Gesellschaft für Interlinguistik (JGI)*. In addition, they can be accessed online: http://www.interlinguistik-gil.de/wb/pages/tagungsakten/jgi2017.php – SF]

200 http://eo.wikipedia.org/wiki/Esperantologia_Konferenco/.

201 Between 1981 and 1986 Tadeusz Ejsmont published in Łódź, Poland, six volumes in the series *Międzynarodowa komunikacja językowa* (see *IntI* 45; *IpI* 43).

202 Unfortunately of the fourteen colloquia the proceedings of only three were published. The *Acta Interlinguistica* of the 11th (1983), 12th (1984) and 13th (1985) interlinguistics symposia were edited by Ryszard Rokicki.

203 They were edited by, among others, Humphrey Tonkin. These and other materials were published in part in the series *Papers of the Center for Research and Documentation on World Language Problems*, also edited by Humphrey Tonkin. By 2002, five volumes had appeared (see Tonkin 1997, and see the other titles in *IpI* 8-9; 48-49; *IntI* 9-11).

204 By the end of 2004, eleven volumes had appeared with the following general topics (in German): translation and planned languages (published

A number of interesting studies, often dealing with problems of specialised terminology in Esperanto, can be found in the series of proceedings of the SAEST symposia (*Simpozio pri Apliko de Esperanto en Scienco kaj Tekniko*)[205,] organised by the Esperanto associations of the Czech Republic and Slovakia.

Recently the proceedings of a historically particularly interesting conference were published – those of the International Auxiliary Language Association (IALA), which brought together, in Geneva in 1930, for a discussion of the problem of an international auxiliary language, such linguists as Earl Babcock, Charles Bally, Otto Jespersen, William Collinson, Albert Debrunner, Otto Funke, Eduard Hermann, Albert Sechehaye, and the brother of Ferdinand de Saussure, René de Saussure (Perrenoud 2002).

Rüdiger Eichholz assembled many studies on Esperanto in the series *Akademiaj Studoj*.[206]

Less well known are the four volumes in the series *Kontribuoj al lingvaj teorio kaj praktiko* (Contributions to language theory and practice) published in 1983-1986 by the Slovak Esperanto Association (edited by Stanislav Košecký: *IpI* 45).

1996), terminological aspects of interlinguistics (1997), *One Language for Science*, a memorial colloquium on Wilhelm Ostwald (1998), sociocultural aspects of planned languages (1998), interlinguistics and lexicography (1999), language policy in Europe (2001), the structure of planned languages (2001), planned languages and their communities (2002), planned languages and electronic media (2003), proceedings of the terminology science and planned languages section of the international conference in honour of Eugen Wüster 1998 (2003), language invention, language planning, planned languages (2004). See also *IpI* 38, *IntI* 40 and the review by Seán Ó Riain in *LPLP* 27 (2003) 3: 269-277.

205 See the survey of the history of the series in Pluhař (1999). In 1998 the series reappeared under the name KAEST (Kolokvo/Konferenco pri Apliko de Esperanto en Scienco kaj Teĥniko, Conference on the Application of Esperanto in Science and Technology). Three volumes of conference proceedings appeared as of 2003 (Malovec 1999, Pluhař 2001, Pluhař 2003).

206 Volumes appeared for 1983 (201 pp.), 1984 (135 pp.), 1985 (318 pp.), 1986 (298 pp.), 1987 (203 pp.) and 1988-90 (560 pp.).

As of 1997 the proceedings of the International Congress University *(Internacia Kongresa Universitato),* held each year as part of the World Congresses of Esperanto, have appeared regularly.[207] Too seldom the proceedings of the Conferences on Esperanto Studies, a series of conferences started in 1978, have been published (see Blanke 2001b).

Additional material from important interlinguistics meetings has been collected by Carlevaro (1998), Chrdle (1995), Gecsö and Varga-Haszonits (1998), Kiselman and Mattos (2001), Košecký (1987, 1990), Koutny and Kovacs (1997), Maitzen, Mayer and Tišljar (1994) and Umeda (1987).

6.6 Theses and advanced textbooks

With increasing frequency, doctoral and other advanced students at universities in numbers of countries are writing dissertations on aspects of our subject. The first bibliography of dissertations, compiled by Symoens (1989, 1995),[208] showed a jump in the numbers of such dissertations as of the mid-1970s. Unfortunately the survey is not complete, because numbers of theses written since the founding in 1969 of the Esperanto Department at Eötvös Loránd University, Budapest, are missing from the list. Several of the more important doctoral dissertations have appeared in published form.[209] Only a few habilitation-level dissertations have been accepted at universities to date.[210]

---

207 See Wandel (1998), Lipari (1999, 2000, 2001, 2003, 2004), McCoy (2002). The latest volume is Wandel 2017.

208 *IntI* and *IpI* (see above) provide information on recent dissertations, when this information is available.

209 There is a growing number of doctoral dissertations. Among those in printed and published form are those of Bak (1991), Blanke (1981a), Corret (1908), Fauvart-Bastoul (1902), Forster (1982), Hagler (1970), Heil (1999), Lloancy (1985), Lobin (2002), Lo Jacomo (1981), Maat (1999), Melnikov (1990) Papaloïzos (1992), Philippe (1991) and the already classic dissertations of Wüster (1931/1970) and Manders (1947).

210 Probably only those of Blanke (1985, Humboldt University), Sakaguchi (1998, Adam Mickiewicz University, Poznan) and Fiedler (1999, Leipzig University), all in German. The writing of a habilitation dissertation, par-

Advanced textbooks for students of interlinguistics have been written by István Szerdahelyi, who taught the subject from 1966 to 1987 in the faculty of applied linguistics at Eötvös Loránd University, Budapest.[211] Textbooks in interlinguistics intended for university instruction have also been written by Barandovská-Frank (1995), Bormann (1995), Jansen (2004, 2012/2013) and Kuznecov (1982b, c).[212]

6.7 Works specifically on Esperanto studies

The first detailed bibliography of Esperanto studies was compiled by Neergaard (1942/1979). It contains works appearing up to the end of the 1930s. From then on, the following basic works on Esperanto studies record the principal contributions, listed as of the 1970s also in the MLA Bibliography.

6.7.1 The language

Among numerous book-length studies of the language, those by the following scholars stand out: Manders (1950), Janton (1973/1994),[213] Wells (1978/1989), Gledhill (2000), Nuessel (2000) and the extensive grammars of Kalocsay and Waringhien (1985) and Wennergren (2005).[214] Specialised studies include those on versification (Kalocsay &

---

ticularly in central Europe, is required following the first doctorate (after the English Ph.D.), to receive the right to teach at the highest level in universities (Facultas docendi or Venia legendi), a condition for nomination to the position of lecturer and subsequently that of university professor.

211 Szerdahelyi's eight textbooks (in Hungarian and Esperanto) deal with the history of planned languages, theoretical problems of interlinguistics, the Esperanto language (grammar, literature), and the methodology of foreign-language instruction. Between 1976 and 1977 there also appeared three volumes of *Esperantologiaj kajeroj*, edited by Szerdahelyi.

212 [See also Gobbo 2009. A new introduction to interlinguistics is currently in preparation by Barandovská-Frank. – HT]

213 The English-language version of Janton's book (1993) was significantly reworked by Tonkin and is far richer than the original.

214 [This work, Wennergren's *Plena manlibro de Esperanta gramatiko*, is available online in a constantly updated version: http://bertilow.com/pmeg/. It essentially replaces the earlier grammar of Kalocsay and Waringhien. – HT]

Waringhien 1932/1968/1982), phraseology (Fiedler 1999, 2015b), word formation (Blanke 1981a; Schubert 2015), wordplay and expressions specific to the Esperanto community (Mel'nikov 2004, 2008, 2015), and rhetorical devices (Dahlenburg 2013). Wera Blanke (2008, 2013) summarises the practice and theoretical problems of terminological work and particularly the development of terminology. Single-language and two-directional dictionaries and glossaries have been registered in print by Ockey and Sutton (2002) and (as of 1980) by Vachey[215] (in electronic form only).

6.7.2 The language community

Handbooks, particularly on the practical use of Esperanto, are rich in material on the beginnings of the language and its progress up to the 1970s. Haupenthal and Haupenthal (2013: 10-11) mention seven publications.

Worthy of particular mention here is the Encyclopaedia of Esperanto (*Encikopedio de Esperanto*: available online), which covers the period from the beginnings of Esperanto (1887) to the beginning of the 1930s (Kökény & Bleier 1933-34/1979). A newer encyclopaedic work appeared in 1974 (Lapenna, Lins & Carlevaro). Also useful is the bilingual collection (Esperanto/English) of various studies, compiled by Eichholz and Eichholz (1982).[216]

The history of the Esperanto language community is fairly well covered: Haupenthal and Haupenthal (2013: 10) note thirty titles.

The sociological aspects of the Esperanto language community has been studied by, among others, Forster (1982), Papaloïzos (1992), Rašić (1994), Stocker (1996) and Galor and Pietiläinen (2015). On Espe-

---

215 Jérôme Vachey: http://www.uea.org/teko/terminaroj_ekde_1980/. On dictionaries for Germans see also Blanke (2006: 249-286).

216 [Much of the material from the Encyclopaedia of Esperanto and elsewhere is now incorporated into the Esperanto Wikipedia (Vikipedio), along with an abundance of more up-to-date information. – HT]

ranto organisations in Eastern Europe until 1989 see Blanke (2007b). An overview of the history of the Universal Esperanto Association, the language community's most important international organisation, is provided by Van Dijk (2012). Lins (1988a, 1988b, 2016, 2016/2017) deals particularly with the persecution of Esperantists under Hitler and Stalin. Current problems of the Esperanto movement are analysed by Tonkin (2006). The workers' Esperanto movement has been studied by Kolbe (1996) and Noltenius (1993).

There are several biographies of the originator of Esperanto, L.L. Zamenhof: Haupenthal and Haupenthal (2013: 11) note twenty titles. The most traditional is that by Privat (2007), first published in the 1920s, and the most current that by Korĵenkov (2011), available also in an abridged English-language edition (Korzhenkov 2010). Also worthy of mention are the German-language Künzli (2010) and the extensive coverage of Zamenhof in Schor (2015) and Garvía (2015).

Zamenhof's works and those originating under his influence were republished and analysed between 1974 and 2004 by the Japanese scholar Itô Kanzi (under the pseudonym Ludovikito) in 58 volumes (see the list in Privat 2007: 173-176). A selection of works by Zamenhof is available in Italian translation (Minnaja 2009).

As regards other interlinguists and Esperantologists Haupenthal and Haupenthal (2013: 11-12) mention eighteen publications, on, among others, Eugène Adam (1879-1947: see Borsboom 1976), Teo Jung (1892-1986: see Jung 1979), Ivo Lapenna (1909-1987: see Minnaja 2001), Kálmán Kalocsay (1891-1976: see Csiszár 1998-2002), Edmond Privat (1889-1962: see Farrokh 1991), and Johann Martin Schleyer (1831-1912: see Haupenthal & Haupenthal 2008).

A bibliography on the historiography of the Esperanto language community is contained in Blanke (2000).

7 Periodicals on Interlinguistics and Esperanto studies

At the end of the nineteenth century the first small journals addressing various planned languages (or projects for planned languages) began to appear. These journals also discussed what linguistic details should characterise a 'perfect' language (Haupenthal & Haupenthal 2013: 14-15)[217]. Among current periodicals, *Language Problems & Language Planning* (*LPLP,* Amsterdam)[218] publishes, in addition to contributions on language policy, also articles on interlinguistics.[219] Work on Esperanto studies can also be found in *Esperantologio* (1949-1961, Copenhagen, ed. Paul Neergaard) and its successor *Esperantologio / Esperanto Studies* (launched 1999, Uppsala, ed. Christer Kiselman)[220].

Electronic journals include *Lingva Kritiko*[221] and, as of 2010, *Interlingvistikaj Kajeroj (InKoj)*.[222] Problems in the teaching of Esperanto are discussed in Szerdahelyi (1965), Rakuša (1971), Kováts (2009), and the journal *Internacia Pedagogia Revuo*.[223] The journal of the Universal Esperanto Association, *Esperanto*,[224] offers information on the practice of the language and on new publications.

---

217 See also Eco (1993).
218 http://benjamins.com/#catalog/journals/lplp/main/.
219 [Another journal publishing articles on interlinguistics and Esperanto studies is *Język Komunikacja Informacja / Language Communication Information* (Poznań, Poland); see: http://jki.amu.edu.pl – SF]
220 All issues are accessible electronically: http://www.cb.uu.se/esperanto/.
221 Edited by Bertilo Wennergren. Between 2008 and autumn 2014, 56 studies in Esperantology (with various subsequent commentaries) have appeared: http://lingvakritiko.com/.
222 http://riviste.unimi.it/index.php/inkoj/index/, editor-in-chief Paolo Valore.
223 The extensive website www.edukado.net, edited by Katalin Kováts, provides information on many specialised and organisational aspects of Esperanto teaching, serves as a forum and credentialling agency for Esperanto teachers and provides current instructional materials.
224 http://www.uea.org/.

7.1 Interlinguistics periodicals

To date, there exist no regularly published scholarly journals dedicated fully to interlinguistics and edited in accordance with the customary rigorous scholarly standards.[225] However, by means of a number of small periodicals, variable in their quality, range, and frequency of publication, we can follow the discussion of interlinguistic issues, particularly as they relate to individual systems of planned languages. Duličenko (1990: 436-437) lists a total of thirty of these periodicals before 1973.

In the final years of the nineteenth century, for only a short period but with abundant material, the journal *Linguist* appeared (Hannover, 1896-1897, approx. 400 pp., editor Max Wahren). In the first half of the twentieth century several important periodicals containing articles on various planned languages were published, among them *Discussiones: Academia pro Interlingua* (Torino 1909-1913, ed. Giuseppe Peano), *Academia pro Interlingua* (Torino, 1921-1927, ed. Giuseppe Peano), *Schola et Vita* (Milan, 1926-1939, ed. Instituto pro Interlingua [Director Nicola Mastropaolo], as of 1928 journal of the Academia pro Interlingua) and *Tolero* (Paris 1928-1935, ed. E. Dayras; 1931-1936 continued as *Interlanguages*, ed. E. Mauney).[226] Also of significance are *Novialiste* (in Jespersen's Novial, Stockholm 1934-1939, ed. Per Ahlberg) and *Mondo* (1912-1929, Stockholm, in Ido and Novial).

After the Second World War, the leading non-Esperanto interlinguistics periodical was *ILR: The International Language Review (A Clearing House for Facts, Theories and Fancies on the History, Science and Bibliography of the International Language Movement)*, published in Denver in fifty issues from 1955 to 1968 by Floyd and Evelyn Hardin.[227] For the

---

225 [*LPLP*, mentioned above, devotes only part of its contents to interlinguistics; *Esperantologio* is published irregularly. – HT]

226 See also Silagi (1996), who published in Budapest (1929-1930) a periodical with a title in Latin: *Communicationes (Libelli pro historia et scientia interlinguarum)*.

227 The successors of *International Language Review*, but with much less

researcher with some knowledge of its background, the bulletin *Union* (1971-1976)[228] also contains some useful material.

From the newsletter published in 1991 on the project for a planned language called *Vorlin* by Richard Harrison (Orlando, USA), the *Journal of Planned Languages* was born. From 1992 to 1996 some 24 issues appeared.[229] Between 1995-2003 six issues of the *Journal of Universal Language* were published by Sejong University, in the Republic of Korea.[230]

More oriented to Esperanto, and edited by Artur Bormann (Reinbek, Hamburg, Germany) from a politicolinguistic and sociological point of view, was *Interlingvistika Informa Servo*, published by the *Gesellschaft für Internationale Sprache e.V.* (Society for International Language). Between 1964 and 1984 a total of 84 issues appeared.

Also significant is the Esperanto-language periodical on the theory of planned languages *Planlingvistiko*, published in La Chaux-de-Fonds, Switzerland, and edited by Jouko Lindstedt (1981-83) and György Nanovfszky (1984-86). A total of 17 issues were published.

---

interlinguistic content, were *International Language Reporter* (1969-1979) and *Eco-logos* (1971-1979), published by John W. Ragsdale, in Denver (see Golden 1993).

228 Organ oficial del *Union International de Interlinguistik Service*, Amsterdam, published by W.J. Visser. The title of the newsletter is in Eurolatin. In *Union* contributions in various planned languages appeared – a total of 22 newsletters with 274 pages.

229 Harrison later resigned and is no longer involved with 'constructed auxlanguages'. His article 'Farewell to Auxiliary languages' (https://archive.is/u5gDO) clearly showed that he does not distinguish between a project – which has of course no culture – and a planned language like Esperanto with its language community, which indeed has a culture. Internet construction and discussion of 'conlangs' (constructed languages) is very active. There is abundant discussion of the linguistic details of the preferred conlang, on which there is no agreement, depending on language knowledge, level of linguistic study and other factors: https://eo.wikipedia.org/wiki/%C4%9Cermolisto_de_planlingvoj, https://en.wikipedia.org/wiki/Constructed_language, https://en.wikipedia.org/wiki/List_of_constructed_languages http://www.omniglot.com/links/conlangs.htm.

230 On the contents see *IntI* 45, 50; *IpI* 48-49.

Planned as a sociolinguistic and politicolinguistic scholarly journal on problems of international communication, the journal *La Monda Lingvo-Problemo, LMLP*, was founded in 1969 and appeared until 1977, in a total of 18 issues, under the editorship first of Victor Sadler, then of Richard Wood. As of 1977, this journal changed its name to *Language Problems & Language Planning, LPLP* (edited by Richard Wood until 1984, then by Humphrey Tonkin (with various collaborators, among them Probal Dasgupta, Klaus Schubert, and Marc van Oostendorp). The current editor-in-chief is Timothy G. Reagan, soon (2019) to be succeeded by François Grin. *LPLP* was published initially in The Hague by Mouton, then in Austin by the University of Texas Press, and, since 1990, in Amsterdam by Benjamins. It regularly contains interlinguistics contributions, under the editorship of first Mark Fettes and more recently Sabine Fiedler, and reviews. Frank Nuessel has served as book review editor throughout its history, along with Federico Gobbo in recent years.

Grundlagenstudien in Kybernetik und Geisteswissenschaft/Humankybernetik, GRKG (ed. Helmar Frank, Miloš Lánský, Manfred Wettler), published as of the 1970s, concentrates on educational cybernetics. *GRKG* and *LPLP* occasionally publish contributions in Esperanto and regularly provide abstracts in Esperanto.

7.2 Periodicals in Esperanto studies

The first journal to appear, before the Second World War, exclusively for the publication of Esperanto studies was *Lingva Kritiko* (*Studoj kaj notoj pri gramatiko, vortaro, stilo*). From 1932 to 1935 some 28 issues appeared as a supplement to *Heroldo de Esperanto* (Köln), under the editorship of Bruno Migliorini and Stefano La Colla (reprinted in 2016 by Edition Iltis).

VI: Paths to the scholarly literature on interlinguistics and Esperanto studies

There have been only two attempts to publish a refereed journal in Esperanto studies. Unfortunately the first such effort did not last long. Paul Neergaard (Copenhagen) edited (1949-1964) a total of five issues of the journal *Esperantologio (Internacia Revuo por la lingvistiko kaj bibliografio de Esperanto)*. Contributions appeared primarily in Esperanto, but also in English and (occasionally) in French. A new departure in the same direction is the previously mentioned journal *Esperantologio – Esperanto Studies (EES)*, founded in 1999 as a continuation of Neergaard's initiative, and edited by Christer Kiselman (Uppsala).

Studies on Esperanto also appeared in the newsletter *La letero de l' Akademio de Esperanto* (Paris), which was published from 1987 to 1995 in 31 issues. It was published by the Amikoj de l' Akademio de Esperanto (Friends of the Esperanto Academy), and edited by Jean Thierry.

Also worthy of mention is *Printempa Kampo (Jara revuo pri esperantologio, Esperanta faklingviko kaj interlingviko)*, a small journal that has appeared irregularly as of 1989 in Dalian, China, and contains contributions to Esperanto studies exclusively by Chinese scholars.[231]

The Japanese Esperanto Institute had plans to publish a journal entitled *Japana Esperantologio: Bulteno de Japana Esperanto-Instituto*, but only two issues appeared (1992, 92pp.; 2003, 70 pp.: see *IpI* 48-49).

The series of *Esperanto-Dokumentoj (Esperanto Documents, Documents sur l'Espéranto)* was in many respects a periodical publication. The series contained studies and documents on the theory and practice of the planned language Esperanto and was published in Rotterdam on an occasional basis by the Universal Esperanto Association. There were series in Esperanto (39 issues as of November 2004), English (47 issues) and French (29 issues).[232]

---

[231] On the contents see *IpI* 12-13.
[232] See the list of titles in *IpI* 17.

Several national Esperanto institutions publish occasional papers, among them the German Esperanto Institute[233] and the Esperantology/Interlinguistics Group of the Italian Esperanto Federation.[234]

Finally, we should mention that various national and international Esperanto periodicals occasionally publish articles in interlinguistics and Esperanto studies, among them *Literatura Foiro, Internacia Pedagogia Revuo, Fonto, La Gazeto, Scienca Revuo*, and *Iltis-Forumo* (1989-1995), also the journals *Esperanto, Esperanto aktuell* and *der esperantist* (1965-1990). Contributions on planned languages occasionally also appear in *Progreso* (Ido), *Panorama in Interlingua* (Interlingua IALA-Gode) and *Cosmoglotta* (Occidental-Interlingue).

8 Libraries and archives specialising in planned languages

Highly significant for the search for interlinguistics materials and their acquisition are those public and private libraries and archives containing collections on planned languages (see Blanke 2008). Marinko Gjivoje (1980) described thirty of the most important. A survey presented by Árpád Máthé at a conference in Vienna in 1992,[235] indicated that at the time a total of one hundred interlinguistics libraries and archives existed around the world in thirty countries. Such collections contain important publications in interlinguistics and Esperanto studies, plus planned-language periodicals and in some cases valuable archives.

Such archives present a special problem. Their conservation often receives less attention than is devoted to printed books – something that overlooks the fact that they are unique, and can be easily lost or 'recycled' (for example letters and unpublished manuscripts by eminent

---

233 See the list of titles in *Esperanto aktuell* 5/2002, p. 2.
234 See the list of publications in *IpI* 31, *IntI* 33.
235 In a lecture in the 15th Conference on Esperanto Studies, 1992, during the 77th World Congress of Esperanto.

interlinguists and specialists in Esperanto studies). In contrast to such materials, lost books are generally replaceable, or can be found in several libraries and collections.[236]

The largest collections[237] are those of the *Internacia Esperanto-Muzeo Vieno* (the planned languages section of the Austrian National Library) [238] and the *Centre de documentation et d'étude sur la langue internationale (CDELI)*,[239] part of the city library of La Chaux-de-Fonds, Switzerland. These libraries contain not only material on and in Esperanto, but also related to Volapük, Latino sine flexione, Occidental-Interlingue, Ido, Novial, Interlingua and other planned languages. Archival materials are particularly abundant at CDELI, where an electronic catalogue is in preparation.[240]

Among the most extensive printed catalogues are those of IEMW (Steiner 1957, 1958, 1969; Hube & März 1975) and of the private collection of Károly Fajszi, now housed in the Budapest Foreign Language Library (Pataki-Czeller 1991, Zsebehásy 2005).

---

236 [The Esperantic Studies Foundation has recently (2017) launched an effort to preserve the archives of local Esperanto groups, in co-operation with the Du Bois Library at the University of Massachusetts Amherst. – HT]

237 Current addresses can be found in UEA 2016.

238 See the now outdated catalogues of Steiner 1957, 1958, 1969, Hube & März 1975. New acquisitions in the period 1950-1984 were announced in the newsletter *Informilo de IEMW*, replaced in 1985-1989 by *Bibliografio de Esperanto (kaj aliaj planlingvoj)*. In more recent times, cataloguing has taken place by means of the electronic data bank TROVANTO, accessible through the Internet. On November 29, 2002, the data bank contained 29,000 entries (see section 7). The Planned Language Collection (Bernhard Tuider, director) now contains 35,000 printed volumes, 2,500 periodical titles, 3,000 museum objects, 2,000 manuscripts, 23,000 photographs, 1,100 posters and 40,000 leaflets.
http://search.obvsg.at/primo_library/libweb/action/search.do?dscnt=0&scp.scps=scope%3A%28ONB_aleph_esperanto%29&tab=onb_sondersammlungen&mode=Basic&vid=ONB.

239 http://www.cdeli.org/ (with over 20,000 bibliographic items; founder and chief archivist Claude Gacond).

240 Part of the collection is now accessible at www.chaux-de-fonds.ch/bibliotheques.

Abundant and particularly up-to-date material is also contained in the Hector Hodler library of the Universal Esperanto Association, Rotterdam[241] (see Lins 1995; Sikosek 2003[242]) and the Butler Library of the Esperanto Association of Britain (housed as of 2002 in Barlaston, Staffordshire).[243]

In rough order of significance, we can also note the following: the Library of the German Esperanto Institute in Aalen,[244] the Spanish Esperanto Museum in Sant Pau d'Ordal (Barcelona), the Károly Fajszi Collection in Budapest (see above; catalogue by Pataki-Czeller 1991, Zsebehásy 2005), the Cesar Vanbiervliet Collection (specialising in periodicals, and part of the city library of Kortrijk, Belgium), the French Esperanto Museum in Gray, and the interlinguistics collection in the library of Istituto Universitario di Lingue Moderne IULM), founded by the Centro Italiano di Interlinguistica.[245] Also worthy of mention are the collections of the Catholic University of Lublin (Poland: see Wojtakowski 1979) and the Amsterdam University Library (see Catalogi 1965a, 1965b), the Alan Connor Collection at the University of Oregon (see Smith & Haake 1978), and the library of the Japanese Esperanto Institute.[246]

Libraries specialising in materials on workers' history include the *Fritz-Hüser-Institut für deutsche und internationale Arbeiter-Literatur* (Fritz Hüser Institute for German and International Workers' Literature) in Dortmund, Germany, which contains a collection on the history of the

---

241 http://de.wikipedia.org/wiki/Bibliothek_Hector_Hodler.

242 http://de.wikipedia.org/wiki/Bibliothek_Hector_Hodler.

243 http://eo.wikipedia.org/wiki/Biblioteko_Butler, https://biblbut.wordpress.com/.

244 In 2002 the Aalen collection contained c. 40,000 titles, including bound volumes of periodicals (*Esperanto aktuell* [2002] 21/4, p.13): https://www.esperanto.de/de/bibliothek.

245 Access to the collection is available by way of www.iulm.it.

246 [Also noteworthy are the William Auld collection at the National Library of Scotland (http://www.nls.uk/collections/rare-books/collections/esperanto), the Esperanto collection of the British Library, and the Allen Boschen Collection at the University of Massachusetts (http://scua.library.umass.edu/umarmot/?s=boschen). – HT]

workers' Esperanto movement (see Lins 1998), and the Internationaal Institut voor Sociale Geschiedenis, IISG (International Institute for Social History) in Amsterdam. In city, regional and provincial archives material can often be discovered on the history of the Esperanto community.[247]

Much needed is a regularly updated master bibliography of titles in interlinguistics and Esperanto studies and, linked to it, a master catalogue. Planning for such a bibliography is now in the discussion stage on the Internet.[248]

9 Interlinguistics in electronic media

The use of electronic media is growing in importance as a source of information on materials in interlinguistics and Esperanto studies.[249] Many catalogues and other aids are available on compact disc.[250] The Internet provides up-to-the-minute information. E-mail links to specialists in the field help in the search for materials. Public library catalogues and data banks are accessible electronically.

---

247 For example, the complete archive and library of the Esperanto Association in the GDR Cultural League (Esperanto-Asocio en Kulturligo de GDR, GDREA, 1965-1991) forms part of the archive of the Cultural League and can be found in Berlin at SAPMO, Stiftung Archive der Parteien und Massenorganisationen der DDR beim Bundesarchiv Deutschlands (Foundation for the Archives of Parties and Mass Organisations of GDR in the Federal Archive of Germany).

248 bibliotekoj@googlegroups.com.

249 On the potential and problems of Internet use for interlinguistics, see articles by Becker (1997b; 2001) and Fettes (1997).

250 The CD *espeRom*, published by the German Esperanto Association (Freiburg), for example, contains scholarly studies on planned languages, language courses and extensive grammars, dictionaries, specialised bibliographies and catalogues of libraries, book catalogues, etc. It also addresses the practical application of Esperanto (e.g. organisations, congresses and other activities, journals) and includes a guide to the steadily increasing services of the Internet. The CD also contains the complete Esperanto translation of the Bible (see *Inti* 23, *IpI* 23).

A growing number of journals are stored on the Internet, for example *Esperantologio – Esperanto Studies (EES)*: http://www.cb.uu.se/esperanto. Rare or obscure publication on the lesser-known planned-language systems have been scanned and are therefore once again accessible. New planned-language projects are presented on the Internet and numerous links to individual projects are easily identified.

Of course, the standard linguistics data bases and lists can be used to identify materials in interlinguistics, for example *Linguistic Abstracts On Line*, available through subscription from *Linguist List Plus* (http://www.linguisticsabstracts.com/).[251]

The following selection of websites offers an overview of interlinguistic activities and provides numerous links to further sites.

1. Esperantic Studies Foundation (ESF): www.esperantic.org (in English and Esperanto).

2. *Gesellschaft für Interlinguistik e.V.*, (GIL, the [German-language] Society for Interlinguistics): www.interlinguistik-gil.de (in German and English), with bibliography, contents pages of GIL publications, and numerous other references.[252]

3. Increasing numbers of interlinguists use their *personal webpages* to list their own publications and other materials, and provide links to other websites, for example the Chinese scholar of informatics and computer linguistics (and interlinguistics) Liu Haitao. His site offers bibliographies and biographies of well-known interlinguists: http://htliu.nease.net. See also the web site of the Swedish linguist Hartmut Traunmüller (www.ling.su.se/staff/hartmut/il.htm) or the author of this study (http://www.blanke-info.de/de).

---

251 I am indebted to Marc van Oostendorp for this reference.
252 See Ulrich Becker's essay on interlinguistics in the Internet (Becker 2001, also published in *IntI* 44).

VI: Paths to the scholarly literature on interlinguistics and Esperanto studies

4. TROVANTO, the catalogue of the *Planned Languages Section of the Austrian National Library* can be accessed at www.onb.ac.at/sammlungen/plansprachen/index.htm. In 2002 the library completed the retrospective entry of all monographs in the collection. A link on its website connects the scholar with the most extensive grammar of Esperanto available on the Internet, *Plena manlibro de Esperanta gramatiko*, by Bertil Wennergren (www.bertilow.com).

5. Martin Weichert has created the Virtual Esperanto Library, Virtuala Esperanto-Biblioteko VEB: www.esperanto.net/veb/ (presently maintained by UEA).

6. A number of professionally oriented websites have recently been established, for example on the pedagogy and teaching of Esperanto and on instructional materials: www.edukado.net.

7. Search engines, for example www.google.com, facilitate the discovery of numerous websites and publications.

8. The most important basis for Esperanto research consists of course of the texts themselves, written or spoken. Lately searches of ever-larger bodies of text have been enabled by electronic means. This is important in researching actual language use for lexicological and lexicographic goals. Bertil Wennergren is assembling a searchable corpus of several million words, accessible at http://bertilow.com .

Along with its many advantages, the Internet also has the disadvantage of instability. Webpages with their URLs and links can change or disappear. Any Internet user can, without restraint, post texts and other collections of data of often dubious quality. For this reason, information gathered by search engines is not always reliable and requires critical examination by experts. Problems of Internet copyright await a definitive solution.

10 Listings of interlinguists

Interlinguists and specialists in Esperanto studies are seldom listed in directories of eminent persons, though there are exceptions. German linguists are presented by Kürschner (1994) in his *Handbook of Linguists*. 'Interlinguistics research on planned languages' is mentioned among the primary fields, and Esperanto appears among the languages. For the linguists in question biographical and bibliographical data are provided.

The 18th edition of *Kürschner's Deutscher Gelehrten-Kalender* (Walter de Gruyter & Co., Berlin, 1996) contains information on interlinguists and presents their detailed bibliographies on CD. The 19th edition in three volumes (München: K.G. Sauer, 2001), contains entries for several interlinguists with brief bibliographies.

Extremely useful is the Who's Who of Esperanto, *Kiu estas kiu en scienco kaj tekniko* (Who's who in science and technology) by Darbellay (1981), which lists 200 Esperanto-speaking scholars in various disciplines across the world, with their most important publications. Among them are interlinguists and scholars of Esperanto studies. An updated and expanded new edition is much needed. It could be compiled quite easily through the Internet.

Somewhat different in character is the directory of scholars with a knowledge of Esperanto in *Internacia Sciencista Dokumentaro* (T. Frank 1996), which is regularly updated in the Internet: www.ais-sanmarino.org.

11 Conclusion

Planned-language theory and observable practice are described in the scholarly literature in relative detail, though not always easily accessed by outside researchers. Much as scholars in the Middle Ages needed a knowledge of Latin, researchers on planned languages should have a command at least of Esperanto, and, if possible, of other planned languages. As we have shown, it is not enough to limit oneself to English-language literature. And, furthermore, simply studying the scholarly literature is insufficient if one wishes to understand planned languages in practice – particularly in the case of Esperanto, with its numerous and multifaceted international activities, radio programs, and representations in the Internet. Attention to planned languages opens up to linguists entirely new aspects of the essential characteristics of languages. For example, it is possible to study, in effect under laboratory conditions, how a language founded by a single individual actually functions and develops. This is a field in which pioneering work is still possible.

Afterword

The year 1985 saw the publication of two pathbreaking books on planned languages: Detlev Blanke's *Internationale Plansprachen: Eine Einführung*, and Andrew Large's *The Artificial Language Movement*. Neither author knew the other. Before Andrew Large there was very little work in English that attempted an overview of the kind represented by *The Artificial Language Movement* (Pei 1958/1968 came closest), and before Detlev Blanke there was nothing comparable in German.

The books were strikingly different. Large's volume offered a broad and literate history of planned language from the seventeenth century to the nineteenth, then turned to the Esperanto movement and its language and history. He discussed the twentieth-century 'challengers' to Esperanto, like Ido, Novial, and Interlingua, and then reviewed the chances of the adoption of any planned, or (as he put it) artificial, language, concluding that these chances were slim: Esperanto, resilient though it had proved to be, had not attracted a mass following, and was in any case regarded with extreme scepticism by the makers of public opinion, who saw it as the province of eccentrics. While other solutions were perhaps less complete, market forces were causing them to prevail.

Large was not himself a member of the Esperanto movement, and thus he relied on secondary sources for much of his information – on Lapenna's comprehensive but selective interpretation of the history of the Esperanto movement and on Forster's analysis of the demographics of the British Esperantists. The book had its errors, even if it was widely cited, and it was decidedly Europocentric. But even as Large was writing, the world of linguistics was rapidly changing: the sub-fields of language planning and language policy were beginning to emerge and Esperanto and other planned languages were finding a niche, even if an insecure one, in these fields. Lapenna had always argued that language was primarily a social phenomenon: as this view gained wider acceptance particularly among sociolinguists, Esperanto and planned languages in general became phenomena worthy of study in themselves. Respectability was less of an issue than fact: if a linguistic phenomenon existed, even outside the canon of standard language, it was worthy of serious study.

Blanke's *Internationale Plansprachen* was a different undertaking from that of Large, in many ways. For Blanke, a planned language was essentially a tool: if it worked it was worthy of study and use; if it failed to work, he was interested in why, though at the same time careful to avoid value judgments. Unlike Large's *The Artificial Language Movement*, Blanke's *Internationale Plansprachen* was written by someone who himself spoke a planned language, namely Esperanto, and who recognised this language and language projects like it as arising out of a coherent theoretical base and addressing a recognisable problem. Essentially independently of the sociolinguistic school in the west, Blanke had reached a similar conclusion: if a language phenomenon exists, it is worthy of scholarly examination in itself. Blanke was particularly interested in how planned languages related to ethnic languages, how the 'artificiality' of, say, Esperanto extended to, indeed was synonymous with, the 'artfulness' of ethnic language, and how planned language could solve taxonomic and terminological problems. His book was an extended classification of planned-language phenomena, drawing on, and going beyond, earlier classifications by European linguists (Couturat and Leau some eighty years earlier, the Soviet linguist Ernest Drezen in the 1920s and 1930s, and various others) and explaining links and overlaps between planned language and ethnic language.

In this detailed work Blanke was relatively unimpeded by the concerns expressed by Large and others: what mattered was the phenomenon, not the question of whether it could or should succeed. Historical determinism would settle that argument. By insisting on the respectability of the phenomenon, he left no room for those who saw it as eccentric. Indeed, as someone active in the Esperanto movement, he had little time for those who simply enjoyed Esperanto for its own sake: he was convinced of its seriousness of purpose and its intellectual potential. Understanding the phenomenon of planned language was the central purpose of his detailed book, with its meticulous description of particular projects, its extensive bibliographies, and its magisterial style.

In addition to his university lecturing, Blanke worked as an official in the Cultural League of the German Democratic Republic, where he had responsibility for the committee to organise a national Esperanto association for the GDR. He understood that the path to success lay in taking Esperanto as an entirely serious intellectual activity and as a potential counterbalance to linguistic imperialism. To argue less was to risk losing the support of the authorities and with it the entire organisational structure. He sought out others, particularly in Eastern Europe and the Soviet Union, with similar intellectual interests, thereby reinforcing the intellectual and political claims both of Esperanto and of the study of interlinguistics. As Esperanto activists, albeit with very different political views, he and I worked together to make the Esperanto organisations of Eastern Europe acceptable to those in the west, discounting the political rhetoric and stressing the common purpose of the promotion of Esperanto – in essence, working to resist those in the west who saw socialism as a kind of contagion ready to infect the unwary. Fortunately, our efforts were generally successful, and the Esperanto movement was never irrevocably split between the socialist East and the capitalist West as so many other movements were.

I first met Detlev in 1963, at an Esperanto youth meeting in Bulgaria. Not only was I impressed by his sense of purpose but I was also won over by his sense of humour: his highly developed self-irony belied, or tempered, his political convictions. We recognised early on that he believed what he believed; I believed what I believed. We were both, after all, adults. At the same time, I was awed by the sheer depth of his knowledge, and not only in his chosen field. We remained firm friends for over fifty years, working together on numerous projects, organising symposia, planning publications, doing our bit to bridge the divide between east and west. He was never fully comfortable in the English-speaking world nor I, for my part, in the German-speaking world, still less that of the GDR; but his thinking informed much of my work in English. We were both conscious of the fact that the English-speaking world suffered from the delusion of self-sufficiency; we sought in our various ways to overcome this delusion. We met at least once a year to bemoan, from our different corners, the state of the world and the apparent inability of the Esperanto movement to articulate its arguments effectively. And, through all this, he continued to write and teach and organise. Most of the articles that form the chapters of this book were my translations, done at his request. They represent only a small part of his scholarly output but they set forth some of his ideas with a clarity that will, I hope, cause us to shift our focus. He, for his part, helped me with scholarly connections in his sphere of activity, I was his guest at Humboldt University, lecturing both to the linguistics and the English departments, and he and a colleague, Ulrich Lins, edited a Festschrift in my honour.

Detlev Blanke's passing was a major loss to scholarship and also the loss of a dear friend. Assembling the present book, along with Professor Sabine Fiedler, was both a labour of love and a homage to Detlev – an expression of thanks and affection for all that he did for us and all that we lived through together.

The present volume brings together some of his English-language publications, which he had begun preparing for publication in a single volume. Had he lived, Detlev would undoubtedly have eliminated duplication from chapter to chapter and brought the chapters up to date. While we have occasionally added relevant updates (signed SF or HT) or adjusted such details as website addresses, we have not attempted to reshape the individual articles that make up the book. Because we have kept the integrity of the original texts, inevitably the reader will find occasional duplications across chapters, for which we apologize.

Humphrey Tonkin

References

Actes. 1933. *Actes du deuxième congrès international de linguistes, Genève 25 - 29 août 1931.* Paris: Libraire d'Amérique et d'orient Adrien Maisonneuve.

Adams, Michael, ed. 2011. *From Elvish to Klingon.* Oxford: Oxford University Press.

Akhmanova, Ol'ga S. 1977. Estestvennye jazyki i postanovka problemy sozdanija iskusstvennogo vspomogatel'nogo jazyka v epochu naučno-techničeskoj revoljucii. In: I. K. Beloded, J. D. Dešeriev, et al., eds., *Naučno-techničeskaja revoljucija i funkcionirovanie jazykov mira.* Moskva: Nauka, pp. 37-41.

Albani, Paolo; Buonarroti, Berlinghiero. 1994. *Aga magéra difúra. Dizionario delle lingue immaginarie.* Bologna: Zanichelli.

Albani, Paolo; Buonarroti, Berlinghiero. 2010. *Dictionnaire des langues imaginaires.* Édition française par Egidio Festa avec la collaboration de Marie-France Adaglio. 2nd edition., Paris: Société d'édition Les Belles Lettres. (Translation from the Italian original *Aga Magéra Difúra: Dizionario delle Lingue Immaginarie.* Bologna: Zanichelli).

Alfandari, Arturo. 1961. *Cours pratique de Neo. Deuxième langue. Dictionnaire français-Neo et Neo-français avec un guide de conversation français-anglais-Neo.* Bruxelles: Brepols.

Ammon Ulrich. 1998. *Ist Deutsch noch internationale Wissenschaftssprache?* Berlin: de Gruyter.

Arnim, W. von. 1896. *Entwurf einer Verkehrssprache, genannt Veltparl.* Oppeln: Maske.

Atanasov, Atanas D. 1983. *La lingva esenco de Esperanto.* Rotterdam: Universala Esperanto-Asocio.

Back, Otto. 1972. Was an Fremdsprachen schwierig ist. *Moderne Sprachen* 16/1-2: 6-26.

Back, Otto. 1979. Über Systemgüte, Funktionsadäquatheit und Schwierigkeit in Plansprachen und ethnischen Sprachen. In: Felber, Helmut; Lang, Friedrich; Wersig, Gernot, eds. *Terminologie als angewandte Sprachwissenschaft. Gedenkschrift für Univ.-Prof. Dr. Eugen Wüster.* München: Saur, pp. 257-272.

Bagger, Preben V. 1980. Terminologiske problemer ved omtale af
Esperanto i danske leksikon- og ordbogsartikler. *Skrifter om
Anvendt og Matematisk Lingvistik* (Copenhagen) 7: 23-38.

Bak, Giŭan. 1991. *Hanguŏwa esuxpheranthouxi hyŏngthae taejo yŏngu.
A Study of Morphological Contrasts of Korean and Esperanto.*
Doctoral diss. Seoul: Konkuk University & Seula Esperanto-
Kulturcentro.

Barandovská-Frank, Věra 1993a. *Kybernetische Pädagogik.
Klerigkibernetiko. Schriften 1973-1992 von Helmar Frank und
Mitarbeitern.* Band 6. Berlin & Paderborn: Institut für Kybernetik;
Dobřichovice/Prag: KAVA-PECH; San Marino: AIEP. (List of
publications of Helmar Frank, pp. 1057-1066).

Barandovská-Frank, Věra 1993b. *Kybernetische Pädagogik.
Klerigkibernetiko. Schriften 1962-1992 von Helmar Frank und
Mitautoren.* Band 7. Berlin & Paderborn: Institut für Kybernetik;
Dobřichovice/Prag: KAVA-PECH; San Marino: AIEP. (List of
publications of Helmar Frank, pp. 1018-1019.)

Barandovská-Frank, Věra. 1995. *Enkonduka lernolibro de
interlingvistiko.* Sibiu: Edítura Universităti din Sibiu. (Also
published in Czech language edition.)

Barandovská-Frank, Věra. 2002. Über die Academia pro Interlingua.
In: Blanke, Detlev, ed. *Plansprachen und ihre Gemeinschaften.*
Beiträge der 11. Jahrestagung der Gesellschaft für Interlinguistik
e.V., 23.-25. November 2001 in Berlin. *Interlinguistische
Informationen*, Beiheft 8. Berlin: Gesellschaft für Interlinguistik
e.V., pp. 6-21.

Barandovská-Frank, Věra. 2009. Interreta lingvokreado kaj
interlingvistiko. *Grundlagenstudien aus Kybernetik und
Geisteswissenschaft/Humankybernetik* (grkg) 50/3: 151-168.

Baudouin de Courtenay, Jan. 1908. *Zur Kritik der künstlichen
Weltsprachen.* Leipzig: Veit.

Baumann, Adalbert. 1915. *Wede. Die Verständigungssprache der
Zentralmächte und ihrer Freunde, die neue Welthilfssprache.* Diessen
vor München: Private edition.

References

Bausani, Alessandro. 1970. *Geheim- und Universalsprachen. Entwicklung und Typologie.* Trans. Gustav Glaesser. Stuttgart: Kohlhammer. (The Italian original appeared after the German translation: *Le lingue inventate. Linguaggi artificiali, linguaggi segreti, linguaggi universali.* Roma: Casa Ed. Astrolabio-Ubaldini Editore, 1974; 2nd edition 1997).

Becker, Ulrich. 1996a. Interlinguistik im Internet. *Interlinguistische Informationen,* 5/3 (21): 2-13.

Becker, Ulrich, ed. 1996b. *Translation in Plansprachen.* Beiträge gehalten auf der 5. Jahrestagung der Gesellschaft für Interlinguistik e. V., November 1995, in Berlin. *Interlinguistische Informationen,* Beiheft 1. Berlin: Gesellschaft für Interlinguistik.

Becker, Ulrich, ed. 1997a. *Terminologiewissenschaftliche Aspekte der Interlinguistik. Beiträge gehalten auf der 6. Jahrestagung der Gesellschaft für Interlinguistik e.V., 15.-17. November 1996 in Berlin. Interlinguistische Informationen,* Beiheft 2. Berlin: Gesellschaft für Interlinguistik.

Becker, Ulrich, ed. 1997b. Interlinguistik im Internet. In: Becker, Ulrich, ed. *Terminologiewissenschaftliche Aspekte der Interlinguistik.* Beiträge gehalten auf der 6. Jahrestagung der Gesellschaft für Interlinguistik e.V., 15.-17. November 1996 in Berlin. *Interlinguistische Informationen,* Beiheft 2. Berlin: Gesellschaft für Interlinguistik, pp. 44-46.

Becker, Ulrich. 2001. Interlinguistik und Internet. In: Fiedler, Sabine; Liu, Haitao, eds. *Studoj pri Interlingvistiko. Studien zur Interlinguistik. Festschrift für Detlev Blanke zum 60. Geburtstag. / Festlibro omaĝe al la 60-jariĝo de Detlev Blanke.* Dobřichovice/Praha: KAVA-PECH, pp. 254-277.

Becker, Ulrich, ed. 2011. *Interlingvistiko kaj Esperantologio. Bibliografio de la publikaĵoj de Detlev Blanke. Kun dulingvaj enkondukoj kaj indeksoj. / Interlinguistik und Esperantologie. Bibliographie der Veröffentlichungen von Detlev Blanke. Mit Einführungen und Registern in Deutsch und Esperanto.* New York: Mondial.

Bednarz, Irena. 1984. *Bibliografio de la enhavo de Scienca Revuo 1949-1978. Suplemento 1979-1982.* Warsaw: Pola Esperanto-Asocio.

Behrmann, Hermann. 1975. *Zur Plansprache Esperanto: Ein rechnererzeugtes Lehrprogramm.* FEOLL-Papier. Paderborn: FEOLL.

Benczik, Maria. 1976. *Literatura Mondo 1922-1949. Kompleta indekso. (Supplement to the reprint of Literatura Mondo vol. 6, 1947-49)* Tokyo: Kooperativo por represo de Literatura Mondo ĉe Teikyo Universitato, Anatomia Instituto de Medicina Fakultato.

Benczik, Vilmos, ed. 1999. *Lingva arto. Jubilea libro omaĝe al William Auld kaj Marjorie Boulton.* Rotterdam: Universala Esperanto-Asocio.

Berger, Ric. 1946. Li sol-re sol. *Cosmoglotta* 25/1: 11-12.

Bibliographia. 1990-1998. *Bibliographia de Interlingua.* Beekbergen: Union Mundial pro Interlingua (UMI).

Bibliographia. 1998. *Bibliographia de Interlingua.* Beekbergen: Union Mundial pro Interlingua (UMI).

Bibliographia. 2002. *Bibliographia de Interlingua 2002,* edition januario, numero 29. Beekbergen: Union Mundial pro Interlingua (UMI).

Bick, Eckhard. 2011. WikiTrans: La angla Vikipedio en Esperanto. In: Nosková, Katarína; Baláž, Peter, eds., *Modernaj teknologioj por Esperanto.* (Aplikoj de Esperanto en Scienco kaj Tekniko). Partizánske, Slovakia: Espero, pp. 28-41.

Bink, Ekkehard, W. D. 1977. Definition der Plansprache und die Ideen der Kriterienkonstanz. In: Behrmann, Hermann, ed. *Interlinguistik in Wissenschaft und Bildung.* Paderborn: FEOLL, pp. 8-13.

Blanke, Detlev. 1975. Kial venkis Esperanto? *der esperantist* 11/5-6 (73-74): 20-22.

Blanke, Detlev. 1976. Pazigrafia. Meždunarodnaja smyslovaja pismennost. In: Isaev, Magomet, ed., *Problemy interlingvistiki. Tipologija i evoljucija meždunarodnych iskusstvennych jazykov.* Moskow: Nauka, pp. 79-91.

Blanke, Detlev. 1977. Interlinguistik und interlinguistische Forschungen. *Zeitschrift für Phonetik, Sprachwissenschaft und Kommunikationsforschung* (ZPSK) 30: 389-398, 619-629.

Blanke, Detlev. 1978. Pri la 'interna ideo' de Esperanto. In: Blanke, Detlev, ed. *Socipolitikaj aspektoj de la Esperanto-movado*. Budapest: Hungara Esperanto-Asocio, pp. 182-208.

Blanke, Detlev. 1981a. *Plansprache und Nationalsprache. Einige Probleme der Wortbildung des Esperanto und des Deutschen in konfrontativer Darstellung*. Linguistische Studien 85, Reihe A, Arbeitsberichte. Doctoral diss. Berlin: Akademie der Wissenschaften, Zentralinstitut für Sprachwissenschaft. (Second edition 1982.)

Blanke, Detlev. 1981b. Kio estas Ilo? *Europa Dokumentaro* 29: 9-10.

Blanke, Detlev. 1985. *Internationale Plansprachen. Eine Einführung*. Berlin: Akademie-Verlag.

Blanke, Detlev. 1986a. 'Esperanto' aŭ 'Internacia Lingvo (Ilo)' – Kiel nomi la lingvon? ['Esperanto' or 'Internacia Lingvo (Ilo)' – How should the language be named?]. *der esperantist* 22/5 (139): 105-112.

Blanke, Detlev, ed. 1986b. *Socipolitikaj aspektoj de la Esperanto-movado*. 2nd edition. Budapest: Hungara Esperanto-Asocio. (1st edition 1978.)

Blanke, Detlev. 1986c: *Esperanto und Wissenschaft. Zur Plansprachenproblematik*. (With contributions by Till Dahlenburg & Martin Schüler). Berlin: Kulturbund der DDR. (2nd edition.)

Blanke, Detlev. 1987. The term 'planned language'. *Language Problems & Language Planning* 11: 335-349.

Blanke, Detlev. 1989. Planned languages – a survey of some of the main problems. In: Schubert, Klaus, ed. *Interlinguistics. Aspects of the Science of Planned Languages*. Trends in Linguistics. Studies and Monographs 42. With Dan Maxwell. Berlin-New York: Mouton de Gruyter, pp. 63-87.

Blanke, Detlev. 1990. Interlinguistik in der DDR. Eine Bilanz. *der esperantist* 26/5 (163): 110-117.

Blanke, Detlev. 1991. Proekty planovych jazykov i planovyj jazyk. In: Isaev, Magomet, ed. *Problemy meždunarodnogo vspomogatel'nogo jazyka*. Moscow: Nauka, pp. 63-69.

Blanke, Detlev. 1994. *Eugen Wüster, la planlingvoj kaj la Enciklopedia Vortaro. Enkonduko al la filmigita manuskripto de la Enciklopedia Vortaro Esperanta-Germana de Eugen Wüster, dua parto: korno-Z.* (Introduction to Wüster 1994: see below.)

Blanke, Detlev. 1996. Wege zur interlinguistischen und esperantologischen Fachliteratur. *Language Problems & Language Planning* 20/2: 168-181.

Blanke, Detlev. 1997a. Zur Plansprache Esperanto und zur Esperantologie im Werk von Eugen Wüster. In: Eichner, Heiner; Ernst, Peter; Katsikas, Sergios, eds. *Sprachnormung und Sprachplanung. Festschrift für Otto Back zum 70. Geburtstag.* 2nd edition. Wien: Edition Praesens, pp. 315-334.

Blanke, Detlev. 1997b. The term 'planned language'. In: Tonkin, Humphrey, ed. *Esperanto, Interlinguistics, and Planned Languages.* Papers of the Center for Research and Documentation on World Language Problems 5. Lanham-New York-Oxford: University Press of America / Rotterdam: Center for Research and Documentation on World Language Problems, pp. 1-20.

Blanke, Detlev. 1998a. Esperanto kiel faklingvo: Terminologiaj kaj fakaplikaj aktivecoj. *Informilo por Interlingvistoj.* 7/1 (24): 9-18.

Blanke, Detlev. 1998b. Terminology science and planned languages. In: Oeser, Erhard; Galinski, Christian, eds. *Eugen Wüster (1898-1977): Leben und Werk – Ein österreichischer Pionier der Informationsgesellschaft; His Life and Work – An Austrian Pioneer of the Information Society.* Vienna: TermNet/InfoTerm, pp. 133-168.

Blanke, Detlev. 1998c. La Enciklopedia Vortaro de Eugen Wüster. *Literatura Foiro* 29 (171): 21-31.

Blanke, Detlev. 1998d. Pri la aktuala stato de interlingvistiko: Kelkaj teoriaj kaj sciencorganizaj problemoj. In: Carlevaro, Tazio, ed. *Domaine de la recherche en linguistique appliquée.* Deuxième Colloque d'Interlinguistique: CDELI, La Chaux-de-Fonds. Contributions. Bellinzona: Hans Dubois, pp. 6-88.

Blanke, Detlev. 2000. Einige methodologische Probleme der Geschichtsschreibung über GDREA. In: *Esperanto und Historiographie. Esperanto-Dokumente* 4. Berlin: Deutsches

Esperanto Institut, pp. 31-62. (With bibliography on the historiography of the Esperanto language community, pp. 55-59.)

Blanke, Detlev. 2001a. Vom Entwurf zur Sprache. In: Schubert, Klaus, ed. *Planned Languages: From Concept to Reality. Interface.* Brussels: Hogeschool voor Wetenschap en Kunst, pp. 37-89.

Blanke, Detlev, ed. 2001b. *Esperanto kaj kulturo – sociaj kaj lingvaj aspektoj: Aktoj de la 19-a Esperantologia Konferenco en la 81-a Universala Kongreso de Esperanto, Prago 1996.* Rotterdam: Universala Esperanto-Asocio.

Blanke, Detlev. 2003a. Interlinguistics and Esperanto studies. Paths to the scholarly literature. *Language Problems & Language Planning* 27/2: 155-192. (Revised German-language translation in Sabine Fiedler 2006. *Interlinguistische Beiträge. Zum Wesen und zur Struktur internationaler Plansprachen.* Frankfurt/Main: Peter Lang, pp. 99-129. Additional versions also in Esperanto, Czech and Chinese languages.)

Blanke, Detlev, ed. 2003b. ProCom '98. Sektion 3 'Terminologiewissenchaft und Plansprachen'. Beiträge der internationalen Konferenz *Professional Communication and Knowledge Transfer* (Wien, 24-26 August 1998). Infoterm/TermNet. *Interlinguistische Informationen*, Beiheft 10. Berlin: Gesellschaft für Interlinguistik e.V.

Blanke, Detlev. 2004. *Interlinguistics and Esperanto Studies: Paths to the Scholarly Literature. Esperanto Documents* 47A. Rotterdam: Universala Esperanto-Asocio.

Blanke, Detlev. 2006. *Interlinguistische Beiträge. Zum Wesen und zur Struktur internationaler Plansprachen.* Ed. Sabine Fiedler. Frankfurt/Main: Peter Lang.

Blanke, Detlev. 2007a. Sprachenpolitische Aspekte internationaler Plansprachen. Unter besonderer Berücksichtigung des Esperanto. In: Blanke, Detlev; Scharnhorst, Jürgen, eds. *Sprachpolitik und Sprachkultur. Sprache – System – Tätigkeit,* 57. Frankfurt/Main: Peter Lang, pp. 205-253.

Blanke, Detlev 2007b. *Esperanto kaj socialismo? Pri la movado sur la 'alia flanko'.* 2nd edition. New York: Mondial.

Blanke, Detlev, ed. 2008. *Plansprachliche Bibliotheken und Archive.* Beiträge der 17. Jahrestagung der Gesellschaft für Interlinguistik e.V., 23.-25. November 2007, in Berlin. *Interlinguistische Informationen,* Beiheft 15. Berlin: Gesellschaft für Interlinguistik.

Blanke, Detlev, ed. 2009a. *Planlingvaj bibliotekoj kaj novaj teknologioj. Aktoj de la kolokvo en Vieno, 19-20 oktobro 2007.* Rotterdam: Universala Esperanto-Asocio.

Blanke, Detlev. 2009b. Causes of the relative success of Esperanto. *Language Problems & Language Planning* 33/3: 251-266.

Blanke, Detlev. 2010. Sprachwandel im Esperanto – gezeigt an Beispielen aus der Lexik. In: Reinke, Kristin; Sinner, Carsten, eds. *Sprache als Spiegel der Gesellschaft. Festschrift für Johannes Klare zum 80. Geburtstag.* München: Verlag Anja Urbanek, pp. 51-77.

Blanke, Detlev. 2011a. Festlibroj – nova fakliteratura ĝenro en Esperanto – kun aparta konsidero pri la festlibro por Humphrey Tonkin. In: Nosková, Katarína; Baláž, Peter, eds. *Modernaj teknologioj por Esperanto. Aplikoj de Esperanto en Scienco kaj Tekniko (KAEST 2010).* Partizánske, Slovakia : Espero, pp. 170-183.

Blanke, Detlev. 2011b. 20 Jahre Gesellschaft für Interlinguistik e.V. – Ergebnisse und Probleme. In: Fiedler, Sabine, ed. *Spracherfindung und ihre Ziele.* Beiträge der 20. Jahrestagung der Gesellschaft für Interlinguistik e.V., 26.-28. November 2010 in Berlin. *Interlinguistische Informationen,* Beiheft 18. Berlin: Gesellschaft für Interlinguistik e.V., pp. 115-150.

Blanke, Detlev. 2013. Zur Rolle des Fachbulletins *Informilo por Interlingvistoj* (IpI). Pri la rolo de la faka bulteno *Informilo por Interlingvistoj* (IpI). In: Barandovská-Frank, Věra, ed. *Littera scripta manet. Serta in honorem Helmar Frank.* Paderborn: Akademia Libroservo / Dobřichovice/Praha: KAVA-PECH, pp. 144-151.

Blanke, Detlev. 2015. How not to reinvent the wheel: The esential scholarly literature in interlinguistics and Esperantology. *INDECS: Interdisciplinary Description of Complex Systems* 13/2: 200-215.

Blanke, Detlev; Blanke,Wera. 1998. Plansprachen als Fachsprachen. In: Hoffmann, Lothar; Kalverkämper, Hartwig; Wiegand, Herbert Ernst, eds. *Fachsprachen. Languages for Special Purposes.* 1. Halbband. Berlin-New York: de Gruyter, pp. 875-880.

Blanke, Detlev; Blanke, Wera. 2015. Is scholarly communication possible in a so-called 'artificial language'? *INDECS: Interdisciplinary Description of Complex Systems*. 13/2: 216-235.

Blanke, Detlev; Haszpra, Ottó ; Felsö, Géza. 1988. *Esperanto – lingvo de la natursciencoj kaj tekniko*. Esperanto-Dokumentoj, 25 E. Rotterdam: Universala Esperanto-Asocio.

Blanke, Detlev; Lins, Ulrich, eds. 2010. *La arto labori kune. Festlibro por Humphrey Tonkin*. Rotterdam: Universala Esperanto-Asocio.

Blanke, Detlev; Lins, Ulrich. 2010. Bibliografio de la verkoj de Humphrey Tonkin. In: Blanke, Detlev; Lins, Ulrich, eds. *La arto labori kune. Festlibro por Humphrey Tonkin*. Rotterdam: Universala Esperanto-Asocio, pp. 878-901.

Blanke, Detlev; Panka, Stefan, eds. 2010. *Karl-Hermann Simon, Lexicon silvestre. Beiträge zum multilingualen Wörterbuch des Forstwesens. Kontribuoj pri la multlingva vortaro de la forstfako* (with preface by Klaus Schubert). Eberswalde: Förderverein Lexicon silvestre e. V.

Blanke, Wera. 1988. Terminologia Esperanto-Centro. Efforts for terminological standardization in the planned language. In: Maxwell, Dan; Schubert, Klaus; Witkam, Toon, eds. New *Directions in Machine Translation. Conference Proceedings, Budapest 18-19 August 1988*. Dordrecht-Providence: Foris, pp. 183-194.

Blanke, Wera. 1989. Terminological standardization – Its roots and fruits in planned languages. In: Schubert, Klaus, ed. *Interlinguistics. Aspects of the Science of Planned Languages*. Trends in Linguistics: Studies and Monographs 42. Berlin-New York: Mouton de Gruyter, 277-292.

Blanke, Wera. 1997. Über den Beitrag von Interlinguisten zur Organization internationaler Terminologiearbeit. In: Becker, Ulrich, ed. *Terminologiewissenschaftliche Aspekte der Interlinguistik*. Beiträge gehalten auf der 6. Jahrestagung der Gesellschaft für Interlinguistik e.V., 15.-17. November 1996 in Berlin. *Interlinguistische Informationen*, Beiheft 2. Berlin: Gesellschaft für Interlinguistik e.V., pp. 4-12.

Blanke, Wera. 2008. *Esperanto – Terminologie und Terminologiearbeit* (with preface by Sabine Fiedler). New York: Mondial.

Blanke, Wera. 2013. *Pri terminologia laboro en Esperanto. Elektitaj publikaĵoj.* New York: Mondial.

Blaschke, Wilhelm. 1950. *Die europäische Sprache entsteht.* Wels: The Author.

Bodmer, Frederic. 1955. *Die Sprachen der Welt.* 2nd edition. Köln: Kiepenheuer.

Böðvarsson, Árni. 1963. *Islensk ordabók.* Reykjavík: Federacio de Islandaj Esperantistoj.

Bormann, Werner. 1995. *Die Hamburger Interlinguistik-Vorlesung.* Kiel: Strigo.

Borsboom, Ed. 1976. *Vivo de Lanti.* Paris: SAT (Sennacieca Asocio Tutmonda).

Brang, Peter; Züllig, Monika. 1981. *Kommentierte Bibliographie zur Slavischen Soziolinguistik. Band II.* Bern: Peter Lang. (Titles on interlinguistics: pp.1142-1157.)

Brown, James C. 1960. Loglan. *Scientific American* 202/6: 53-63.

Brugmann, Karl 1913 - 1914. Die künstlichen Weltsprachen und ihre Aussichten. *Akademische Rundschau* (Leipzig) 6: 290-309.

Busch, Johann Georg. 1787. *Ueber die Frage: gewinnt ein Volk in Absicht auf seine Aufklaerung dabey, wenn seine Sprache zur Universal-Sprache wird.* Berlin.

Bußmann, Hadumod. 2002. *Lexikon der Sprachwissenschaft.* Dritte aktualisierte und erweiterte Auflage. 3rd edition, Stuttgart: Kröner.

Carlevaro, Tazio, ed. 1998. *Domaine de la recherche en linguistique appliquée.* Deuxième Colloque d'interlinguistique. Contributions. CDELI, La Chaux-de-Fonds. Bellinzona: Hans Dubois.

Carlevaro, Tazio; Haupenthal, Reinhard. 1999. *Bibliografio de Ido.* Bellinzona: Hans Dubois / Saarbrücken: Edition Iltis.

Catalogi Kunsttalen I. 1969. Esperanto. *Catalogus van de boekerij de Nederlandse Esperantisten-vereniging 'La Estonto estas nia' en van de Esperanto-collectie in de Universiteitsbibliotheek.*

Eerste Deel. Speciale Catalogi, Nieuwe Serie, No. 5. Amsterdam Universiteitsbibliotheek.

Catalogi Kunsttalen II. 1969. *Esperanto. Catalogus van de boekerij de Nederlandse Esperantisten-vereniging 'La Estonto estas nia' en van de Esperanto-collectie in de Universiteitsbibliotheek. Tweede Deel. Tijdschriften – en Serietitels.* Speciale Catalogi, Nieuwe Serie, No. 5. Amsterdam: Universiteitsbibliotheek.

Černyšev, Vasilij A. 1968. K probleme jazyka-posrednika. In: *Jazyk i obščestvo.* Moskva: Nauka.

Chrdle, Petr, ed. 1995. *La stato kaj estonteco de la internacia lingvo Esperanto.* Prelegokolekto de la unua simpozio de la Akademio de Esperanto (Praha 1994-07-07-14). Dobřichovice/Praha : KAVA-PECH.

Collinder, Björn. 1938. *La problemo de lingvo internacia.* Purmerend; Muuses.

Corret, Pierre. 1908. *Utilité et possibilité de l'adoption d'une langue internationale auxiliaire en médecine.* Doctoral diss. Paris: Presa Esperantista Societo.

Corsetti, Renato; La Torre, Mauro; Vessella, Nino. 1980. Pliriĉiĝo de la morfemaro en Internacia Lingvo. In: Szerdahelyi, István, ed. *Miscellanea Interlinguistica.* Budapest: Tankönyvkiadó, pp. 368-379.

Corsetti, Renato; La Torre, Mauro. 1995. Quale lingua prima? Per un esperimento CEE che utilizzi l'esperanto. *Language Problems & Language Planning* 19: 26-46.

Corsetti, Renato; La Torre, Mauro. 2001. Ĉu klara strukturo estas instrua? In: Schubert, Klaus, ed. *Planned Languages. From Concept to Reality, Part II.* Special issue of *Interface: Journal of Applied Linguistics* 15: 179-202.

Couturat, Louis. 1910. *Étude sur la dérivation dans la langue internationale.* Paris: Delagrave.

Couturat, Louis. 1911. Des rapports de la logique et de la linguistique dans le problème de la langue internationale. *Revue de métaphysique et de morale* 19: 509-516.

Couturat, Louis & Leau, Léopold. 1979 (=1903+1907). *Histoire de la langue universelle (1903). Les nouvelles langues internationales (1907). Mit einem bibliographischen Nachwort (deutsch-französisch) von Reinhard Haupenthal.* 3rd ed. Hildesheim-Zürich-New York: Olms. (Reprint.)

Couturat, Louis; Leau, Léopold. 1903+1907/2001. *Histoire de la langue universelle (1903). Les nouvelles langues internationales (1907). Mit einem bibliographischen Nachwort (deutsch-französisch) von Reinhard Haupenthal.* Hildesheim-Zürich-New York: Olms. (Reprint.)

Csiszár 1998-2002. *Omaĝe al Kálmán Kalocsay.* 7 vols. Budapest: KAL-ĈI Dokumentaro.

Dahlenburg, Till-Dietrich. 2006. '*Pli lume la mallumo zumas...' Stilfiguroj en la poezio de Esperanto.* New York: Mondial. (2nd edition 2013: *Figuroj retorikaj en beletro esperanta. Vortaro kun difinoj kaj ilustraĵoj el la internacia literaturo.* New York: Mondial.)

Dalgarno, George. 1661. *Ars signorum, vulgo character universalis et lingua philosophica* (The art of signs, that is, a universal character, and a philosophical language). London: J. Hayes.

Darbellay, Christian. 1981. *Kiu estas kiu en scienco kaj tekniko.* Neuss: Author.

Dehler, Wera. 1985. Terminologiaj principoj de Esperanto. *der esperantist* 21/4 (132): 83-89.

Denissow, P. N.; Kostomarow, Vitalij G. 1977. Die Weltbedeutung der russischen Sprache im 20. Jahrhundert und ihre Stellung unter den anderen Weltsprachen. In: Filin F.P.; Kostomarow, V.G.; Skworzow, L.L., eds. *Die russische Sprache der heutigen Welt.* Leipzig: Enzyklopädie-Verlag.

Desmet, Petro; Horvath, Jozefo. 2012. *Bildvortaro.* Antverpeno: Flandra Esperanto-Ligo.

Dominte, Constantin; Nagy, Jozefo. 2000. Interlingvistiko kaj esperantologio en Rumanio. Bibliografia skizo. *Informilo por Interlingvistoj* 9/2 (33): 4-19.

References

Dorren, Gaston. 2014. *Lingo. A Language Spotter's Guide to Europe.* London: Profile Books.

Dr Esperanto (= L.L. Zamenhof), 1887. *Meždunarodnyj jazyk. Predislovie i polnyj učebnik.* Warszawa: Kelter.

Draskau, Jennifer Kewley; Picht, Heribert, eds. 1994. *International Conference on Terminology Science and Terminology Planning. In Commemoration of E. Drezen (1892-1992),* Riga 17-19 August 1992, and *International IITF Workshop Theoretical Issues of Terminology Science,* Riga 19-21 August 1992. Wien: TermNet.

Drezen, Ernest K. 1931/1991. *Historio de la mondolingvo.* 2nd Esperanto edition. Leipzig: EKRELO. (4th Esperanto edition revised by Sergej N. Kuznecov. Moskva: Progreso, 1991.)

Drezen, Ernest K. 1935/1983. *Pri problemo de internaciigo de science-teknika terminaro. Historio, nuna stato kaj perspektivo.* Raporto akceptita de la Komisiono por Teknika Terminologio će Sovetunia Akademio de Sciencoj kaj de la Konferenco de ISA (Internacia asocio de normigasocioj) en Stockholm, 1934. Trans. A. Samojlenko. Moskva: Standartizacija i Racionalizacija / Amsterdam: EKRELO. (Reprint 1983, with afterword by Alfred Warner, Saarbrücken: Artur E. Iltis.)

Drezen, Ernest K. 2004. *Za vseobščim jazykom. Tri veka iskannij.* Moskva: URSS. Izdateľstvo naučnoj i učebnoj literatury.

Duc Goninaz, Michel, ed. 1987. *Studoj pri la Internacia Lingvo. Études sur la langue internationale. Studies on International Language.* Ghent: AIMAV.

Duličenko, Aleksandr Dmitrievič. 1976. Iz istorii interlingvističeskoj mysli v Rosii (From the history of the interlinguistic idea in Russia). In: Isaev, Magomet I., ed. *Problemy interlingvistiki. Tipologija i evoljucija meždunarodnych iskusstvennych jazykov.* (Problems of interlinguistics). Moscow: Nauka, pp. 114-130.

Duličenko, Aleksandr Dmitrievič. 1983. *Sovetskaja interlingvistika. Annotirovannaja bibliografija za 1946-1982 gg.* Tartu: Tartuskij gosudarstvennyj universitet.

Duličenko, Aleksandr Dmitrievič. 1990: *Meždunarodnye vspomogateľnye jazyki.* Tallin: Valgus.

Duličenko, Aleksandr Dmitrievič. 1997. Esperanto: A unique model for general linguistics. In: Tonkin, Humphrey, ed. *Esperanto, Interlinguistics, and Planned Language* (Papers of the Center for Research and Documentation on World Language Problems 5). Lanham-New York-Oxford: University Press of America / Rotterdam, Hartford: Center for Research and Documentation on World Language Problems, pp. 66-69.

Duličenko, Aleksandr Dmitrievič. 2003. *V pouskach vsemirnogo jazyka, ili interlingvistika dlja vsech.* Tartu: Universitas Tartuensis. (Esperanto translation: Duličenko 2006.)

Duličenko, Aleksandr Dmitrievič. 2006. *En la serĉado de la mondolingvo aŭ interlingvistiko por ĉiuj.* Kaliningrad: Sezonoj. (Esperanto translation of Duličenko 2003.)

Eckardt, André. 1952. *Die Neue Sinnschrift 'Safo' als Einheitszeichenschrift der Völker.* 4th edition. Starnberg: The Author.

Eco, Umberto. 1993. *La ricerca della lingua perfetta nella cultura europea.* Roma-Bari: Laterza. (English translation 1995: *The Search for the Perfect Language*, trans. James Fentress. Oxford: Blackwell. German translation 1994: *Die Suche nach der vollkommenen Sprache.* München: Beck. Esperanto translation 1996: *La serĉado de la perfekta lingvo*, trans. Daniele Mistretta. Pisa: Edistudio.)

Eichholz, Rüdiger. 1986. *Terminologia Vortaro. Provtraduko de la Rekomendo R 1087 de ISO.* Bailieboro, Ontario: Esperanto Press.

Eichholz, Rüdiger. 1988. *Esperanta Bildvortaro.* Bailieboro, Ontario: Esperanto Press.

Eichholz, Rüdiger. 1992. *Perkomputora termino-kolekto* (Pekoteko). 1985-1990, Vol. I-III. Bailieboro, Ontario: Esperanto Press.

Eichholz, Rüdiger; Eichholz, Vilma Sindona, eds. 1982. *Esperanto in the Modern World. Studies and Articles on Language Problems, the Right to Communicate, and the International Language.* Bailieboro, Ontario: Esperanto Press.

Einstein, Leopold. 1855. Zur Geschichte der weltsprachlichen Versuche von Leibniz bis auf die Gegenwart. *Bayrische Lehrerzeitung* 13: 130-132, 142-143.

Ejsmont, Tadeusz, ed. 1981. *Międzynarodowa komunikacja językowa. Internacia lingva komunikado. Konferencaj materialoj.* Łódź: Uniwersytet Łódski.

Esperanto-Katalogo. 2001. *Esperanto-katalogo – Libroservo de Universala Esperanto-Asocio.* Rotterdam: Universala Esperanto-Asocio. (Now accessible in updated form at www.uea.org).

Fantini, Alvino E.; Reagan, Timothy G. 1992. *Esperanto and Education: Towards a Research Agenda.* Washington: Esperantic Studies Foundation.

Farrokh, Mohammad. 1991. *Pensée et l'action d'Edmond Privat (1889-1962). Contribution à l'histoire des idées politiques en Suisse.* Bern: Peter Lang.

Fauvart-Bastoul, Marcelle L. 1902. *D'Une langue auxiliaire internationale au point de vue du droit des gens.* Doctoral diss. Dijon: Rey.

Felber, Helmut; Lang, Friedrich Hans. 1979. Würdigung der Person und des Wissenschaftlers. In: Felber, Helmut; Lang, Friedrich; Wersig, Gernot, eds. *Terminologie als angewandte Sprachwissenschaft. Gedenkschrift für Univ.-Prof.Dr. Eugen Wüster.* München: Saur, pp. 15-28.

Ferenczy, Imre. 2010. Esperanto kaj medicino. In: Blanke, Detlev; Lins, Ulrich, eds. *La arto labori kune. Festlibro por Humphrey Tonkin.* Rotterdam: Universala Esperanto-Asocio, pp. 612-618.

Fettes, Mark. 1997. Interlinguistics and the Internet. *Language Problems & Language Planning* 21: 170-176.

Fettes, Mark; Bolduc, Suzanne. 1998. *Al lingva demokratio. Towards Linguistic Democracy. Vers la démocratie linguistique.* Rotterdam: Universala Esperanto-Asocio.

Fiedler, Sabine. 1999. *Plansprache und Phraseologie: Empirische Untersuchungen zu reproduziertem Sprachmaterial im Esperanto.* Doctoral diss. Frankfurt/Main: Peter Lang.

Fiedler, Sabine. 2002. *Esperanta frazeologio.* Rotterdam: UEA.

Fiedler, Sabine. 2010. The English-as-a-lingua-franca approach: Linguistic fair play? *Language Problems & Language Planning* 34/3: 201-221.

Fiedler, Sabine. 2011. Das Thema Plansprachen (Esperanto) in der aktuellen sprachpolitischen Fachliteratur. In: Brosch, Cyril; Fiedler, Sabine, eds. *Florilegium Interlinguisticum. Festschrift für Detlev Blanke zum 70. Geburtstag.* Frankfurt/Main: Peter Lang, pp. 79-105.

Fiedler, Sabine. 2012. The Esperanto denaskulo: The status of the native speaker of Esperanto within and beyond the planned language community. *Language Problems & Language Planning* 36/1: 69-84.

Fiedler, Sabine. 2015a. The topic of planned languages (Esperanto) in the current specialist literature. *Language Problems & Language Planning* 39/1: 84-104.

Fiedler, Sabine. 2015b. Esperanto phraseology. *Interdisciplinary Description of Complex Systems (INDECS)* 13/2: 250-263.

Fiedler, Sabine; Liu, Haitao. 2001. *Studoj pri Interlingvistiko. Studien zur Interlinguistik. Festschrift für Detlev Blanke zum 60. Geburtstag. Festlibro omaĝe al la 60-jariĝo de Detlev Blanke.* Dobřichovice/Praha: KAVA-PECH. (With summaries in German, English and Esperanto. Accessible also at http://www.lingviko.net/db/Bib_Blanke.htm.)

Fieweger, Julius. 1893. *Internationale Verkehrssprache DIL oder bestes Verständigungsmittel zwischen den Nationen nach dem System des Dr. Gül in Bagdad: Grammatik.* Breslau: Aderholz.

Fodor, István. 2000. *A világ nyelvei / foszerk XVI.* Budapest: Akadémiai K.

Forster, Peter G. 1982. *The Esperanto Movement.* Contributions to the Sociology of Languages 32. Doctoral diss. The Hague-Paris-New York: Mouton.

Fössmeier, Reinhard; Tuĥvatullina, Liana, eds. 2005. *Internacia sciencista dokumentaro de la Akademio de la Sciencoj (AIS) San Marino.* 5th edition, San Marino: AIS.

Foster, Edward P. 1908. *Ro.* Cincinnati, Ohio: The Author.

Frank, Helmar. 1975. Plansprachliche Dokumentation. *Nachrichten für Dokumentation* 26: 17-21.

Frank, Helmar. 1993. Die Internationale Akademie der Wissenschaften (AIS) San Marino. In: Barandovská-Frank, Věra, ed. *Kybernetische Pädagogik. Klerig-kibernetiko. Schriften 1973-1992 von Helmar Frank und Mitarbeitern*. Band 6. Bratislava: Esprima / San Marino: AIEP, pp. 911-916.

Frank, Tilo. 1996. *Internacia sciencista dokumentaro 1996-1999. Registro de la internacilingvaj sciencistoj konataj al Akademio Internacia de la Sciencoj San Marino*. 3rd edition. Paderborn: Institut für Kybernetik.

Frohne, Günter. 1976. Zu den Kriterien der soziolinguistischen Kategorie 'Weltsprache'. *Wissenschaftliche Zeitschrift der Pädagogischen Hochschule Karl-Liebknecht, Potsdam*, 20/5: 723-733.

Gajić, R. 1980. *Zhivij jezik Eseji a komunikacijama i planskim ćjezicima*. Nil: Gradina.

Galinski, Christian; Budin, Gerhard; Krommer-Benz, Magdalena; Manu, Adrian. 1994. Internacia kunlaboro en la terminologio-planado. *Scienca Revuo* 45/1 (164): 18-27.

Galor, Zbigniew; Pietiläinen, Jukka. 2015. *UEA en konscio de esperantistoj*. Dobřichovice/Praha: Kava-Pech.

Garvía, Roberto. 2015. *Esperanto and Its Rivals: The Struggle for an International Language*. Philadelphia: University of Pennsylvania Press.

Gazzola, Michele. 2012. The linguistic implications of academic performance indicators: General trends and case study. *International Journal of the Sociology of Language* 216: 131-156.

Gecső, Tamás; Varga-Haszonits, Zsuzsa, eds. 1998. *Memorlibro. Kolekto de prelegoj dum la solena internacia konferenco organizita okaze de la tridekjariĝo de la universitata fako Esperantologio (Budapeŝto, 17/18-04-1997)*. Budapest: Universitato Eötvös Loránd.

Gjivoje, Marinko. 1980. *Konsultlibro pri Esperantaj bibliotekoj kaj muzeoj*. Zagreb: The Author. (Introductions in English, German, French, Croatian, Russian, Hungarian.)

Gledhill, Christopher. 2000. *The Grammar of Esperanto. A corpus-based description.* 2nd edition, München-Newcastle: Lincom Europa. (1st edition 1998.)

Glück, Helmut. 2005. *Metzler Lexikon Sprache.* 3rd edition, Stuttgart, Weimar: Metzler.

Gobbo, Federico. 2009. *Fondamenti di interlinguistica ed esperantologia. Pianificazione linguistica e lingue pianificate.* Milano: Liberia Cortina.

Gobbo, Federico. 2015a. La holivudaj planlingvoj. *Esperanto* (Rotterdam) 108/5: 112-113.

Gobbo, Federico. 2015b. Machine translation as a complex system: The role of Esperanto. . *INDECS: Interdisciplinary Description of Complex Systems* 13/2: 264-274.

Gode, Alexander, et al. 1951. *Interlingua-English, A Dictionary of the International Language.* New York: Ungar. (2nd edition 1971a).

Gode, Alexander; Blair, Hugh E. 1951. *Interlingua, A Grammar of the International Language.* New York: Ungar. (2nd edition 1971b).

Gold, David L. 1982. What kind of language is Esperanto? *Language Problems & Language Planning* 6: 340-341.

Golden, Bernard. 1993. De *The International Language Review* ĝis *Eco-logos* – La historio de interlingvistika periodaĵo. *Periodaĵoj. Bibliografia organo de Rondo Takács* (Budapest) 3 (Sept.): 2.

Gordin, Michael D. 2015. *Scientific Babel: How Science Was Done Before and After Global English.* Chicago-London: University of Chicago Press.

Gorecka, Halina; Korĵenkov, Aleksander. 2005. *Bibliografio de Esperantaj kaj interlingvistikaj libroj eldonitaj en Ruslando kaj Sovetunio.* 4th edition. Kaliningrad: Sezonoj.

Grimm, August Theodor von. 1976. Programm zur Bildung einer allgemeinen Sprache. In: Haupenthal, Reinhard, ed. *Plansprachen. Beiträge zur Interlinguistik.* Darmstadt: Wiss. Buchgesellschaft, pp. 7-11.

Grosselin, Augustin. 1836. *Systéme de langue universelle*. Paris: Roret.

Gubbins Paul, ed. 2012. *Star in a Night Sky: An Anthology of Esperanto Literature*. London: Francis Boutle.

Guchman, Mirra M. 1973. Die Literatursprache. In: Serébrennikow, Boris, ed. *Allgemeine Sprachwissenschaft*, vol. 1. Berlin: Akademie Verlag, pp. 412-454.

Gulyás, István. 2010. Pri la faka agado de la fervojistaj esperantistoj. In: Blanke, Detlev; Lins, Ulrich, eds. *La arto labori kune. Festlibro por Humphrey Tonkin*. Rotterdam: Universala Esperanto-Asocio, pp. 619-626.

Guérard, Albert Léon. 1922. *A Short History of the International Language Movement*. London: Fisher Unwin.

Guérard, Albert Léon. 1934. For an international auxiliary language. *Books Abroad* 8: 259-262.

Haarmann, Harald. 1973. *Sprachenregelung: Grundfragen der Sprachenregelung in den Staaten der Europäischen Gemeinschaft*. Hamburg: Deutscher Taschenbuch Verlag.

Haarmann, Harald. 2001. *Kleines Lexikon der Sprachen. Von Albanisch bis Zulu*. München: C.H. Beck. (Esperanto: pp. 115-118.)

Haferkorn, Rudolf. 1954. Teknikaj kaj sciencaj terminaroj en Esperanto. *Scienca Revuo* 6 (26): 42-52.

Haferkorn, Rudolf. 1962. Sciencaj, teknikaj kaj ceteraj fakvortaroj en Esperanto. *Scienca Revuo* 12 (47-48): 111-128.

Haferkorn, Rudolf. 1966. Suplementa indekso de la sciencaj, teknikaj kaj ceteraj fakvortaroj en Esperanto. *Scienca Revuo* 16 (63-64): 131-134.

Hagler, Margaret C. 1970. *The Esperanto Language as a Literary Medium: A Historical Discusion of Esperanto Literature 1887 - 1970 and a Stylistic Analysis of Translated and Original Esperanto Poetry*. Doctoral diss. Bloomington: Indiana University.

Hallig, Rudolf; Wartburg, Walter von. 1952. *Ein Begriffssystem als Grundlage für die Lexikographie*. Abhandlung der Deutschen

Akademie der Wissenschaften, Berlin, Klasse Sprache, Literatur, Kunst, no. 4.

Haselhuber, Jakob. 2012. *Mehrsprachigkeit in der Europäischen Union*. Frankfurt/Main: Peter Lang.

Haupenthal, Esther. 1995. *Bibliografio de la verkaro de Reinhard Haupenthal*. Saarbrücken: Iltis.

Haupenthal, Reinhard. 1968. *Enkonduko en la librosciencon de Esperanto. Bibliografia gvidilo kun komento*. Nürnberg: Pickel.

Haupenthal, Reinhard, ed. 1976. *Plansprachen. Beiträge zur Interlinguistik*. Darmstadt: Wissenschaftliche Buchgesellschaft.

Haupenthal, Reinhard. 1982. *Volapük-Bibliographie*. Beigebunden in: Schleyer, Johann Martin (1982), *Volapük. Die Weltsprache*. Hildesheim: Olms.

Haupenthal, Reinhard, ed. 1985. *Li kaj Ni. Festlibro por la 80a naskiĝtago de Gaston Waringhien (1901-29 julio 1981)*. Antwerpen: TK / La Laguna: Stafeto.

Haupenthal, Reinhard. 1991. Lexikographie der Plansprachen. In: Hausmann, Franz Josef; Reichmann, Oskar; Wiegand, Herbert Ernst; Zgusta, Ladislav, eds. *Wörterbücher. Dictionaries. Dictionnaires. Ein internationales Handbuch zur Lexikographie. An International Encyclopedia of Lexicography. Encyclopédie internationale de lexicographie*. Vol. 3. Berlin-New York: de Gruyter, pp. 3120–3137.

Haupenthal, Reinhard. 2009. *Gaston Waringhien (1901-1991). Bibliographie seiner Veröffentlichungen. Bibliografio de liaj publikaĵoj*. Bad Bellingen: Edition Iltis.

Haupenthal, Reinhard, ed. 2014. *Laudationes: In honorem Gaston Waringhien (1901-1991), André Albault (1923), Adolf Burkhardt (1929-2004), Claude Gacond (1931)*. Bad Bellingen: Edition Iltis.

Haupenthal, Irmi; Haupenthal, Reinhard, eds. 2000. *De A al B. Festlibro por André Albault*. Schliengen: Edition Iltis.

Haupenthal, Irmi; Haupenthal, Reinhard, eds. 2003. *Klaro kaj elasto. Fest-libro por la 80a naskiĝ-tago de Fernando Diego*. Schliengen: Edition Iltis.

Haupenthal, Irmi; Haupenthal, Reinhard, eds. 2004. *Esperante kaj ekumene. Fest-libro por la 75a naskiĝ-tago de Adolf Burkhardt*. Schliengen: Edition Iltis.

Haupenthal, Irmi; Haupenthal, Reinhard, eds. 2008. *Studien zu Leben, Wirken und Werk von Johann Martin Schleyer (1831-1912): Pfarrer, Schriftsteller, Autor des Volapük*. Prälat-Schleyer-Jahrbuch 1. Saarbrücken: Edition Iltis.

Haupenthal, Irmi; Haupenthal, Reinhard, eds. 2011. *Instrui dokumenti organizi: Fest-libro por la 80a naskiĝ-tago de Claude Gacond*. Bad Bellingen: Edition Iltis.

Haupenthal, Irmi; Haupenthal, Reinhard. 2013. *Auswahlbibliographie zur Interlinguistik und Esperantologie. Selekta Bibliografio pri Interlingvistiko kaj Esperantologio*. Bad Bellingen: Edition Iltis.

Häusler, Frank. 1981. Weltsprachen, Plansprachen und internationale sprachliche Kommunikation. *Wissenschaftliche Zeitschrift der Pädagogischen Hochschule Erich Weinert, Magdeburg* 18/2: 162-178.

Heil, Anett. 1999. *Grammatische Reduktion in Franko-kreolsprachen und Plansprachen*. Doctoral diss. Rostocker Romanistische Arbeiten, Band 2. Frankfurt/Main: Peter Lang.

Herbert, Jean. 1952. *Handbuch für den Dolmetscher*. Genf: Georg.

Hernández Yzal, Luis M.; Máthé, Árpád; Molera, Ana Maria. 2010. *Bibliografio de periodaĵoj en aŭ pri Esperanto*. Budapest: Bibliografia Fondaĵo Luis M. Hernández Yzal.

Hoffmann, Lothar. 1984. *Kommunikationsmittel Fachsprache. Eine Einführung*. Berlin: Akademie-Verlag.

Hoffman, Lothar 1985. *Kommunikationsmittel Fachsprache*. Revised edition, Tübingen: Narr.

Hoinix. P. [Pseudonym of George Henderson]. 1889. *Anglo-Franca, an compromis language engl.-fr. (an nouveau plan) for the facilitation of international communication*. London: Trübner.

Holmström, J. E., ed. 1958. *Scientific and Technical Translating and Other Aspects of the Language Problem*. Paris: UNESCO.

Hošek, Ignaz. 1907. *Grammatik der neuslavischen Sprache. Eine Vermittlungssprache für die Slaven der Österreichisch-Ungarischen Monarchie.* Kremsier: The Author.

Hube, Walter; März, Herbert. 1975. *Alfabeta katalogo pri la kolektoj de Internacia Esperanto-Muzeo en Wien. Parto II (M-Z).* Wien: Internacia Esperanto-Muzeo en Wien / Österreichische Nationalbibliothek. (First part = Steiner 1969.)

Hübler, Axel. 1985. *Einander verstehen. Englisch im Kontext internationaler Kommunikation.* Tübingen: Gunter Narr.

Hüllen, Werner. 1984. Bischof John Wilkins und die Fachsprachen unserer Zeit. *Special Language/Fachsprache* 6/3-4: 115-122.

IALA. 1927. *Provisional Committee on Auxiliary Language Survey. A Preliminary Investigation of the Teaching of Auxiliary Languages in Schools: A Report to the Council of the Parents League of New York.* Report of the International Auxiliary Language Association, New York.

IALA. 1945. *General Report.* New York: International Auxiliary Language Association.

IEC. 1938/1950. *Vocabulaire electrotechnique international / International Electrotechnical Vocabulary.* First edition 1938, reprinted 1950. Geneva : Commission Electrotechnique Internationale / International Electrotechnical Commission.

Isaev, Magomet Ismailovič, ed. 1976. *Problemy interlingvistiki. Tipologija i evoljucija meždunarodnych iskusstvennych jazykov.* (Problems of interlinguistics). Moskva: Nauka.

Isaev, Magomet Ismailovič. 1981. *Jazyk Esperanto.* Moskva: Nauka.

Isaev, Magomet Ismailovič. 1991. *Problemy meždunarodnogo vspomogatel'nogo jazyka.* (Problems of the international auxiliary language). Moskva: Nauka.

Jacob, Henry. 1946. *On the Choice of a Common Language.* London: Pitman.

Jacob, Henry. 1947. *A Planned Auxiliary Language.* London: Dobson.

Jansen, Wim. 2004. *Elementen uit de interlinguïstiek*. Amsterdam: Universiteit van Amsterdam.

Jansen, Wim. 2012/2013. *Inleiding in de interlinguïstiek. Syllabus bij de keuzemodule Interlinguïstiek*. Amsterdam: Universiteit van Amsterdam, Studiejaar 2012-2013.

Janton, Pierre. 1973. *L'Espéranto* (Que sais-je? 1511). Paris: Presses universitaires de France. (4th revised edition 1994. Translations exist in English [see below], German, Dutch, Spanish, and Esperanto.)

Janton, Pierre. 1993. *Esperanto: Language, Literature, and Community*. Ed. Humphrey Tonkin. Trans. Humphrey Tonkin, Jane Edwards, & Karen Johnson-Weiner. Albany: State University of New York Press. (Extended and revised edition of Janton 1973.)

Jespersen, Otto. 1894. *Progress in Language*. London: Swan Sonnenschein / New York: Macmillan.

Jespersen, Otto. 1928a. *Eine internationale Sprache*. Heidelberg: Winter.

Jespersen, Otto. 1928b. *An International Language*. London: Allen and Unwin.

Jespersen, Otto. 1930/1931. A new science, interlinguistics. *Psyche* 11: 57-67.

Jones, William. 1769. *The Philosophy of Words, Containing Among Other a Plan for a Universal and Philosophical Language*. London: n. p.

Jung, Teo. 1979. *Ĉiu ĉiun. Sep jardekojn de la Esperanto-movado: memorajoj de 86-jara optimisto*. Antverpeno: TK/Stafeto.

Jüttner, Irmtraud, ed. 1990. *Bibliographie zur Sprachwissenschaft der DDR für das Jahr 1989 (mit einem Nachtrag für 1988)*. Sprachwissenschaftliche Informationen 14. Berlin: Akademie der Wissenschaften der DDR, Zentralinstitut für Sprachwissenschaft.

Jirkov, Lev Ivanovič. 1931. *Kial venkis Esperanto?* Leipzig: EKRELO.

Kalocsay, Kálmán; Waringhien, Gaston. 1932. *Kiel fariĝi poeto aŭ Parnasa gvidlibro*. Budapest: Literatura Mondo.

Kalocsay, Kálmán; Waringhien, Gaston; Bernard, Roger. 1968. *Parnasa gvidlibro.* (2nd revised and expanded edition of Kalocsay & Waringhien 1932. 3rd edition, Pisa: Edistudio, 1982).

Kalocsay, Kálmán; Waringhien, Gaston. 1985. *Plena analiza gramatiko de Esperanto.* 5th revised edition. Rotterdam: Universala Esperanto-Asocio.

Kennedy, Hubert C. 1980. *Peano. Life and Works of Giuseppe Peano.* Dordrecht-Boston-London: D. Reidel.

Kiselman, Christer; Mattos, Geraldo, eds. 2001. *Lingva planado kaj leksikologio. Kontribuaĵoj al internacia simpozio, Zagrebo 2001 07 28-30. Language Planning and Lexicology. Proceedings of an international symposium.* Chapecó, Brasilia-DF: Fonto.

Klare, Johannes. 2012. André Martinet (1908-1999): An outstanding linguist and interlinguist of the twentieth century. *Language Problems & Language Planning* 36/3: 273-293.

Klaus, Georg. 1972. *Semiotik und Erkenntnistheorie.* Berlin: Deutscher Verlag der Wissenschaften.

Knöschke, Linde; Kolbe, Ino 1997. *Der Esperantist 1(1965)-164(1990). Register Teil I.* Berlin: Gesellschaft für Interlinguistik e.V.

Knowlson, James R. 1975. *Universal Language Schemes in England and France 1600-1800.* Toronto-Buffalo: University of Toronto Press.

Kökény, Lajos; Bleier, Vilmos, eds. 1933-34/1979. *Enciklopedio de Esperanto.* 2 vols. Budapest: Literatura Mondo. (2nd edition 1979, 1 vol. Budapest: Hungara Esperanto-Asocio.)

Kolbe, Ino. 1996. *Zur Geschichte des Deutschen Arbeiter-Esperanto-Bundes in Leipzig (Westsachsen), Teil I und II. Von den Anfängen bis zum Verbot (1933).* Eine kommentierte Dokumentation. Ed. with commentary Detlev Blanke. Leipzig: Landesverband Sachsen im Deutschen Esperanto-Bund e.V.

Kolbe, Ino. 1998. *Der Esperantist 1(1965)-164(1990). Register Teil II.* Berlin: Arbeitsgruppe Geschichte des Esperanto-Verbandes der DDR.

Kolker, Boris. 1978. Lev Tolstoj kaj la internacia lingvo. *Esperanto* (Rotterdam) 71: 172-175.

Korĵenkov, Aleksandr. 2011. *Homarano. La vivo, verkoj kaj ideoj de d-ro L.L. Zamenhof.* 2nd revised and extended edition, Kaliningrad: Sezonoj / Kaunas: Litova Esperanto-Asocio. (1st edition 2009).

Korzhenkov, Aleksander. 2010. *The Life of Zamenhof.* Trans. Ian M. Richmond, ed. Humphrey Tonkin. New York: Mondial. 99pp.

Košecký, Stanislav, ed. 1987. *Problémy interlingvistiky. Zborník materiálov z interlingvistického seminára (Vysoké Tatry 20.-22. mája 1987).* Bratislava: Jazykovedný ústav L. Štúra SAV; Slovenský esperantský sväz; Český esperantský svaz.

Košecký, Stanislav, ed. 1990. *Problémy interlingvistiky II.* Bratislava: Jazykovedný ústav L. Štúra SAV; Slovenský esperantský sväz.

Koutny, Ilona. 2001. Speech processing and Esperanto. In: Schubert, Klaus, ed. *Planned Languages: From Concept to Reality.* Brussel: Hogeschool voor Wetenschap en Kunst, pp. 99-120.

Koutny, Ilona, ed. 2009. *Abunda fonto. Memorlibro omaĝe al prof. István Szerdahelyi.* Poznań: ProDruk & Steleto.

Koutny, Ilona; Kovács, Márta, eds. 1997. *Struktura kaj socilingvistika esploro de Esperanto. Memore al profesoro István Szerdahelyi.* Budapest: Steleto & Internacia Ligo de Esperantistaj Instruistoj.

Kováts, Katalin, ed. 2009. *Manlibro pri instruado de Esperanto.* 3rd edition. Den Haag: Internacia Ligo de Esperantistaj Instruistoj.

Krause, Erich-Dieter. 1999. *Großes Wörterbuch Esperanto-Deutsch.* Hamburg: Buske.

Krause, Erich-Dieter. 2007. *Großes Wörterbuch Deutsch-Esperanto.* Hamburg: Buske.

Künzli, Andreas. 2006. *Universalaj Lingvoj en Svislando. Svisa Enciklopedio Planlingva. Schweizer Plansprachen-Lexikon. Encyclopédie suisse des langues planifiées. Enciclopedia svizzera delle lingue pianificate (Volapük, Esperanto, Ido, Occidental-Interlingue, Interlingua).* La Chaux-de-Fonds: Svisa Esperanto-Societo & CDELI (Centre de documentation et d'étude sur la langue internationale), Bibliothèque de la Ville de La Chaux-de-Fonds.

Künzli, Andreas. 2010. *L.L. Zamenhof (1859-1917). Esperanto, Hillelismus (Homaranismus) und die 'jüdische Frage' in Ost- und Westeuropa*. Wiesbaden: Harrassowitz.

Kürschner, Wilfried, ed. 1994. *Linguistenhandbuch. Biographische und bibliographische Daten deutschsprachiger Sprachwissenschaftlerinnen und Sprachwissenschaftler der Gegenwart*. 2 vols. Tübingen: Narr.

Kuznecov, Sergej Nikolaevič. 1976. K voprosu o typologičeskoj klassifikacii meždunarodnych iskusstvennych jazykov (On a typological classification of international artificial languages). In: Isaev, Magomet Ismailovič, ed. *Problemy interlingvistiki. Tipologija i evoljucija meždunarodnych iskusstvennych jazykov* (Problems of interlinguistics). Moscow: Nauka, pp. 60-78.

Kuznecov, Sergej Nikolaevič. 1982a. *Osnovnye ponjatja i terminy interlingoistiki*. Moskva: Universitet Patrice Lumumba.

Kuznecov, Sergej Nikolaevič. 1982b. *Osnovy interlingvistiki*. Moscow: Izd. Univ. Družby narodov.

Kuznecov, Sergej Nikolaevič. 1982c. *Osnonvye ponjatija i terminy interlingvistiki*. Moscow: Izd. Univ. Družby narodov.

Kuznecov, Sergej Nikolaevič. 1984. *Napravlenija sovremennoj interlingvistiki*. Moscow: Izd. Univ. Družby narodov.

Kuznecov, Sergej Nikolaevič. 1987. *Teoretičeskie osnovy interlingvistiki*. Moscow: Izd. Univ. Družby narodov.

Kuznecov, Sergej Nikolaevič. 1991. Drezen, lia verko, lia epoko. In: Drezen, Ernest K. (1931/1991): *Historio de la Mondolingvo*. 4th Esperanto edition, ed. Sergej N. Kuznecov. Moskva: Progreso, pp. 3-40. (2nd Esperanto edition, Leipzig: EKRELO, 1931.)

Lang, Anneliese; Lang, Friedrich H.; Reiter, Rosa. 1979. Bibliographie der Arbeiten Wüsters auf den Gebieten der Terminologie, Dokumentation, Klassifikation, Normung und Sprachwissenschaft. In: Felber, Helmut; Lang, Friedrich; Wersig, Gernot, eds. 1979. *Terminologie als angewandte Sprachwissenschaft. Gedenkschrift für Univ.-Prof. Dr. Eugen Wüster*. München: Saur, pp. 29-57.

Lapenna, Ivo; Lins, Ulrich; Carlevaro, Tazio. 1974. *Esperanto en perspektivo. Faktoj kaj analizoj pri la Internacia Lingvo* (Esperanto in perspective. Facts and analyses concerning the International Language). London-Rotterdam: Universala Esperanto-Asocio.

Large, Andrew. 1985. *The Artificial Language Movement*. Oxford, New York: Basil Blackwell / London: André Deutsch.

Le Hir, Jean-Louis. 1867. *Langue auxilaire universelle*. S. Pol de Léon.

Libert, Alan. 2000. *A Priori Artificial Languages*. München: Lincom Europa.

Libert, Alan. 2003. *Mixed Artificial Languages*. München: Lincom Europa.

Lindstedt, Jouko. 1981. Science studi planlingvojn: Komencaj notoj. *Planlingvistiko* 1: 2-3.

Lins, Ulrich. 1988a. *Die gefährliche Sprache. Die Verfolgung der Esperantisten unter Hitler und Stalin*. Gerlingen: Bleicher.

Lins, Ulrich. 1988b. *La dangera lingvo. Studo pri la persekutoj kontraŭ Esperanto*. Gerlingen: Bleicher. (2nd edition 1990, Moscow: Progreso. 3rd revised edition: see Lins 2016. Translated editions also in English [Lins 2016/2017], German, Italian, Korean, Russian, Lithuanian, Japanese.)

Lins, Ulrich. 1995. Die Hodler-Bibliothek in Rotterdam. *Interlinguistische Informationen* 4/5-6 (17-18): 8-11.

Lins, Ulrich. 1998. Das Esperanto-Archiv im Fritz-Hüser-Institut. *Mitteilungen des Förderkreises Archive und Bibliotheken zur Geschichte der Arbeiterbewegung* 13 (March): 2-4.

Lins, Ulrich. 2008. Esperanto as language and idea in China and Japan. *Language Problems and Language Planning* 32/1: 47-60.

Lins, Ulrich. 2016. *La dangera lingvo. Studo pri la persekutoj kontraŭ Esperanto*. Revised edition. Rotterdam: Universala Esperanto-Asocio.

Lins, Ulrich. 2016/2017. *Dangerous Language*. Vol I: *Esperanto Under Hitler and Stalin*. Vol. II: *Esperanto and the Decline of Stalinism*. Trans. Humphrey Tonkin. London: Palgrave Macmillan.

Lipari, Michela, ed. 1999. *IKU. Internacia Kongresa Universitato. Berlino 31 julio – 7 aŭgusto 1999.* Rotterdam: Universala Esperanto-Asocio.

Lipari, Michela, ed. 2000. *IKU. Internacia Kongresa Universitato. Tel Avivo 26 julio-1 aŭgusto 2000.* Rotterdam: Universala Esperanto-Asocio.

Lipari, Michela, ed. 2001. *IKU. Internacia Kongresa Universitato. Zagrebo 21-28 julio 2001.* Rotterdam: Universala Esperanto-Asocio.

Lipari, Michela, ed. 2003. *IKU. Internacia Kongresa Universitato. Gotenburgo 26 de julio-2 aŭgusto 2003.* Rotterdam: Universala Esperanto-Asocio.

Lipari, Michela, ed. 2004. *IKU. Internacia Kongresa Universitato. Pekino, 24-31 julio 2004.* Rotterdam: Universala Esperanto-Asocio.

Liptay, Albert. 1892. *Langue catholique. Projet d'un idiome internationale sans construction grammaticale.* Paris: Bouillon. (Reprinted Hildesheim: G. Olms 1979.)

Liu, Haitao. 2001. Informadika aspekto de interlingvistiko. In: Fiedler, Sabine; Liu, Haitao, eds. *Studoj pri Interlingvistiko. Studien zur Interlinguistik. Festschrift für Detlev Blanke zum 60. Geburtstag. Festlibro omaĝe al la 60-jariĝo de Detlev Blanke.* Dobřichovice/Praha: KAVA-PECH, pp. 147-171.

Ljudskanov, Alexander. 1975. *Mensch und Maschine als Übersetzer.* Halle: Niemeyer.

Lo Bianco, Joseph. 2004. Invented languages and new worlds. *English Today* 20/2:8-18.

Lo Jacomo, François. 1981. *Liberté ou autorité dans l'évolution de l'espéranto.* Doctoral diss. University of Paris (Sorbonne). Pisa: The Author.

Lloancy, Marie-Thérèse. 1985. *Esperanto et jeu de mots dans l'œuvre de Raymond Schwartz (1894-1973).* Doctoral diss. Paris: Université René Descartes, U.E.R. de Linguistique Générale et Appliquée.

Lobin, Günter. 2002. *Ein Sprachmodell für den Fremdsprachenunterricht. Der propädeutische Wert einer Plansprache in der Fremdsprachenpädagogik.* Doctoral diss. Aachen: Shaker.

Lott, Julius. 1888. *Ist Volapük die beste und einfachste Lösung der Weltsprachenprobleme?*. Wien: The Author.

Maat, Jaap. 1999. *Philosophical Languages in the Seventeenth Century: Dalgarno, Wilkins, Leibniz*. Amsterdam: University of Amsterdam, Institute for Logic, Language and Computation.

Maimieux, Joseph de. 1797a. *Pasigraphie, ou premiers éléments du nouvel art-science d'écrire et d'imprimer en une langue de manière à être lu et entendu dans toute autre langue sans traduction*. Paris: Bureau de Pasigraphie.

Maimieux, Joseph de [Pseudonym: J. von Morath]. 1797b. *Pasigraphie. Anfangsgründe der neuen Kunst-wissenschaft in einer Sprache alles so zu schreiben und zu drucken, dass es in jeder anderen ohne Übersetzung gelesen und verstanden werden kann*. Paris-Altona: Bureau de Pasigraphie.

Maitzen, Hans Michael; Mayer, Herbert; Tišljar, Zlatko, eds. 1994. *Aktoj de Internacia Scienca Simpozio Esperanto 100-jara. Universitato de Vieno, 28-30.10.1987*. Vienna: Pro Esperanto / Maribor: Interkulturo.

Malovec, Miroslav, ed. 1999. *Modernaj rimedoj de komunikado (Aplikoj de Esperanto en scienco kaj tekniko)*. Dobřichovice/Praha: KAVA-PECH.

Manders, W[ilhelmus] J[ohannes] A[rnoldus]. 1947. *Vijf kunsttalen. Vergelijkend onderzoek naar de waarde van het Volapük, Esperanto, Ido, Occidental en Novial*. Doctoral diss. Purmerend: Muusses.

Manders, W[ilhelmus] J[ohannes] A[rnoldus]. 1950. *Interlingvistiko kaj esperantologio*. Purmerend: Muusses. (Partial German translation [of pp. 12-19] in Haupenthal, Reinhard, ed. 1976. *Plansprachen. Beiträge zur Interlinguistik*. Darmstadt: Wiss. Buchgesellschaft, pp. 234-242; reprinted 1980, Saarbrücken: Iltis.)

Manders, W[ilhelmus] J[ohannes] A[rnoldus]. 1953-1954. Review of J. Nordano, *Une langue se construit*, Helsinki, 1951. *Synthèse* 9: 123-124.

Mangold, Max. 1979. Das Esperanto-Lautsystem in Afrika. In: Felber, Helmut; Lang, Friedrich; Wersig, Gernot, eds. *Terminologie als angewandte Sprachwissenschaft. Gedenkschrift für Univ.-Prof. Dr. Eugen Wüster*. München: Saur, pp. 247-256.

Mannewitz, Cornelia. 1997. Zur Rolle von Kunstsprachen in Gesellschaftsutopien. In: Ulrich Becker, ed. *Terminologiewissenschaftliche Aspekte der Interlinguistik*. Beiträge gehalten auf der 6. Jahrestagung der Gesellschaft für Interlinguistik e.V., 15.-17. November 1996 in Berlin. *Interlinguistische Informationen*. Beiheft 2. Berlin: Gesellschaft für Interlinguistik, pp. 35-43.

Maradan, Mélanie. 2010. *Terminologie des Doppler-Effekts (Deutsch-Englisch-Spanisch, Esperanto-Französisch)*. Master's thesis. Genève: Université de Genève, École de traduction et d'interprétation.

Marr, Nikolaj Ja. 1928. K voprosu ob edinom jazyke (On the question of a unified language). In: Drezen, Ernest K. *Za vseobscim jazykom. Tri veka iskanij*. Moskva-Leningrad: Gosudarstvennoe izdatel'stvo, pp. 3-9.

Martinet, André. 1946. La linguistique et les langues artificielles. *Word* 2: 37-47.

Martinet, André. 1991. Sur quelques questions d'interlinguistique. Une interview de François Lo Jacomo et Detlev Blanke. *Zeitschrift für Phonetik, Sprachwissenschaft und Kommunikationsforschung* 44/6: 675-687.

Máthé, Árpád. 1993. Bibliografio de planlingvaj periodaĵoj. *Periodaĵoj. Bibliografia organo de Rondo Takács*, Budapest. 1 (julio): 2.

Mattos, Geraldo, ed. 1987. *Centjara Esperanto*. Chapéco: Fonto,

Mattusch, Max Hans-Jürgen. 1999. *Vielsprachigkeit: Fluch oder Segen für die Menschheit? Zu Fragen einer europäischen und globalen Fremdsprachenpolitik*. Frankfurt/Main: Peter Lang.

Mayrhofer, Manfred; Dressler, Wolfgang. 1969. Zur Problematik künstlicher Welthilfssprachen (Plansprachen). *Anzeiger der phil.-hist. Klasse der Österreichischen Akademie d. Wissenschaften* 106: 263–274.

McCoy, Roy, ed. 2002. *IKU. Internacia Kongresa Universitato. Fortalezo, Brazilo. 3-10 aŭgusto 2002*. Rotterdam: Universala Esperanto-Asocio.

Mel'nikov, Alexandr S. 1990. *Principy postroenija i funkcional'nogo razvitija planogo meždunardonogo jazyka v sovremennoj interlingvistika*. Doctoral diss. Tartu/Minsk.

Mel'nikov, Alexandr S. 1992. *Specifaj kulturaj scioj de la esperantista kvazaŭetno kaj ilia respeguliĝo en la koncerna lingvajo*. Rostov-na-Donu: The author.

Mel'nikov, Alexandr S. 2004. *Lingvokul'turologičeskie aspekty planovych meždunarodnych jazykov (na fone etničeskich jazykov)*. Rostov-na-Donu: Izdatel'stvo Rostovskogo gosudarstvennogo pedagogičeskogo universiteta.

Mel'nikov, Alexandr S. 2008. *Vortludoj kaj luda komunikado*. San-Marino: AIS / Moskvo: Eŭropa Universitato Justo.

Mel'nikov, Alexandr S. (Melnikov, Aleksandro S.). 2015. *Gvidlibro tra Esperantio: Konciza leksikono de la Esperanto-kulturo*. Rostov-na-Donu: The author.

Menade. 1998. *Menade bal, püki bal. Festschrift zum 50. Geburtstag von Reinhard Haupenthal*. Saarbrücken: Iltis.

Meyer, Anna-Maria. 2014. *Wiederbelebung einer Utopie. Probleme und Perspektiven slavischer Plansprachen im Zeitalter des Internets*. Bamberger Beiträge zur Linguistik 6. Bamberg: University of Bamberg Press.

Meyer, Anna-Maria. 2016. Slavic constructed languages in the internet age. *Language Problems & Language Planning* 40/3: 287-315.

Meyer, Richard Moritz. 1901. Künstliche Sprachen. *Indogermanische Forschungen* 12: 33–92, 242–318.

Minnaja, Carlo, ed. 2001. *Eseoj memore al Ivo Lapenna*. Copenhagen: T. Kehlet.

Minnaja, Carlo, ed. & trans. 2009. *Le grandi personalità dell'UNESCO: Lazaro Ludoviko Zamenhof. Antologia*. Milano: Federazione Esperantista Italiana.

Minnaja, Carlo; Silfer, Giorgio. 2015. *Historio de la esperanta literaturo*. La Chaux-de-Fonds, Switzerland: Literatura Foiro.

Mistrík, Jozef. 1985. *Basic Slovak*. Bratislava: Slovenské Pedagogické Nakladateľstvo.

MLA. *International Bibliography of Books and Articles on the Modern Languages and Literatures*, New York: The Modern Language Association of America. Database available online.

MNL. 1973. *Meyers Neue Lexikon*. 2nd edition. Vol. 6. Leipzig: Bibliographisches Institut.

Molee, Elias. 1902. *Tutonish or Anglo-German Union Tongue*. Chicago: Scroll.

Monnerot-Dumaine, Marcel. 1960. *Précis d'interlinguistique générale et speciale*. Paris: Librairie Maloine.

Motsch, Wolfgang. 1974. *Zur Kritik der sprachwissenschaftlichen Strukturalismus*. Berlin: Akademie Verlag.

Müller, Kurt. E., ed. 1992. *Language as Barrier and Bridge*. Lanham, New York, London: University Press of America.

Nedobity, Wolfgang. 1982. Key to international terminology. In: Nedobity, Wolfgang, ed. *Terminologies for the Eighties. With a special section: 10 years of Infoterm*. Infoterm Series 7. München: Saur, pp. 306-313.

Neergaard Paul. 1942/1979. La esperantologio kaj ties disciplinoj. Taskoj kaj rezultoj. In: *Tra densa mallumo*, Copenhagen, pp. 37-64. (Reprint: Saarbrücken: Sarlanda Esperanto-Ligo, 1979.)

Neergaard, Paul; Kiselman, Christer, eds. 1992. *Aktoj de Internacia Scienca Akademio Comenius*. Vol. I. Pekino: Ĉina Esperanto-Ligo.

Nevelsteen, Yves. 2012. *Komputiko. Prikomputila terminokolekto*. 2nd edition. Partizánske, Slovakia: Espero.

Noltenius, Rainer, ed. 1993. *Den Arbeitern aller Länder eine Sprache! Illustrierte Geschichte der Arbeiter-Esperanto-Bewegung. Al la laboristoj en ĉiuj landoj unu lingvon! Ilustrita historio de la Laborista Esperanto-Movado*. Informationen 37/93. Katalog zur Ausstellung des Fritz Hüser-Instituts Dortmund. Dortmund: Fritz-Hüser-Institut für deutsche und ausländische Arbeiter-Literatur.

Nosková, Katarína; Baláž, Peter, eds. 2011. *Modernaj teknologioj por Esperanto*. KAEST 2010. Partizánske, Slovakia: Espero.

Nosková, Katarína; Baláž, Peter, eds. 2013. *Modernaj edukaj metodoj kaj teknologioj*. KAEST 2012. Partizánske, Slovakia: Espero.

Nuessel, Frank. 2000. *The Esperanto Language*. New York-Ottawa-Toronto: Legas.

Ockey, Edward. 1982. *A Bibliography of Esperanto Dictionaries. Bibliografio de Vortaroj*. Banstead, England: The Author. (2nd edition, *Bibliografio de vortaroj kaj terminaroj en Esperanto 1887-2002*, revised by Geoffrey Sutton. Rotterdam: Universala Esperanto-Asocio, 2002.)

Oeser, Erhard; Galinski, Christian, eds. 1998. *Eugen Wüster (1898-1977). Leben und Werk – Ein österreichischer Pionier der Informationsgesellschaft. His Life and Work – An Austrian Pioneer of the Information Society*. Wien: TermNet/Infoterm.

Ogden, Charles Kay. 1931. *Basic English. A General Introduction with Rules of Grammar*. London: Routledge.

Ogden, Charles Kay. 1968. *Basic English. International Second Language*. New York: Orthological Institute.

Okrent, Arika. 2009. *In the Land of Invented Languages*, New York: Spiegel & Grau.

Ölberg, Hermann. 1954. Zur Grundlegung der Interlinguistik. *Innsbrucker Beiträge zur Kulturwissenschaft* 2/2: 64-70.

Ó Riain, Seán. 2003. The German interlinguistics society Gesellschaft für Interlinguistik e.V (GIL). *Language Problems & Language Planning* 27/3: 269-277.

Papaloïzos, Lilli. 1992. *Ethnographie de la communication dans un milieu social exolingue. Le Centre Culturel Espérantiste de La Chaux-de-Fonds (Suisse)*. Doctoral diss. Bern: Peter Lang.

Pabst, Bernhard. 2003. EBEA: Retrobibliographierung nicht monographischer Literatur zum Esperanto. In: Blanke, Detlev, ed. *Plansprachen und elektronische Medien. Beiträge der 12. Jahrestagung der Gesellschaft für Interlinguistik. 6.-8. Dezember 2002 in Berlin*, pp.64-76.

Pataki-Czeller, Mária. 1991. *Katalogo de la Esperanto-kolektajo de Károly Fajszi Budapest. Libroj. Parto I.* Budapest: Országos Idegennyelvü Könyvtár.

Paul, Hermann. 1937. *Prinzipien der Sprachgeschichte.* 5th edition. Halle: Niemeyer.

Peano, Giuseppe. 1903. De Latino sine flexione, lingua ausiliare internazionale. *Revue de mathématique* 8/3: 71.

Peano, Giuseppe. 1915. *Vocabulario Commune ad Latino-ltaliano-Français-English-Deutsch. Pro usu de interlinguistas* (Common vocabulary for Latin-Italian-French-English-German. For the use of interlinguists). Torino: Cavoretto.

Pei, Mario. 1958/1968. *One Language for the World, and How to Achieve It.* New York: Devin-Adair. (Reprint: New York: Biblio & Tannen 1968.)

Perrenoud, William, ed. 2002. *IALA: Conférence de recherches linguistiques / Meeting of Linguistic Research – Procès-verbaux, Genève, 20 mars-2 avril 1930.* With introduction and bibliography by Reinhard Haupenthal. Schliengen: Iltis.

Philippe, Benoît. 1991. *Sprachwandel bei einer Plansprache am Beispiel des Esperanto.* Doctoral diss. Konstanz: Hartung-Gorre.

Phillipson, Robert. 1992. *Linguistic Imperialism.* Oxford: Oxford University Press.

Phillipson, Robert. 2003. *English-Only Europe?* London-New York: Routledge. (*IntI* 46, *IpI* 45; Esperanto edition: *Nur-angla Eŭropo?* Trans. István Ertl, Rotterdam: Universala Esperanto-Asocio, 2004.)

Phillipson, Robert. 2009. *Linguistic Imperialism Continued.* New York-London: Routledge.

Pigal, Engelbert, ed. 1930. *Occidental. Die Weltsprache.* 3rd edition. Stuttgart: Franckh'sche Verlagsbuchhandlung.

Pinter, Ana-Maria, ed. 1999. *Kybernetische Pädagogik. Klerigkibernetiko. Einführende, weiterführende und wertende Schriften.* Introductory, intermediate and evaluative texts by Helmar G. Frank. Dobřichovice/ Praha: KAVA-PECH / München: KoPäd. (Includes list of publications of Helmar Frank.)

Piron, Claude. 1994. *Le défi des langues: Du gâchis au bon sens.* Paris: L' Harmattan.

Pirro, Jean. 1868. *Universal Language-Universalsprache.* Paris: Retaux.

Plehn, Hans-Joachim. 1985. *Biografio de duona vortaro aŭ – Kial Esperantujo perdis sian gvidantan Esperantologon.* Saarbrücken: Iltis.

Pluhař, Zdeněk. 1999. Iom da historio de AEST. In: Malovec, Miroslav, ed. *Modernaj rimedoj de komunikado.* Aplikoj de Esperanto en scienco kaj tekniko. Dobřichovice/Praha: KAVA-PECH, pp. 9-13.

Pluhař, Zdeněk, ed. 2001. *Fakaj aplikoj de Esperanto.* Aplikoj de Esperanto en scienco kaj tekniko 2. Dobřichovice/Praha: KAVA-PECH.

Pluhař, Zdeněk, ed. 2003. *Fakaj studoj en Esperanto.* Aplikoj de Esperanto en scienco kaj tekniko 3. Dobřichovice/Praha: KAVA-PECH.

Pluhař, Zdeněk, ed. 2005. *Fake pri Esperanto kaj Esperante pri sciencoj.* Aplikoj de Esperanto en scienco kaj tekniko 4. Dobřichovice/Praha: KAVA-PECH.

Pluhař, Zdeněk, ed. 2007. *Lingvo kaj Interreto kaj aliaj studoj.* Aplikoj de Esperanto en scienco kaj tekniko 5. Dobřichovice/Praha: KAVA-PECH.

Pluhař, Zdeněk, ed. 2009. *Esperanto – instrumento de fakuloj.* Aplikoj de Esperanto en scienco kaj tekniko 6. Dobřichovice/Praha: KAVA-PECH.

Pokrovskij, Sergio. 1995. *Komputika leksikono.* Jekaterinburg: Sezonoj.

Pompiati, Karl. 1918. *Die neue Weltsprache: Nov Latin Logui.* Wien: Private edition.

Privat, Edmond. 2007. *Vivo de Zamenof.* 6th edition, ed. Ulrich Lins. Rotterdam: Universala Esperanto-Asocio.

Rakuša, Rudolf. 1971. *Metodiko de la Esperanto-instruado.* 2nd edition. Ljubljana: Mladinska Knjiga.

Raporto 2013. *Raporto pri Publika Prelegkunveno de la 100-a Japana Esperanto-Kongreso.* Tokyo: Japana Esperanto-Instituto. (In Japanese and Esperanto.)

Rašić, Nikola. 1994. *La rondo familia. Sociologiaj esploroj en Esperantio.* Pisa: Edistudio.

Rátkaj, Árpád. 1978. Socialismaj teorioj kaj la internacia laborista asocio pri la universala lingvo. In: Blanke, Detlev, ed. *Socipolitikaj aspektoj de la Esperanto-movado.* Budapest: Hungara Esperanto-Asocio, pp. 13-30.

Rátkaj, Árpád. 1980. Sistemo de la transnacia lingvouzo. In Szerdahelyi, István, ed. *Miscellanea interlinguistica.* Budapest: Tankönykiadó, pp. 197-204.

Régulo Pérez, Juan. 1992. *Rikolto.* Ed. Reinhard Haupenthal & Gaston Waringhien. Chapecó (SC), Brazil: Fonto.

Roget, Peter Mark; Browning, D.C. 1966. *Everyman's Thesaurus of English Words and Phrases.* London: Dent / New York: Dutton.

Rollet de l' Isle, Maurice. 1911. *Konsilaro por la farado de la sciencaj kaj teknikaj vortoj.* Kötzschenbroda-Dresden: H.F. Adolf Thalwitzer.

Romančik, Romaš Ėrlend. 2006. *Ordinaryj Professor Aleksandr Dimitrievič Duličenko: bibliografia.* Tartu: Universitas Tartuensis.

Rónai, Paulo. 1969. *Der Kampf gegen Babel oder das Abenteuer der Universalsprachen.* München: Ehrenwirth. (Translation of Ronai 1967.)

Rondo Takács. 1992. *Inventaro de planlingvistikaj periodajoj.* Sant Pau d'Ordal: Hispana Esperanto-Muzeo.

Rosenberger, Woldemar. 1902. *Wörterbuch der Neutralsprache (Idiom neutral) Neutral-Deutsch und Deutsch-Neutral.* Leipzig: Haberland.

Sack, Friedrich L. 1951. *The Problem of an International Language.* Washington-Edinburgh: World Organisation of the Teaching Profession.

Sadler, Victor. 1991. Machine translation project reaches watershed. *Language Problems & Language Planning* 15/1: 78-83.

Sakaguchi, Alicja. 1998. *Interlinguistik. Gegenstand, Ziele, Aufgaben, Methoden.* Frankurt/M.: Peter Lang.

Salzmann, Oswald. 1915. *Das vereinfachte Deutsch. Die Sprache aller Völker.* Leipzig: Salzmann.

Samarin, William J. 1970. Lingua francas of the world. In: Fishman, Joshua Aaron, ed. *Readings in the Sociology of Language.* The Hague: Mouton, pp. 660-672.

Sandelin, Bo. 2001. The de-Germanization of Swedish economics. *History of Political Economy* 33/3: 517-539.

Sapir, Edward. 1931. The function of an international auxiliary language. *Psyche* 11, 4-15.

Saussure, Ferdinand de. 1967. *Grundfragen der allgemeinen Sprachwissenschaft.* Hrsg. von Charles Bally und Albert Sechehaye. Übers. v. Hermann Lommel. 2. Aufl. Berlin: de Gruyter.

Saussure, René de. 1910a. *La construction logique des mots en Espéranto. Réponse à des critiques.* Geneva: Kündig.

Saussure, René de. 1910b. *La logika bazo de vortfarado en Esperanto de Antido.* Propono al la Akademio Esperantista okaze de la Sesa Universala Kongreso de Esperanto en Washington 1910. Genf: Universala Esperantista Librejo.

Schremser-Seipelt, Ulrike. 1990. *Das Projekt Internationaler Terminologieschlüssel von Eugen Wüster.* Doctoral diss. Universität Wien. Geisteswissenschaftliche Fakultät.

Schippan, Thea. 1984. *Lexikologie der deutschen Gegenwartssprache.* Leipzig: Enzyklopädie-Verlag.

Schleicher, August. 1873. *Die Darwinsche Theorie und die Sprachwissenschaft.* 2nd edition. Weimar: Böhlau.

Schleyer, Johann Martin. 1881. *Grammatik der Universalsprache für alle gebildeten Erdbewohner.* Konstanz: Feyel.

Schleyer, Johann Martin. 1982. *Volapük. Die Weltsprache. Entwurf einer Universalsprache für alle Gebildete der ganzen Erde.* Hildesheim/New York: Olms. (Reprint of 1st edition 1880.)

Schmidt, Johann. 1981. *Erste vollstandige Zeitschriftenliste des Volapük und Literatur-Liste des Volapük*. Saarbrücken: Edition Iltis.

Schmidt, Johann. 1986. *Geschichte der Universalsprache Volapük*. Saarbrücken: Edition Iltis.

Schmidt, Johann. 2005. *Liste der Volapük-Verbände und Vereine*. Saarbrücken: Edition Iltis.

Schmitt, Alfred. 1936. Review: Eugen Wüster, *Enzyklopädisches Wörterbuch Esperanto-Deutsch*. *Indogermanische Forschungen* 54: 294-295.

Schneider, Wolf. 1979. *Wörter machen Leute*. Reinbeck: Rowohlt.

Schor, Esther. 2015. *Bridge of Words: Esperanto and the Dream of a Universal Language*. New York: Metropolitan Books/Henry Holt.

Schremser-Seipelt, Ulrike. 1990. Das Projekt internationaler Terminologie-Schlüssel von Eugen Wüster. Diss. University of Vienna.

Schubert, Klaus. 1988. Ausdruckskraft und Regelmäßigkeit: Was Esperanto für automatische Übersetzungen geeignet macht. *Language Problems & Language Planning* 12/2: 130-147.

Schubert, Klaus, ed. 1989a. *Interlinguistics. Aspects of the Science of Planned Languages*. Trends in Linguistics. Studies and Monographs 42. With Dan Maxwell. Berlin-New York: Mouton de Gruyter.

Schubert, Klaus. 1989b. Interlinguistics – Its aims, its achievements, and its place in language science. In: Schubert, Klaus, ed. *Interlinguistics. Aspects of the Science of Planned Languages*. Trends in Linguistics. Studies and Monographs 42. With Dan Maxwell. Berlin-New York: Mouton de Gruyter, pp. 7-44.

Schubert, Klaus. 1992. Esperanto as an intermediate language for machine translation. In: Newton, John, ed. *Computers in Translation. A Practical Appraisal*. London-New York: Routledge, pp. 78-95.

Schubert, Klaus. 1993. Semantic composity: Esperanto word formation for language technology. *Linguistics* 31: 311-365.

Schubert, Klaus. 1996. Zum gegenwärtigen Stand der maschinellen Übersetzung. In: Becker, Ulrich, ed. *Translation in Plansprachen*. Beiträge gehalten auf der 5. Jahrestagung der Gesellschaft für Interlinguistik, November 1995, in Berlin. Beiheft 1. Berlin: Gesellschaft für Interlinguistik e.V., pp. 14-33.

Schubert, Klaus. 1999. DLT: Resuma raporto. *Informilo por Interlingvistoj* 8 (28): 1-3.

Schubert, Klaus, ed. 2001. *Planned Languages: From Concept to Reality*. Interface. Brussels: Hogeschool voor Wetenschap en Kunst.

Schubert, Klaus. 2011. Zum bewussten Eingreifen in die Sprache. In: Brosch, Cyril; Fiedler, Sabine, eds. *Florilegium Interlinguisticum. Festschrift für Detlev Blanke zum 70. Geburtstag*. Frankfurt/Main: Peter Lang, pp. 47-60.

Schubert, Klaus. 2015. Word-formation and planned languages. In: Müller, Peter O.; Ohnheiser, Ingeborg; Olsen, Susan; Rainer, Franz, eds. *Word-Formation. An International Handbook of the Languages of Europe*. Teilbd. 3. Handbücher zur Sprach- und Kommunikations-wissenschaft 40.3. Berlin-Boston: De Gruyter Mouton, pp. 2210-2225.

Schuchardt, Hugo. 1888. *Auf Anlass des Volapük*. Berlin: Oppenheim.

Schweder, Sandra. 1999. *Entwicklung und Akzeptanz technischer Terminologien in der Plansprache Esperanto*. M.A. Thesis. Hildesheim: Universität Hildesheim, Fachbereich III – Sprachen und Technik, Institut für Angewandte Sprachwissenschaft.

Selinker, Larry. 1972. Interlangue. *International Review of Applied Linguistics in Language Teaching (IRAL)* 10: 209-231.

Serta. 1987. *Serta gratulatoria in honorem Juan Régulo*. Vol. 2: *Esperantismo*. La Laguna: Universidad de la Laguna.

Sexton, Brian C. 1993. *Kio estas Interlingua?* Sheffield: British Interlingua Society.

Sikosek, Ziko Marcus. 2003. *Esperanto sen mitoj*. 2nd revised edition. Antverpeno: Flandra Esperanto-Ligo.

Silagi, Denis. 1996. Der Name Interlingua. *Interlinguistische Informationen* 5/2 (20): 6-10.

Skutnabb-Kangas, Tove. 2000. *Linguistic Genocide in Education – or Worldwide Diversity and Human Rights?* Mahwah, New Jersey: Erlbaum.

Slaughter, Mary M. 1982. *Universal Languages and Scientific Taxonomy in the Seventeeth Century.* Cambridge: Cambridge University Press.

Smith, Karin; Haake, Susan. 1978. *Catalog of the George Alan Connor Esperanto Collection.* Oregon: University of Oregon Library, Special Collections Division.

Spitzhardt, Harry. 1973. Zur Frage der Sprachplanung in den jungen Nationalstaaten. *Zeitschrift für Phonetik, Sprachwissenschaft und Kommunikationsforschung* (ZPSK, Berlin) 26: 533-554.

Stalin, Josef W. 1951. *Der Marxismus und die Fragen der Sprachwissenschaft.* Berlin: Dietz.

Starrenburg, Diego. 1922. *Grammatica di la mundolingua 'Menimo'.* Valencia: Barranco.

Steiner, Hugo. 1957. *Katalogo pri la kolektoj de Internacia Esperanto-Muzeo en Wien. Parto I. Sistema katalogo pri la Esperanto-presaĵoj laŭ la Internacia Dekuma Klasifiko.* Wien: Internacia Esperanto-Muzeo/Österreichische Nationalbibliothek.

Steiner, Hugo. 1958. *Katalogo pri la kolektoj de Internacia Esperanto-Muzeo en Wien. Parto II. Sistema katalogo pri la presaĵoj de la ne-Esperanto-artefaritaj lingvoj (Volapük, Ido, Interlingue, Interlingua ktp.) laŭ la Internacia Dekuma Klasifiko.* Wien: Internacia Esperanto-Muzeo/Österreichische Nationalbibliothek.

Steiner, Hugo. 1969. *Alfabeta katalogo pri la kolektoj de Internacia Esperanto-Muzeo en Wien. Parto I, A-L.* Wien: Internacia Esperanto-Muzeo Wien/Österreichische Nationalbibliothek.

Stenström, Ingvar. 1997. *Occidental-Interlingue. Factos e fato de un lingua international.* Varberg: Societate Svedese pro Interlingua. (The bibliographical section was reprinted in *Informilo por Interlingvistoj* 12/2 (2003): 2-10.)

Stepanova, Maria D. 1971. Die 'Innere Valenz' des Wortes und das Problem der linguistischen Wahrscheinlichkeit. In: Helbig, Gerd, ed. *Beiträge zur Valenztheorie.* Halle: Niemeyer, pp. 133-142.

Stillman, Robert E. 1995. *The New Philosophy and Universal Languages in Seventeenth Century England: Bacon, Hobbes, and Wilkins.* Lewisburg: Bucknell University Press / London: Associated University Presses.

Stocker, Frank. 1996. *Wer spricht Esperanto? Kiu parolas Esperanton?* München-Newcastle: Lincom Europa.

Stojan, Petr Efstaf'evič. 1973. *Bibliografio de la internacia lingvo. Kun bibliografia aldono de Reinhard Haupenthal* (Bibliography of the international language. With a bibliographical Supplement by Reinhard Haupenthal). 2nd edition, Hildesheim-New York: Olms. (Reprint of the 1929 edition: Genève: Universala Esperanto-Asocio).

Stoppoloni, Silvio. 1982. Plansprachliches Rechner-Dialogsystem (PREDIS). Pritakso kaj perspektivoj. In: Koutny, Ilona, ed. *Homa lingvo kaj komputilo. Prelegoj de Interkomputo.* Budapest: Komputoscienca Societo Johano Neumann, pp. 88-101.

Strasser, Gerhard F. 1988. *Lingua Universalis. Kryptologie und Theorie der Universalsprachen im 16. und 17. Jahrhundert.* Wiesbaden: Harrassowitz.

Sudre, Jean-François. 1862. *Langue musicale universelle. Double dictionnaire.* Paris. (2nd edition 1866).

Suonuuti, Heidi. 1997. *Guide to Terminology.* Nordterm 8. Helsinki: Tekniikan sanastokeskus ry/Nordterm.

Suonuuti, Heidi. 1998. *Terminologia gvidilo.* Ed. Wera Blanke. Trans. Sabine Fiedler. Rotterdam: Universala Esperanto-Asocio.

Sutton, Geoffrey. 2008. *Concise Encyclopedia of the Original Literature of Esperanto.* New York: Mondial.

Symoens, Edward. 1989. *Bibliografio de universitataj kaj altlernejaj diplomverkoj, disertacioj kaj tezoj pri Esperanto kaj interlingvistiko. Bibliographie: Thèses et dissertations universitaires ou d' instituts superieurs sur l'espéranto et l'interlinguistique. Dissertations and Theses on Esperanto and Interlinguistics: A Bibliography.* Rotterdam: Universala Esperanto-Asocio.

Symoens, Edward. 1995. *Bibliografio de disertacioj pri Esperanto kaj interlingvistiko. Suplemento.* Rotterdam: Universala Esperanto-Asocio.

Svadost, Ermar P. 1968. *Kak vozniknet vseobshcij jazyk?* Moskva: Nauka.

Szerdahelyi, István. 1965. *Metodologio de lingvoinstruado kaj parolalproprigo.* Budapest: Tankönyvkiadó.

Szerdahelyi, István. 1977. *Babeltöl a világnyelvig* (The world language problem). Budapest: Gondolat.

Szerdahelyi, István, ed. 1980. *Miscellanea interlinguistica.* Budapest: Tankönyvkiadó.

Szerdahelyi, István. 1981. Interlingvistiko nocio kaj fako. *Planlingvistiko* 1: 4-6.

Takács, Jozefo. 1934. *Katalogo de la Esperanto-gazetaro.* Jablonné n. Orl.: Ant. Pražák.

Tauli, Valter. 1968. *Introduction to a Theory of Language Planning.* Uppsala: Almquist & Wiksells.

Tonkin, Humphrey. 1977. *Esperanto and International Language Problems: A Research Bibliography.* Washington: Esperantic Studies Foundation.

Tonkin, Humphrey, ed. 1997. *Esperanto, Interlinguistics, and Planned Language.* Papers of the Center for Research and Documentation on World Language Problems 5. Lanham-New York-Oxford: University Press of America/ Rotterdam, Hartford: Center for Research and Documentation on World Language Problems.

Tonkin, Humphrey. 2006. *Lingvo kaj popolo. Aktualaj problemoj de la Esperanto-movado.* Rotterdam: Universala Esperanto-Asocio.

Tonkin, Humphrey. 2007. Recent studies in Esperanto and interlinguistics: 2006. *Language Problems & Language Planning* 31/2: 169-196.

Tonkin, Humphrey. 2009. *Una lingua e un popolo: Problemi attuali del movimento esperantista.* Ed. Carlo Minnaja. Trans. Elvia Belluco. Venafro: Edizioni Eva. (Italian translation of Tonkin 2006.)

Tonkin, Humphrey. 2010. Navigating and expanding the MLA Bibliography. *Journal of Scholarly Publishing* 41/3: 340-353.

Tonkin, Humphrey. 2011. Plansprachen als Modelle der Sprachplanung. In: Brosch, Cyril; Fiedler, Sabine, eds. *Florilegium Interlinguisticum. Festschrift für Detlev Blanke zum 70. Geburtstag.* Frankfurt/Main: Peter Lang, pp. 60-68.

Tonkin, Humphrey. 2012. Language rights and linguistic justice. *Język. Komunikacja. Informacja / Language. Communication. Information* (Poznań) 7: 9-22.

Tonkin, Humphrey. 2015. Language planning and planned languages: How can planned languages inform language planning? *Interdisciplinary Description of Complex Systems* (INDECS) 13/2 (special issue: The Phenomenon of Esperanto): 193-199. http://indecs.eu/index.php?s=13_2&y=2015.

Tonkin, Humphrey; Fettes, Mark. 1996. *Esperanto Studies: An Overview.* Esperanto Documents 43A. Rotterdam: Universala Esperanto-Asocio.

Trischen, H. 1906. *Mondlingvo: Provisorische Aufstellung einer internationalen Verkehrssprache.* Dresden: Pierson.

Trubetzkoy, Nikolai S. 1939. Wie soll das Lautsystem einer künstlichen internationalen Hilfssprache beschaffen sein? *Travaux du Cercle Linguistique de Prague* 8: 5-21.

UEA 1994 = Libroservo de Universala Esperanto-Asocio. *Esperanto-Katalogo: Libroj kaj aliaj eldonajoj.* Rotterdam: Universala Esperanto-Asocio.

UEA 2016. *Jarlibro 2016.* Rotterdam: Universala Esperanto-Asocio.

Umeda, Yosimi, ed. 1987 *Plena raporto. Socilingvistikaj aspektoj de la Internacia Lingvo – kun aparta konsidero pri la lingva diverseco en la mondo.* Internacia simpozio honore al la centjara jubileo de Esperanto, 5-7.8.1986, Tokio. Tokyo: Japana Esperanto-Instituto. (In Japanese and Esperanto.)

Usui, Hiroyuki. 2008. Interlinguistics and Esperanto studies in the social context of modern Japan. *Language Problems & Language Planning* 32/2: 181-202.

Vallon, Hervé, ed. 2015. *Reinhard Haupenthal. Bibliographie seiner Veröffentlichungen zur Esperantologie und Interlinguistik.* Bad Bellingen: Edition Iltis.

Van Dijk, Ziko. 2012. *Historio de Universala Esperanto-Asocio.* Partizánske, Slovakia: Espero.

Van Parijs, Philippe. 2011. *Linguistic Justice for Europe and for the World.* Oxford: Oxford University Press.

Vatré, Henri. 1988. *Indekso por la Nica Literatura Revuo (1955/56-1961/62).* Saarbrücken: Iltis.

Vatré, Henri. ed. 1998.

Verax, Charles. 1911/1912. Propono pri terminologiaj fundamentaj principoj por la scienca lingvo en Esperanto. *Oficiala gazeto esperantista* 4 (junio 1911 – majo 1912): 378-382.

Veuthey, Francisco, ed. 2014. *Jarlibro.* Rotterdam: Universala Esperanto-Asocio.

Volk, A.; Fuchs, R. 1883. *Die Weltsprache, entworfen auf der Grundlage des Lateinischen.* Berlin: Kühl.

Vossler, Karl. 1923. *Gesammelte Aufsätze zur Sprachphilosophie.* München: Hueber.

Vossler, Karl. 1925. *Geist und Literatur in der Sprache.* Heidelberg: Winter.

Vraciu, Ariton. 1980. *Lingvistică generală şi comparată.* Bucureşti: Editura Didactica si Pedagogica.

Wandel, Amri, ed. 1998. *Internacia Kongresa Universitato, 1-7 aŭgusto 1998, Montpeliero, Francio.* Rotterdam: Universala Esperanto-Asocio.

Wandel, Amri. 2010. Du jardekoj de Internacia Kongresa Universitato. In: Blanke, Detlev; Lins, Ulrich, eds. *La arto kunlabori. Festlibro por Humphrey Tonkin.* Rotterdam: Universala Esperanto-Asocio, pp. 636-643.

Wandel, Amri. ed. 2017. *Internacia Kongresa Universitato, 70-a Sesio, Seulo, Suda Koreio, 22-29 julio 2017.* Rotterdam: Universala Esperanto-Asocio.

Wandruszka, Mario. 1971. *Interlinguistik. Umrisse einer neuen Sprachwissenschaft.* München: Piper.

Waringhien, Gaston, ed. 1970. *Plena ilustrita vortaro de Esperanto.* Paris: Sennacieca Asocio Tutmonda (SAT).

Waringhien, Gaston. 1989. *Lingvo kaj vivo. Esperantologiaj eseoj.* 2nd revised edition with appendix. Rotterdam: Universala Esperanto-Asocio. (1st edition 1959).

Waringhien, Gaston; Duc Goninaz, Michel, eds. 2005. *Nova plena ilustrita vortaro de Esperanto.* Paris: Sennacieca Asocio Tutmonda (SAT).

Wells, John C. 1978/1989. *Lingvistikaj aspektoj de Esperanto.* Rotterdam: Universala Esperanto-Asocio. (2nd edition 1982, reprinted 1989. German translation: *Linguistische Aspekte der Plansprache Esperanto*, trans. Günther Becker, Saarbrücken: Saarländischer Esperanto-Bund. Also translated into Danish.)

Wennergren, Bertilo. 2005. *Plena manlibro de esperanta gramatiko.* El Cerrito: Esperanto-Ligo por Norda Ameriko. (http://bertilow.com/pmeg/elshutebla/index.html)

Werner, Jan. 1986. *Terminologia kurso.* Roudnice nad Labem: Sdružený Klub ROH / Praha: Ĉeĥa Esperanto-Asocio.

Werner, Jan. 2004. *Terminologiaj konsideroj.* Dobřichovice/Praha: KAVA-PECH.

Whorf, Benjamin Lee. 1956. *Language, Thought and Reality.* Ed. J. B. Carroll. New York: Wiley.

Wilkins, John. 1668. *An Essay Towards a Real Character and a Philosophical Language.* (Reprint: Menston: Scolar Press 1968.)

Will, Georg A. 1755. *De lingua universali.* Altona: Meyer.

Wit, Bert de. 1981. *Esperanto, utopie of realiteit?* Rotterdam: Federacio de Laboristaj Esperantistoj.

Witkam, Toon. 1983. *DLT: Distributed Language Translation – A Multlingual Facility for Videotext Information Networks.* Utrecht: Buro for Systeemontwikkeling (BSO).

Wjuster, E. 1935. *Meždunarodnaja standardizacija jazyka v technike*. Perevod c nemeckogo i obrabotka O. I. Bogomolovoj pod redakciej E. K. Drezena, prof. L. I. Žirkova, inž. A. F. Lecochina i prof. M. F. Malikova. Leningrad-Moskva: Standartgiz.

Wojtakowski, Edward T. 1979. *Decimala katalogo de la planlingva literaturo ĉe universitata biblioteko de la Katolika Universitato en Lublino (K.U.L.). Katalog dziesiętny księgozbioru esperanckiego w bibliotece uniwersyteckiej K.U.L.* Rome-Lublin: IKUE-Centro.

Wood, Richard E. 1982. *Current Work in the Linguistics of Esperanto.* Esperanto Documents 28A. Rotterdam: Universala Esperanto-Asocio.

Wüster, Eugen. 1921. Esperanto-Deutsch, ein Versuch zum synthetischen Esperanto-Wörterbuch. *Esperanto-Praktiko* 3/6: 99-100.

Wüster, Eugen. 1923-1929. *Enzyklopädisches Wörterbuch Esperanto-Deutsch. Mit besonderer Aufweisung des Zamenhof'schen Sprachgebrauchs. Versuch auf dem Wege zum internationalen synthetischen Esperanto-Wörterbuch. / Enciklopedia Vortaro Esperanta-Germana. Kun speciala elmontro de la Zamenhofa lingvuzo. Provo sur la vojo al la internacia sinteza vortaro de Esperanto. A-Korno.* 4 volumes. Leipzig: Hirt & Sohn. (1923, 1925, 1926, 1929.)

Wüster, Eugen. 1931/1970. *Internationale Sprachnormung in der Technik besonders in der Elektrotechnik. Die nationale Sprachnormung und ihre Verallgemeinerung.* Berlin: VDI. (2nd edition Bonn: Bouvier 1966; 3rd edition Bonn: Bouvier, 1970, with supplementary report 'Fünfunddreißig Jahre später' (35 years later).)

Wüster, Eugen. 1934. *Grundzüge der Sprachnormung.* Berlin: VDI.

Wüster, Eugen. 1935. See Wjuster.

Wüster, Eugen. 1936a. *Konturoj de la lingvonormigo en la tekniko.* Trans E. Pfeffer. Budapest: Literatura Mondo. (Reprint 1975: Aabyhøj, Dansk Esperanto-Forlag.)

Wüster, Eugen. 1936b. Über das Projekt eines ISA-Codes. Bericht für die Besprechung im ÖNA am 12. Dezember 1935. *Sparwirtschaft* 14/1: 10-16.

Wüster, Eugen. 1955/1976. Die Benennungen 'Esperantologie' und 'Interlinguistik'. In: Haupenthal, Reinhard, ed. 1976. *Plansprachen. Beiträge zur Interlinguistik*. Darmstadt: Wiss. Buchgesellschaft, pp. 271-277. Reprinted from *Esperantologio* (Copenhagen) 1 (1949/55): 209-214.

Wüster, Eugen. 1971. Internacia terminologio en la servo de la informatiko (Inaŭgura parolado por la Internacia Somera Universitato, Vieno 1970). *Scienca Revuo* 22/1 (87): 3-10.

Wüster, Eugen. 1978. *Esperantologiaj studoj. Memorkolekto*. Ed. Reinhard Haupenthal, Antverpeno / La Laguna: Stafeto / TK.

Wüster, Eugen. 1991. *Einführung in die Allgemeine Terminologielehre und Terminologiosche Lexikographie*. 3rd edition. Bonn: Romanistischer Verlag.

Wüster, Eugen. 1994. *Enciklopedia Vortaro Esperanto-Germana. Korno-Z (Enzyklopädisches Wörterbuch Esperanto-Deutsch Korno-Z)*. Manuskript. Mit einer Einführung von Detlev Blanke. Darin enthalten: Plehn, Hans-J., *Enciklopedia Vortaro Esperanto-Germana. Korno-L.* Bearbeitung des Manuskripts von Eugen Wüster. Wien: Österreichische Nationalbibliothek/IEMW (32 Microfiches).

Zamenhof, Ludwig L. 1903/1992. *Fundamenta krestomatio de la lingvo Esperanto*. 18th edition, with notes by Gaston Waringhien. Rotterdam: Universala Esperanto-Asocio.

Zamenhof, Ludwig L. 1929. *Originala Verkaro*, ed. Johannes Dietterle. Leipzig: Ferdinand Hirt.

Zamenhof, Ludwig L. 1948. *Leteroj. Vol. II 1907-1914*, ed. Gaston Waringhien. Paris: Sennacieca Asocio Tutmonda (SAT).

Zamenhof, Ludwig L. 1972. *Hilelismo*. Trans. Adolf Holzhaus. Helsinki: Fondumo Esperanto.

Zamenhof, Ludwig L. 1991. *Fundamento de Esperanto*. 10th edition, ed. André Albault, Pisa: Edistudio.

Zsebehásy, György. 2005. *Katalogo de la Esperanto-kolektajo de Károly Fajszi Budapest. Libroj. Parto II*. Budapest: Országos Idegennyelvü Könyvtár.

www.ingramcontent.com/pod-product-compliance
Lightning Source LLC
Chambersburg PA
CBHW032023230426
43671CB00005B/186